Mary Lincoln's Insanity Case

Mary Lincoln's Insanity Case

A Documentary History

JASON EMERSON

University of Illinois Press

Urbana, Chicago, and Springfield

Frontispiece: Photograph of First Lady Mary Lincoln
in mourning gown and bonnet, probably around 1862,
after son Willie Lincoln's death. Courtesy Allan County
Public Library, Fort Wayne, Indiana.

Library of Congress Cataloging-in-Publication Data
Emerson, Jason, 1975–
Mary Lincoln's insanity case : a documentary history /
Jason Emerson.
p. cm.
Includes bibliographical references and index.
ISBN 978-0-252-03707-8 (hardcover : alk. paper) —
ISBN 978-0-252-09417-0 (e-book) 1. Lincoln, Mary Todd,
1818–1882—Mental health. 2. Lincoln, Mary Todd,
1818–1882—Trials, litigation, etc. 3. Newspapers—United
States—History—19th century—Sources. 4. Presidents'
spouses—United States—Biography. 5. Lincoln, Abraham,
1809–1865—Family. 6. Mental illness—
United States—Case studies. I. Title.
E457.25.L55E47   2012
973.7092—dc23   2011052789

Contents

Illustrations follow page 166

Acknowledgments

Numerous people assisted me in locating and compiling the documents in this book, and I owe them all a debt of thanks.

Kara Vetter, registrar, Indiana State Library, Indianapolis, Indiana; Cindy Van Horn, curator, Lincoln Financial Foundation Collection, Allen County Public Library, Fort Wayne, Indiana; James Cornelius, Lincoln Collection curator, and Glenna Schroeder-Lein, manuscripts librarian, Abraham Lincoln Presidential Library, Springfield, Illinois; Holly Snyder, North American history librarian, John Hay Library, Brown University, Providence, Rhode Island; Daniel Meyer, associate director, Special Collections and Research Center, University of Chicago Library; Lynn Eaton, research services librarian, Rare Book, Manuscript and Special Collections Library, Duke University, Durham, North Carolina; John L. Popolis Jr., museum technician, Lincoln Home National Historic Site, Springfield, Illinois; Michelle Ganz, archivist and special collections librarian, Abraham Lincoln Library and Museum, Harrogate, Tennessee; and Deborah Emerson, my stepmother and executive director, Central New York Library Resources Council.

The articles, "Mary Todd Lincoln: Patient at Bellevue Place, Batavia," by Rodney A. Ross, and "New Mary Lincoln Letter Found," by Jason Emerson, were published previously by the *Journal of the Illinois State Historical Society,* and I thank the society for permission to republish selections from those works.

Thanks also to my good friend and fellow Lincoln enthusiast Jonda Anderson, who read over the manuscript and offered excellent feedback.

Introduction

Shortly before Mary Lincoln was declared insane by a Chicago jury in May 1875, one resident summed up the public knowledge and feeling in the city about the former first lady in a letter to a friend:

> We are sorry to hear that poor Mrs. Abraham Lincoln, who lives here, has had a nervous breakdown. One can hardly wonder at it, with all she has been through. Being in the White House during the civil war was enough of a strain, even without the tragic death of her husband, to which she was a witness. It must have been awful for her. Poor woman. They say she is haunted by the fear that Chicago is to be destroyed by fire again, and she has gone to the bank and removed all her valuables, in order to take them out of the city, in case the dreaded conflagration comes. Her son, Robert T. Lincoln, a lawyer here, is most kind and attentive to her. One hears nothing but praise for his conduct.[1]

In fact, Mary Lincoln's life and mental health in the decade after her husband's assassination was far more complex, pitiable, and worrisome than anyone except her oldest son truly understood. The one thing that nearly the entire country agreed on, however, was that Abraham Lincoln's murder had driven his wife insane. This belief followed her the rest of her life, and was remarked on often at the time of her death. Even Rev. James A. Reed, during Mary Lincoln's funeral in July 1882, said, "It is no reflection upon either the strength of her mind or the tenderness of her heart, to say that when Abraham Lincoln died, she died. The lightning that struck down the strong man, unnerved the woman. The sharp iron of this pungent grief went to her soul. The terrible shock, with its quick following griefs, in the death of her children, left her mentally and physically a wreck, as it might have left any of us in the same circumstance."[2]

But even then most people truly did not know Mary's history in the years following April 1865.

After leaving the White House, Mary lived in Chicago with her remaining sons Robert and Tad. In 1868 she took Tad to Europe to travel, but specifically to improve his education. They returned to America in 1871, but shortly after their arrival in

Chicago seventeen-year-old Tad died of pleurisy. After the death of her youngest child, her "troublesome little sunshine" as she once called him, Mary Lincoln's long-remarked-on eccentricities became even more pronounced. Robert Lincoln, Mary's oldest and last surviving son, was so concerned over his mother's health and safety that he hired a personal nurse, Ellen Fitzgerald, to be her constant companion as she traveled restlessly around the United States and Canada. Robert was, in 1872, not yet thirty years old, married and with a three-year-old daughter, and a partner in his own law firm in Chicago.

In 1873 Mary Lincoln began medical care under Dr. Willis Danforth for what he diagnosed as "fever and nervous derangement of the head." By March 1875, Mary Lincoln was suffering from mental troubles including hallucinations, delusions, paranoia, and depression. Her statements and actions had become so bizarre and worrisome to her oldest son that he consulted seven of the Midwest's best medical experts and three of his father's closest friends seeking advice. They all advised him that his mother was insane and needed medical treatment.[3] Since Mary would never voluntary acquiesce to psychiatric care, Robert followed Illinois state law and had his mother tried in county court on the charge of insanity.

Mary Lincoln's insanity trial on May 19, 1875, lasted for three hours during which time eighteen witnesses—doctors, hotel employees, and shopkeepers—testified that she was mentally impaired and needed medical attention. Robert himself took the stand, explained his mother's history, and declared that he had "no doubt" she was insane. "She has been of unsound mind since the death of father; has been irresponsible for the past ten years," he said amidst multiple tearful breakdowns.[4] The jury took less than ten minutes to declare Mary Lincoln insane and a fit person to be committed to a sanitarium for medical treatment. Robert was subsequently named the conservator of his mother's estate and had total control of her property and finances.

Robert arranged for his mother's treatment at Bellevue Place sanitarium, a private asylum in Batavia, Illinois, run by Dr. Richard J. Patterson. During the first weeks and months of her residence in Batavia, both Dr. Patterson and Robert Lincoln believed Mary to be improving. After two months, however, Mary, believing herself perfectly sane and imprisoned against her will, hatched a plot to secure her freedom. She enlisted the help of her old friends and legal advisors, James and Myra Bradwell, and with them she launched a campaign—both public and private—for her release.[5]

By September 1875, after only four months at Bellevue Place, Mary was allowed to leave Batavia and live instead with her older sister (who also was a mother figure) and brother-in-law, Elizabeth and Ninian Edwards, in Springfield, Illinois. Neither Dr. Patterson nor Robert Lincoln believed that Mary was cured by this time, but she was so distraught over her situation—goaded considerably by Myra Bradwell—that both men knew no further good could come of her remaining at Bellevue Place. Robert considered his mother's move to Springfield (under supervision of a nurse) to be an "experiment," to see how she would handle her freedom.

Mary spent the next twelve months at the Edwardses' home. During most of this time Robert was his mother's court-appointed conservator and controlled all her finances. As time passed, Mary's mental condition, according to her sister and brother-in-law, was better than it had been in years—except on the subject of her finances. On that subject, she was nearly obsessed and completely infuriated that Robert controlled her money. She grew more and more embittered at him every day, and even threatened to kill him at one point. Robert gave his mother everything she asked of him during this time—money, clothing, and property of hers stored in his possession—but could not legally return to her power over her finances.

Mary became so intractable and agitated over the money issue that she began to revert to her presanitarium ways. At one point Robert even threatened to send her back to the asylum. He told his uncle, "[My mother] has always been exceedingly generous to me," for which he was grateful, "but being grateful merely will not discharge my duty to her even if necessary against her will."[6] Robert was legally bound as his mother's conservator for one year after his appointment. When that year expired in June 1876, Robert agreed to allow his mother the return of her estate.

Mary Lincoln's second trial declared her restored to reason and a fit person to control her own property. Although Robert did not consider his mother returned to sanity, he did not fight the trial or any of the court's judgments. Immediately after the verdict, Mary demanded that Robert return to her everything of hers that was stored in his possession (including items she gave his family as gifts, which she now declared he had stolen); then she broke off all contact with him. Mary subsequently fled to Europe in a self-imposed exile where she stayed for four years. She did not speak to her only living son during that entire period. Their estrangement was so thorough that Robert even admitted to a correspondent in 1877 that he did not know his mother's address, only that she was "somewhere in Europe."[7]

Mary and Robert's reconciliation finally occurred in May 1881. Mary was again living at the Edwardses' home in Springfield after returning to the United States in October 1880 due to deteriorating health. Robert was, at that time, President James A. Garfield's secretary of war. In May Secretary Lincoln left Washington for an official visit to Fort Leavenworth, Kansas, and on his way stopped in Springfield where he spent an entire day with his mother at the Edwardses' home. The rapprochement most likely was arranged by Mary's sister, Elizabeth Edwards, who long had encouraged both Mary and Robert to mend fences.

Over the remaining fourteen months of Mary Lincoln's life, Robert and his family visited her in Illinois every few weeks; when Mary stayed in New York City for medical treatment in fall 1881 the Lincolns traveled up from Washington every week to see her. Mary Lincoln died on July 16, 1882. Robert Lincoln, her sole heir, arranged her funeral and burial, and inherited her entire estate.

For the rest of his life, Robert Lincoln was the guardian and the curator of not only his father's historical legacy but also his mother's. But as conscientious—even unyielding—as Robert was to defend and promote his father's greatness, he was even more determined to downplay, suppress, and even expunge his mother's story during her "period of mental derangement," as he called it.

Robert considered Mary's insanity an embarrassment not only to himself, but, more importantly, to her own legacy and her husband's memory. This was why Robert attempted at one point in his life to collect and destroy all of his mother's letters written during the insanity period. He quickly discovered, however, that his mother was such a prolific letter writer that the task was impossible, and so he gave it up. Strangely, while attempting to destroy all of his mother's own words, Robert simultaneously kept a complete documentary record of the insanity period, including the medical and legal documents and correspondence, as well as his own correspondence dealing with his mother during the year as her conservator. While he never explained why he collected and kept this "Insanity File" as he labeled it, the logical explanation is that he believed the documents would one day (whether to his descendants or to general posterity) vindicate his actions.

Robert Lincoln probably never could have conceived the degree to which he has come to be viewed as a mustache-twirling villain in regards to his mother's insanity case. It is ironic that the currently prevalent conception of him and his actions in 1875 is that of an utterly ruthless, rapacious, and heartless son, while at the time of the trial the support and understanding of his position and actions were nearly unanimous around the country. The difference between this contemporary assessment and the opinions of later historians could not be more antithetical. And yet, the vast gulf between attitude and understanding of the event persists.

I often am asked why I am so fascinated by Mary Lincoln's insanity case and why I continue to write books and articles about it. Quite simply, I find the subject has not been sufficiently researched and examined and, to fully understand this person and this event in her life, more historical sleuthing and focused consideration are necessary.

Mary Lincoln was an extraordinary woman, yet she also had very real personal problems and character flaws. That she suffered from an inherited mental illness, with the more serious symptoms being hallucinations, delusions, and depression, is apparent.[8] These symptoms are well documented, as are the nearly universal beliefs by her family, friends, acquaintances, newspaper reporters, and the general public that she was—quite understandably from all she suffered—in the parlance of the times, "insane." Likewise, that her oldest son, Robert T. Lincoln, being a quintessential

Victorian gentleman, did what he thought was both necessary and proper given his duty as the "head" of the family to protect his mother from herself and from other people, is apparent. Again, the evidence for this, and the nearly universal beliefs by Mary's family, friends, and acquaintances, as well as newspaper reporters and the general public, that Robert acted correctly and admirably, is vastly documented.

And yet, given this immense amount of primary documentation offering evidence of Mary's mental illness and Robert's altruistic sense of duty, why has the notion remained so prevalent that Mary Lincoln was the perfectly sane victim of a male chauvinist society and a cold-hearted rapacious bastard of a son who wanted to shut her away and steal her money? How can this be such a popular interpretation of the insanity case when there truly is no evidence to sustain the charges? There are multiple reasons, the two most important being the use of a revisionist (specifically feminist) historical philosophy by most of Mary's modern biographers, and the generally poor historical reputation of Robert Lincoln, who, as a millionaire captain of industry and an intensely private individual, has been dubbed a callous and aristocratic prig.

More than any other cause, however, the one overwhelming and disheartening reason that Mary Lincoln's mental illness and insanity case is so misunderstood is that practically nobody has actually gone to the primary evidence for the answers— not even the historians who would purport to write about the subject. And even those writers who have looked at the evidence have not really considered it beyond their own particular political, social, or historical agendas.

This great historical tragedy—and travesty—is the reason for the present book.

While the objectivity of any author or editor is suspect, I believe I have gathered here all the documents necessary to keep future debates on Mary's case grounded in the historical record. If I have overlooked anything of importance, I trust the diligence of other Lincoln scholars to bring it forward.

This collection is a documentary history of Mary Lincoln's mental illness and insanity case, and is a compilation of every possible primary source on the subject, including 138 letters by participants, forty-six contemporary newspaper articles and editorials, six legal documents, the Bellevue Place sanitarium daily patient progress report during Mary Lincoln's incarceration, as well as multiple reminiscences, interviews, and diaries of people who knew Mary Lincoln or were involved in the case, including one recollection by a member of the 1875 insanity trial jury. Thankfully, this is an almost completely two-sided record, having not only letters but also their responses, even letters and related newspaper articles. Happily, most of the later recollections and reminiscences also refer back to primary documentation on the case.

The documents in this collection come from numerous sources stored in archives around the country, but the three main sources come from the personal papers of Robert T. Lincoln. Robert kept Letterpress copies (onion skin transfers) of all his correspondence from 1867–1920; these eighty volumes of correspondence were discovered in his Vermont home in the 1970s by historian James T. Hickey and taken to Illinois. The volumes are now part of the Lincoln Collection in the Abraham Lincoln Presidential Library in Springfield, Illinois. Robert also kept an exhaustive documentary record of his mother's insanity case, including all the correspondence and legal documents he had access to, and even some newspaper clippings. This cache, which Robert himself labeled, "MTL Insanity File," also was discovered in his Vermont home in the 1970s and removed by Hickey. These documents are now part of the Lincoln Financial Foundation Collection in the Allen County Public Library in Fort Wayne, Indiana (which was previously in the now-defunct Lincoln Museum of the same city).

The majority of the documents of the case reside in these two collections. A third major cache of insanity case papers, however, was discovered by this author in 2005. These contained the correspondence between Mary Lincoln and her friend and accomplice Myra Bradwell, which had been missing for nearly one hundred years. Then in 2010 a few previously missing insanity documents were shown on *Antiques Roadshow* and subsequently auctioned and purchased by a museum in Louisville, Kentucky. These documents are minor documents that add nothing to the story and have been previously published in an article from the *Aurora Beacon-News* in the 1930s.[9] They are not included here for lack of space and their nominal importance. Otherwise, nearly every *known* letter and document on the case is accounted for and included in this collection.

Very few of the following documents have been previously published. Some have appeared in books on the subject, such as my book *The Madness of Mary Lincoln*, Mark E. Neely and R. Gerald McMurtry's *The Insanity File: The Case of Mary Todd Lincoln*, and Justin and Linda Turner's *Mary Todd Lincoln: Her Life and Letters*. The Bellevue Place sanitarium daily patient reports were previously published in full in a journal article. The rest may have been mentioned, cited, or quoted from in articles or books, but never printed in totality.

Biographer William Herndon once wrote of Abraham Lincoln, "I feel it is my duty to state to all people my ideas of Lincoln and my knowledge of the facts of his life so far as I know them. . . . I want the world to know Lincoln."[10] I feel the same way about Mary Lincoln in general, and her insanity case in particular. In living with, discussing, even arguing about my conclusions and interpretations concerning her case for many years, the thought I forever return to is that I wish everyone could see the original letters, reminiscences, and documents that I have seen.

The aim of this book, therefore, is neither to accuse nor defend Mary Lincoln, Robert Lincoln, or anyone involved in the insanity case, nor to pass judgment on the merits of the evidence. My interpretation of this event and all persons involved in it has previously been published in my book *The Madness of Mary Lincoln,* and readers can look there for my specific opinions and interpretations. This book, rather, is intended to give to students and enthusiasts of Mary Lincoln's insanity case access to all the existing documents.

There always will be differing interpretations of history, as there should be. My conception of Mary and Robert Lincoln and the insanity case is antithetical to those of Mary's most recent and sympathetic biographers Catherine Clinton and Jean Baker, both of whom see Mary as a sane woman railroaded into the asylum by evil doctors and a heartless son. And yet interpretation is based on the historical evidence. A person cannot make an educated decision on what to believe is the historical truth if the facts one is given are incomplete or distorted. To understand Mary Lincoln's insanity case, one must go to the original evidence—in doing so, the most balanced view will be obtained of what actually occurred and why.

And so I urge those with an interest and eagerness to understand Mary's plight to read through the documents in this book. Do not blindly accept my opinions, or Baker's, or Clinton's, or any one historian's. Do that most glorious and noble action a person can do—inform yourself, and make up your own mind.

Editorial Note

The format of this book is chronological. It begins in April 1865, in the immediate aftermath of Abraham Lincoln's murder, and concludes in 1959, with the last primary piece of evidence published concerning Mary Lincoln's mental health. The assassination was chosen as the starting point because it typically is regarded as the catalyst for Mary Lincoln's mental deterioration, although references to her pre-1865 behavior also are included as context throughout the book.

Each item presented here is consistently formatted with document identifiers placed at the beginning of the text and source location placed at the bottom. For newspaper articles, for example, the title is given at the beginning and the newspaper's full name and date of publication are given at the bottom. Newspaper articles with no title, or titled simply "Mrs. Lincoln," have had identifiers added to avoid repetitious confusion. In the former case, titles have been created based on the article text and enclosed in brackets; in the latter case, the first subhead has been moved up and made part of the title, or a few distinguishing words from the text have been added. In letters, the name of the writer and recipient, and place and date of writing, are given at the beginning of the text; the archival location of the letter is given at the bottom. All archival locations have been written out, with the exception of one: the Robert Todd Lincoln Letterpress Books, which are held in the Abraham Lincoln Presidential Library, Springfield, Illinois. To save space, this source has been abbreviated to LB, which is then followed by volume, microfilm reel, and page numbers separated by colons. For example, a letter in volume 33, microfilm reel 54, on page 247, would be abbreviated as LB, 33:54:247.

Practically every document in this book is printed in full. The only omissions or elisions concern items not relevant to the overall topic, such as concluding paragraphs in personal letters inquiring about or offering news on personal matters. A handful of letters written during the insanity period, and included in the Mary Todd Lincoln Insanity File, have been omitted from this work because of their nominal contents—such as the hiring of a nurse for Mary when she moved into the Edwardses' home in September 1875—and the need to keep this book to a manageable word count.

Editorial comments have been limited to basic context and scene-setting to help string together the narrative. Luckily, the documents tell the story on their own exceedingly well. Annotations have been made where necessary to explain people, places, or events, and generally to allow the reader a better understanding and evaluation of the document contents.

In terms of editing style, I have avoided the use of *sic,* turned dashes into periods or commas where necessary, and generally updated punctuation and nineteenth-century grammar. Any editorial insertions in the text appear in brackets; any use of parentheses was done by the respective authors. Any text emphasized by italics is original to the respective authors. Handwriting that was illegible (mostly by Robert Lincoln, who had atrocious penmanship and many of whose Letterpress copies have faded terribly through the years) is noted in brackets, as are some portions of text where my translations of handwriting were fairly certain but not definite.

The newspaper articles included in this volume were chosen based on their content and not on their titles or political affiliations or leanings. Since Mary Lincoln's insanity trial, and most of the events before and after it, occurred in Chicago, the majority of the newspaper articles reproduced herein are from Chicago newspapers that had correspondents at the scene of an event or interview, or the articles were written by actual participants. The Chicago-based reports were published in major and minor newspapers across the United States; any reprints have been included only where the original reporting could not be obtained.

Many of the newspaper articles included herein—although they concern the same topic and were published on the same dates—come from different newspapers. While this may seem repetitive to the reader, it ensures complete coverage regardless of a newspaper's political affiliations because each account offers viewpoints and facts that differ slightly from or augment the others. Reading all of these articles not only fills out the picture, but shows readers where certain pieces of information regarding Mary's insanity case originate.

For example, the Republican-leaning *Chicago Tribune*'s articles on the insanity trial (from which most previous writers on the subject get their information) state that Mary Lincoln did not speak during the entire three-hour ordeal and that her attorney put up no palpable defense; the likewise Republican-leaning *Chicago Inter Ocean* (which had the best overall coverage of the trial but is often ignored as a source) states that Mary Lincoln repeatedly spoke to her attorney and even to the judge, and also lists numerous instances where her attorney objected or offered rebuttals to the testimony; the Democrat-leaning *Chicago Times* states that Mary vehemently, but softly, denounced the proceedings to her attorney, especially as Robert testified. In this case, as in many others, the *politics* of who spoke when and how often is unimportant, but the historic value of depictions, their differences and similarities of the scene, is important.

It is only by reading every Chicago newspaper article concerning the trial that a reader can see the complete and balanced story—or the ability to make the best possible generalization based on a preponderance of the evidence—of what happened.

Chapter 1

April 1865–May 1875

The specific time and cause of the onset of Mary Lincoln's mental troubles is debated and debatable, but, until the late twentieth century, the general consensus by citizens, journalists, family and friends, and even Robert Lincoln, was that President Lincoln's assassination on April 14, 1865, was the catalyst that drove Mary Lincoln insane.

The first three selections, written within a month after the shooting, were penned by two Lincoln family friends (Anson Henry and Horatio Taft) and by the commissioner of public buildings (Benjamin French); the latter encountered Mary Lincoln on a nearly daily basis.

DR. ANSON G. HENRY TO HIS WIFE
Washington, D.C., April 19, 1865

My Dear Wife,

Today has been the saddest day of my life, if indeed one can be sadder than another of the sad days that has shrouded the nation in gloom. . . .

I was in Richmond on the night of the assassination. The next day in the afternoon I went down to City Point and met the sad news. I was so stunned by the blow that I could not realize that he was dead until I saw him lying in the [White House] Guest's chamber cold and still in the embrace of Death. Then the terrible truth flashed upon me and the fountain of tears was broken up and I wept like a child refusing to be comforted. . . .

After recovering my composure I sought the presence of poor broken hearted Mrs. Lincoln. I found her in bed more composed than I had anticipated, but the moment I came within her reach she threw her arms around my neck and wept most hysterically for several minutes, and this completely unmanned me again, but my sympathy was to her most consoling, and for half an hour she talked very composedly about what had transpired between her and her husband the day and evening of his death, which I will tell you when we meet. She says he was more cheerful and joyous that day and evening than he had been for years. When at dinner he complained of being worn out with the incessant toils of the day, and proposed to go to the Theater and have a laugh over the Country Cousin. She says she discouraged going, on account of a bad headache, but he insisted that he must go, for if he stayed home he would have no rest for he would be obliged to see company all evening as usual.

Finding that he decided to go, she could not think of having him go without her, never having felt so unwilling to be away from him. She sat close to him and was leaning in his lap looking up in his face when the fatal shot was fired, his last words being in answer to her question "What will Miss Harris think of my hanging on you so"—"She won't think anything about it"—and said accompanied with one of his kind and affectionate smiles. Yes, that look and expression is stamped upon her soul so indelibly to ever be effaced by time, and its recollection will never fail to soothe and comfort her in her hours of darkest affliction.

Lincoln Miscellaneous manuscripts,
University of Chicago library

HORATIO NELSON TAFT
Diary entry, April 30, 1865

The President of the United States has been *assassinated.* Abraham Lincoln, the good and kind hearted, was shot while sitting in his box at Ford's Theatre on the night of the 14th inst., at about half past ten o'clock. . . .

When the shot was fired Mrs. Lincoln was sitting near her husband with her hand on his knee. She says she saw the flash and heard the report of the pistol, thinking it was in some way connected with the play. She leaned forward to see what it *was,* and then looked to Mr. Lincoln to see *where he* was *looking.* He was sitting with his head drooped down and eyes shut. She was not alarmed at this, he sometimes held his head in that way when in deep thought, but she put her hand on his forehead and *he* not stirring she put it on the back of his head and feeling it wet she immediately withdrew it covered with blood. She then screamed and that is the last she remembered that took place in the Theatre. She says, as she put her hand on his head she recollects that something suddenly brushed past her *and* rubbing off her shawl. It was *Booth* as he jumped from the box. The president made no noise, nor attempted to speak, nor stirred a limb after he was shot, nor was he conscious for one moment from that time until he died. When his skin was touched or his hand was taken, there was a slight quiver or tremor of the muscles, but that was all. . . .

[Lincoln was taken across the street to the Petersen house.] The room [he was placed in] is at the end of the entrance hall about 9 feet by 15, with two windows and three doors, one door entering from the hall, one at the left as you enter, opening to an open porch or piazza, and the other at the farther end of the room, opening into another small room from which stairs descended to the basement. Some few individuals came in to the room through that door clandestinely. Mrs. Lincoln occupied a room near by with some of her friends who were there. She went in frequently to see the president with Doct. *Gurley* (The family pastor) who had been sent for about 3 o'clock. She was not in the room when *he* died. Robert Lincoln was there and Dr. Gurley, the two private secretaries of the president *Nicolay* and *Hay*. Upon one occasion when Mrs. L went in and saw her husband she fainted and was carried out insensible. It was thought *best for her not* to be there when he died. Dr. Gurley prayed by the bedside of the president when he first arrived (at 3 o'clock). Then went into the room where Mrs. Lincoln was and prayed with her, and remained with her most of the time, accompanying her and supporting her into the room of the dying president when she visited it. . . .

After the president died Dr. Gurley went to Mrs. L and told her "the president is dead." O—*why* did you not let me know? *Why did* you not *tell* me? "Your friends thought it was not *best*. You must be resigned to the will of God. You must be calm and trust in God and in your friends." She soon after left, with Dr. G. for her home.

Diary of Horatio Nelson Taft

BENJAMIN FRENCH TO PAMELA FRENCH
Washington, D.C., May 21, 1865

I think I sent you a printed account of the week's events [after the assassination of President Lincoln], which I wrote for the *Republican*, so I need not write it here. . . . Mrs. Lincoln expects to start for Chicago tomorrow. I think the tragical death of her husband has made her *crazyer* than she used to be—but the most unaccountable thing she ever did was to purchase about a thousand dollars worth of mourning goods the month before Mr. Lincoln died. What *do* you suppose possessed her to do it! Please keep that fact in your own house. I will sometime tell you what I have gone through since Mr. L's death. I cannot write it.

Benjamin Brown French Family Papers

After the assassination, Mary and her sons Robert and Tad moved to Chicago to begin a new life. Robert began studying law with the firm of Scammon, McCagg, and Fuller; and Tad, for the first time in his life, began attending school. Mary, during these first years of her widowhood, was consumed not only with grief but also with her finances. She left the White House carrying a debt of tens of thousands of dollars. The income from her husband's estate was modest, so Mary lobbied Congress for her husband's full four years of presidential salary—although she received recompense for only one year—and also requested she be paid a pension as a widow whose husband died in the performance of official duty.

By 1867, having received no pension, Mary believed herself to be on the brink of poverty. Using a pseudonym, she tried to raise money with a sale of her old White House gowns and jewelry in New York City. Her true identity quickly was uncovered and her entire effort was derided and ridiculed in the national press as an embarrassment to the memory of the Great Emancipator. Some commentators found her actions more than just humiliating and indelicate; they declared them unbalanced.

"MRS. LINCOLN [FINANCIAL CONDITIONS]"
Illinois State Journal, Oct. 10, 1867

A special dispatch from Chicago to the St. Louis *Democrat* in referring to Mrs. Lincoln's recent mortifying statements in regard to her financial condition, says:

> "Her conduct has greatly distressed her intimate friends and relatives in this city, and the most charitable construction that they can put upon her strange course is that she is insane, which I fear is the case."

The same explanation of her conduct, we understand, has been suggested by those who are acquainted with her in this place. Indeed an impression generally pervades our community that she has not been entirely in her right mind for several years. In this view, she deserves pity and commiseration instead of harsh and uncharitable judgment for her singular behavior.

Illinois State Journal, October 10, 1867, 1

Family friend and Lincoln estate executor David Davis called Mary's attempted clothing sale "an act of insanity" and when he confronted her about it he found that "she really had the insane delusion that poverty stared her in the face."[1] Mary's oldest son, Robert, agreed, as can be seen in a letter he wrote to his fiancée at the time.

ROBERT T. LINCOLN TO MARY HARLAN
Oct. 16, 1867

I suppose you have seen some of the papers so there is no need of detailing what I was told they were full of. I did not read them. The simple truth, which I cannot tell anyone not personally interested, is that my mother is on one subject not mentally responsible. I have supposed this for some time from various indications and now have no doubt of it. I have taken the advice of one or two of my friends in whom I trust most and they tell me I can do nothing. It is terribly irksome to sit still under all that has happened and say nothing, but it has to be done. The greatest misery of all is the fear of what may happen in the future. This is, of course, not to be foreseen and is what troubles me most. I have no doubt that a great many good and amiable people wonder why I do not take charge of her affairs and keep them straight but it is very hard to deal with one who is sane on all subjects but one. You could hardly believe it possible, but my mother protests to me that she is in actual want and nothing I can do or say will convince her to the contrary. Do you see that I am likely to have a good deal of trouble in the future, do what I can to prevent it.

> This original manuscript letter no longer exists,
> but is transcribed in Helm, *True Story of Mary*,
> 267–77, a book in which she was assisted with
> family materials by Robert Lincoln.

Mary's youngest son, Tad, died in 1871 at age seventeen from pleurisy. The loss of the third of her four children to another early death was difficult, although Mary handled it better than Robert expected.[2] Mary lived with Robert and his wife and daughter in their Chicago home for a few months after Tad passed. Then Mary and her daughter-in-law had a falling out and the widow left Chicago. After that she became a homeless wanderer, roaming around America visiting various health spas and spiritualist retreats. Robert hired a nurse to accompany his mother.

It was during this time that Mary's physical and emotional conditions deteriorated to a noticeable and worrisome level. "From that time [of Tad's death], Mrs. Lincoln, in the judgment of her most intimate friends, was never entirely responsible for her conduct. She was peculiar and eccentric, and had various hallucinations," later wrote family friend Isaac N. Arnold.[3] Mary's personal nurse stated the widow suffered from "periods of mild insanity" and "had strange delusions" in the years after Tad's death.[4] In 1873, Mary Lincoln began medical care from Chicago physician Willis Danforth, who later characterized her troubles as "fever and nervous derangement of the head."[5] And yet within these troubles, she was at times quite rational, as many of her letters, such as those to her friend Myra Bradwell, show.

MARY LINCOLN TO MYRA BRADWELL
May 6, 1874

My dear Mrs. Bradwell,

Your kind note from Mobile was received several days since and I would have sent you an earlier reply had it not been for quite a severe attack of illness and this is the first day I am out of bed for five days. Such terrible weather we have had! I am delighted that you are enjoying yourself so very much and trust that you will return to us with your health entirely restored. Today is lovely here and I am even anticipating the Dr.'s afternoon call with his sugar pellets and harmless draughts as a pleasant variety to the monotony of the day. Our good friend, Mrs. Swisshelm, has been confined to the house with severe quinzy and you may be sure that I am missing her greatly. Her quaint style is perfectly charming to me and such a relief to me from my *remembrance* of the artificial world, with which in former and *so much* happier days I was constantly surrounded. This note I fear will scarcely reach—ere you are leaving for C. [Chicago]

With a world of love, believe me, your devoted friend,

Mary Lincoln

Robert Todd Lincoln Family Papers

[MRS. LINCOLN: CONFINED TO HOUSE]
Chicago Inter Ocean, Oct. 15, 1874

Mrs. Abraham Lincoln, being confined to her house in this city by nervous exhaustion, will be unable to be in attendance at the ceremonies at Springfield today in honor of the memory of her distinguished husband. She has been confined to her room for the past five months by a severe illness, from which she is just now slowly recovering.

Chicago Inter Ocean, October 15, 1874, 4

MARY LINCOLN TO MYRA BRADWELL
St. Augustine, Fla., February 20, 1875

My dear Mrs. Bradwell,

Your kind letter was received some time since and although I have not replied to it, believe me truly that you are very frequently in my thoughts—and I, have so often wished we could be together in this "Sunny clime." I am now looking down upon a yard with its roses, white lilacs and other flowers. (Although it is raining and we have had a good deal of rain in its soft, dreamy, light fashion,) since the middle of January, I remained too much out, on my balcony, took a severe cold, had much inward and outward fever for three weeks and one day when it was raging at its height I told my nurse to pack up a small trunk and valise and we would leave town. So, on the 11th of Feb. we started for this place five hours distant from Jacksonville by boat and railway. On board the steamer I met three or four choice Philadelphia friends, ladies and gentlemen and they insisted on my joining them and instead of a modest journey of five hours to St. A. it proved four days and nights on the boat. If these *comme il faut* persons from the north generally and the most charming scenery on the celebrated Ochlawahs river could give pleasure, then it certainly was mine. Words would fail in description going from the broad St. John's into the narrow streams. With scenery such as is seldom met with in this world such pens as W. C. Bryant and others have given minute details of the voyage. Scribner's November monthly speaks of it and Harper dwells at great length upon it. How much we will have to say to each other when we meet. From this most unexpected excursion I came here. I have been here five days, three of which have been passed in bed. For you may be well assured that the fever in my veins, must run its course. But two bright days I have emerged from it wandering over this quaint and most interesting place. My first visit was of course to the ancient Fort* and my wondering head was in every prison nook until we came to the one whose entrance was excavated I believe, in 1835, where two iron cages were found, one, now said to be in the Smithsonian Institute in Wash. Hooked to the wall, where history records, and the Sergeant repeats, the story that two prisoners were enclosed in these same cages walled in, left to their fate, with God alone to be merciful to them! The prison of course is in darkness except the dim light held by the sergeant. I entered the fearful place and how I came out of it and how I have suffered in mind since our merciful Heavenly Father alone knows the wrongs of time will be redressed in a brighter world! My son writes me that the winter has been terribly cold and my good friend and your dear husband, how is he getting along and how is his health this winter? What would I not give to see you again. My pen *as you perceive,* refuses its office.

With much love to you and yours believe me, most
affectionately yours,
Mary Lincoln

Robert Todd Lincoln Family Papers

In early March 1875, while Mary Lincoln was wintering in Jacksonville, Florida, she suddenly became convinced that Robert, her last remaining son, was deathly ill, and she would not be persuaded otherwise. She sent a flurry of telegrams to her son and his law partner Edward Isham in Chicago, and got on the first train north. Robert, knowing her mental condition and concerned for her safety, had his mother observed during her journey.

MARY LINCOLN TO EDWARD ISHAM
Jacksonville, Fla., Mar. 12, 1875

My belief is my son is ill. Telegraph me at once without a moments delay of receipt of this. I start for Chicago when your message is received.
Mrs. A. Lincoln

---

* Castillo de San Marcos, later renamed Fort Marion.

MARY LINCOLN TO EDWARD ISHAM

Jacksonville, Fla., Mar. 12, 1875

My dearly beloved son Robert T. Lincoln rouse yourself and live for my sake all I have is yours from this hour. I am praying every moment for your life to be spared to your mother.

Mrs. A. Lincoln

Deliver tonight without fail.

J. J. S. WILSON, SUPT. TO STATION MANAGER

Jacksonville, Fla., undated

Please make inquiry and let it be strictly confidential if Mrs. Abraham Lincoln now at Jacksonville is in any trouble mentally or otherwise and advise me at once. Do not allow her under any circumstances to know of this and please give me prompt reply.

J. J. S. Wilson

**JOHN COYNE, MANAGER, TO J. J. S. WILSON,
FOR ROBERT T. LINCOLN**

Jacksonville, Fla., Mar. 12, 1875

I have tried every hotel and all the principal boarding houses and cannot find Mrs. Lincoln. She will call in the morning. When in the office this evening she appeared nervous and somewhat excited. Will telegraph you more definitely tomorrow.

John Coyne

MARY LINCOLN TO ROBERT LINCOLN

Jacksonville, Fla., Mar. 13, 1875

Start for Chicago this evening. Hope you are better today. You will have money on my arrival.

Mrs. Lincoln

JOHN COYNE, MANAGER, TO J. S. S. WILSON, SUPT.

Jacksonville, Fla., Mar. 13 1875

Mrs. Lincoln and nurse left this evening for Chicago. She will not be convinced that her son is not dangerously ill. Nurse thinks Mrs. L should be at home soon as possible.

John Coyne, manager

J. C. WILSON TO ROBERT LINCOLN
Indianapolis, Ind., Mar. 16, 1875

Left here via Kankakee twelve twenty five. Occupies parlor car.
J. C. Wilson

All telegrams from Folder 3, Box 1, Mary Todd
Lincoln Insanity File

Mary arrived in Chicago to find her son in perfect health. She stayed in the city and over the ensuing two months her mental condition deteriorated rapidly. Robert was so concerned that he consulted seven medical experts and three of his father's closest friends—David Davis, Leonard Swett, and John Todd Stuart—and, upon all their advice, he decided to commit his mother to an insane asylum.

ELIZABETH J. TODD GRIMSLEY BROWN
TO ROBERT LINCOLN
Mar. 16, 1875

My dear Robert,

Yours of the 15th received today. Regret to know that you have even anticipated trouble, and hope, with you, it may "blow over."[*] But if you feel that I, more than anyone else, can aid you, and you find you need me, I will hold myself in readiness to answer your summons promptly. I can imagine your fears and sympathize with you. Your request "confidential" shall be regarded.

As ever,
Your loving cousin
E. J. Brown

Folder 10, Box 2, Mary Todd Lincoln Insanity File

JOHN TODD STUART TO ROBERT LINCOLN
May 10, 1875

My dear cousin: I received your telegram of this day and answered that I could not meet you tomorrow. I have business engagement for the week which require me to remain at home. My wife's health had grown so much worse since Saturday that I ought not to leave her.

---

[*] Robert Lincoln's original letter, which Brown here quotes from, has not survived.

I have carefully examined your two letters, and the facts, which you detail, in connection with those coming under my observation and related to me while at Chicago leave no doubt of the propriety of the appointment of a conservator for your mother. I am not so sure about the necessity of *personal restraint* but is it not probable that if a conservator was appointed that she would consent to remain at some private hospital?

I have no doubt but that she is insane and Cousin Lizzie Brown expresses the same opinion. John Bunn's[*] information was derived through a lady boarding at the Pacific who attained her information through the servants at the Hotel. The same is true of Judge Edwards.

Yourself and mother both have my sincere sympathy in this great affliction but I think it best for both of you and for all friends that she should be treated as an insane person.

You can make whatever use of this letter you think proper.

Yours affectionately,

John T. Stuart

Folder 26, Box 2, Mary Todd Lincoln Insanity File

The Ayer & Kales law firm asked physicians Richard J. Patterson, Nathan Smith Davis, Ralph N. Isham, James Stewart Jewell, Hosmer Allen Johnson, and Charles Gilman Smith each to review Mary Lincoln's mental state. (At the suggestion of family friend and eminent attorney Leonard Swett, Robert Lincoln hired the Chicago firm to represent him.)

All six physicians wrote similar one-page responses to the Ayer and Kales consult/ questions: yes, Mary Lincoln is insane; yes, she needs confinement to an asylum. The only physician to elaborate further was Nathan Smith Davis.

NATHAN SMITH DAVIS TO AYER & KALES LAW FIRM
May 18, 1875

The character of her insanity is such that she may, at times, appear perfectly sane in ordinary conversation; and yet she is constantly subject to such mental hallucinations as to render her entirely unsafe if left to herself.

Folder 24, Box 2, Mary Todd Lincoln Insanity File

---

[*] Lincoln family friend and Springfield, Illinois, banker.

DAVID DAVIS TO LEONARD SWETT

Indianapolis, Ind., May 19, 1875

My Dear Swett,

Your communication of May 16th in relation to Mrs. Lincoln was received a few moments ago and I hasten to reply.

As you are aware, Robert, Mr. Stuart and I have had a protracted consultation on the subject. Your letter has in no wise changed the opinion which I entertained at the time of the consultation. On the contrary, the statement of the eminent physicians named by you, "that Mrs. Lincoln is insane and ought to be confined" has confirmed it. I believe her to be a fit subject for personal restraint and fear the consequences unless action is taken soon. Indeed, my fears are greatly increased by your statement that she now talks of leaving for California or Europe. A departure from Chicago at all, in her present condition would be very embarrassing, and it seems to me, should not be permitted. I trust that you may see your way clear to prevent it. If the physicians affirm in writing what they have verbally stated to you and Mr. Ayer, that Mrs. Lincoln is insane and ought to be confined, you would be justified in taking immediate action. If you and Mr. Ayer as lawyers, are satisfied there is evidence enough to warrant you in expecting a favorable verdict from a jury, then proceedings should be commenced at once. I am aware that an unfavorable verdict would be disastrous in the extreme, but this must be risked, if after maturely considering the subject your fixed opinion is that you ought to proceed. I do not see how Robert can get along at all, unless he has the authority to subject his mother to treatment. The appointment of a conservator, without the confinement, will not answer the purpose. It might do with persons of different temperament from Mrs. Lincoln, but with her it would not do at all. Like you I have been satisfied for years that her unsoundness of mind affords the proper explanation for all the vagaries she has developed.

You and I were devoted friends of her husband, and in this crisis it is our duty to give to Robert the support which he so much needs. [*crossed out: in the terrible ordeal through which he has passed*] And I doubt not that he will receive the support from his relatives in Springfield. I know that he has the support of Mr. Stuart. I do not see the propriety of waiting until the commission of some act which [would] arrest public attention. It may be that medical attention, in a retreat for insane persons, would operate favorably upon her. This chance should not be lost. After all the whole case turns on the sufficiency of the evidence to procure a favorable verdict. If you are satisfied on this point, believing as I do that Mrs. Lincoln is insane and should be placed under treatment, I see no other course than judicial action. Of course this is painful to us all and especially so to Robert, but like all other painful duties, it must be met and discharged. Thoughtful and right minded men will approve and under the circumstances, it is hoped newspapers will forbear to criticize.

Robert has my deepest sympathy in this terrible ordeal. That he may have strength given him to bear it, is my earnest prayer.

Although I do not wish anything I write to be published, yet I wish it distinctly understood that Robert has my support, and approval. I sincerely hope that Mr. Stuart will think it advisable to be with Robert during the trial.

Be pleased to let me know what is done.

Your friend,

David Davis

Folder 15, Box 2, Mary Todd Lincoln Insanity File

Chapter 2

Trial of 1875
Newspaper Reports

On May 19, 1875, former First Lady Mary Lincoln was tried in Cook County Court on the charge of insanity. Leonard Swett and B. F. Ayer—two of Chicago's most eminent attorneys—acted for Robert; Isaac N. Arnold, former congressman and a friend of Abraham Lincoln, represented Mary. Under the Illinois State insanity statute, a defendant (Mary) was not legally required to have an attorney, but Robert Lincoln and Leonard Swett procured one for her anyway. During the three-hour trial, eighteen witnesses testified against Mary Lincoln: physicians, shopkeepers, hotel employees, and her own son. The jury, comprising twelve of the most successful and respected men in the city—including one doctor and one congressman—took less than ten minutes to declare her guilty and fit for removal to an insane asylum.

"MRS. LINCOLN INSANE"
Chicago Post and Mail, May 19, 1875

The Ex-Hostess of the White House
Before the County Court

—————

Eminent Doctors Pronounce Her of Unsound Mind

—————

To the multitude of the American people who so loved Abraham Lincoln, it will come as a painful surprise that his widow, Mrs. Lincoln, has been sent to the insane asylum. But such is the fact, or is, at least, so ordered by the County Court. The growing fact that she was fast passing under a mental malady came to a direct issue in the County Court at 3 o'clock this afternoon.

At that time the veritable late hostess of the White House came into court leaning upon the arm of Mr. Samuel Turner, [manager] of the Grand Pacific [Hotel], where she has been boarding.

Twelve as eminent and capable men as the city affords were sworn as the jurors to sit in the inquisition. They were: L. J. Gage, S. M. Moore, C. B. Farwell, T. A. Moran, S. C. Blake, C. M. Henderson, H. C. Durand, S. B. Parkhurst, Wm. Stewart, D. R. Cameron, J. M. Adams, and Thomas Coggswell.

Mrs. Lincoln was dressed in plain black, took a chair and readily recognized Hon. I. N. Arnold, rose and shook hands with him, when he came near her, he having offered to appear for her.

Such care had been exercised in keeping the matter quiet that but few were present beyond jurors and witnesses.

By her side sat Robert Lincoln, who naturally feels great grief at the necessity of being compelled to do this thing.

B. F. Ayers and Leonard Swett appeared for the friends.

Dr. Willis Danforth testified that he was her physician as far back as 1873, when he thought she showed symptoms of insanity; she thought an Indian was pulling wires out of her head; she set the day when she said she was going to die. And he gave it as his professional opinion that the symptoms of insanity were increasing.

Mr. Ayers stated that it was the desire of the friends that she should be treated at some private hospital for the insane, and not sent to the State Asylum [as assumed in the statue].

Sam Turner testified that she had been at the Grand Pacific since March 15; had taken her meals in her room; had come one morning, April 1, to the office with uncombed hair and told him that everything was going wrong about the hotel; and the city was all on fire on the South Side; made him go with her to every room in the hotel having a "7" in its number in search of Mr. Shoemaker; she appeared very wild; it was the prevailing opinion about the hotel that she was very much deranged; that it was unsafe for her to be left there alone.

During the testimony Mrs. Lincoln gave direct but somewhat wild attention, yet said nothing.

Mrs. Allen, housekeeper of the Pacific, testified that she had slept in the room with Mrs. Lincoln for a few nights; that Mrs. Lincoln mixed together four or five different medicines; that she had made so many purchases that her closet, about four feet by ten feet, was piled so full of unopened packages that the door could be opened only a few inches. She did not think her of sane mind.

Mary Gavin [hotel maid] gave similar testimony.

There was still at 4 P.M., many witnesses, Drs. Isham and N. S. Davis among others, to be examined. But the doctors have examined her case in advance, and no doubt remains that she will be found insane by the jury and sent to some retreat for insane people.

Chicago Post and Mail, May 19, 1875, 1. Reprinted in
Illinois State Journal, May 21, 1875, 2.

Trial of Mrs. Abraham Lincoln for Insanity.

———

Why Her Relatives and Friends Were Driven to This Painful Course.

———

Testimony of Physicians as to Her Mental Unsoundness.

———

Hearing Strange Voices—Fears of Murder— Sickness of Her Son.

———

What Was Seen by the Employees of the Hotel.

———

Tradesmen Testify Concerning Her Purchases of Goods.

———

She is Found Insane, and Will Be Sent to Batavia.

———

Scenes in Court.

———

The death of President Lincoln was one of the nation's saddest misfortunes,—a misfortune that it has not yet outlived. The fact that he had fallen by the hand of the assassin only tended to intensify the public grief, and to add to the gloom which settled upon the popular heart. From North, South, East, and West, the popular wail of regret came up, and a distracted country was united in sympathy at the great calamity. Even from across the waters, where he was known only as President, and not as the type of the American citizen, came expressions of the deepest sadness. In the general grief, regret, and humiliation, his native State, Illinois, and the great City of Chicago, which had ever been proud to honor him, were foremost. But to none was the calamity so painful, and upon none were its traces so continuous and marked, as his immediate family and intimate personal friends. The nation put on the garb of mourning, to be worn off by time or effaced by the rapid succession of great national events; but the hearts of his family were pierced, deeply and eternally. Especially was this true with

HIS WIDOW

and eldest son, the former of whom, at the time, it was feared, would lose her mind. In fact, the effect was visible in her subsequent life and conduct, which time seemed to heighten and increase. The death of a son[*] was one of the inflictions which her

———

[*] Tad Lincoln in 1871.

mind, then failing, was soon called upon to endure. Travel, change of scenes and associations, the best of medical care, all failed to arrest the premonitions of a failing mind. The lavish affection of her children, and the consolation of friends, and the nation's sympathy, failed to arrest the symptoms of insanity or to lighten her mind of the immense burden it was tottering beneath. She continued to decline, not only in vigor of mind, but in physical condition, nothing seeming to avail her in her grief and declining years.

So feeble had become the state of her mind, and as a consequence so eccentric her nature, and habits of life, that, Saturday last

A COUNCIL OF THE LEADING PHYSICIANS

of the city and her personal friends was held to consider what was best to be done for her. She was stopping at the Grand Pacific Hotel, and from the uncertainty of her demeanor it was felt that something was necessary to be done to protect her life from her own hands, and to secure her from bodily harm.

The result of the council was an agreement to petition Judge Wallace, of the county court, to make an order of warrant and venire to try the question of her sanity. The warrant was accordingly issued yesterday, when

A JURY

composed of Dr. S. C. Blake, C. B. Farwell, C. M. Henderson, S. M. Moore, L. J. Gage, H. C. Durand, S. B. Parkhurst, William Stewart, D. R. Cameron, J. A. Mason, J. McGregor Adams, and Thomas Coggswell, was impaneled for the sad trial, and Mrs. Mary Lincoln was

BROUGHT INTO COURT.

The unfortunate lady entered the court-room scarcely observed, and certainly without her sad mission being known, except by the friends who accompanied her, and the large number of witnesses who had been summoned. The lady was pallid, her eye was watery and excited, and her general appearance that of one suffering from nervous excitement. She was attired in a plain black suit, and was neat and comely of appearance. In the party accompanying her was her son, whose every feature was marked with sadness. His eyes, too, were suffused with tears, as were also those of several of the party. The persons entering the court-room had more the appearance of a funeral procession than anything else, and their appearance was the signal for a breathless silence among the few in the room at the time.

IN COURT.

She took a seat facing his Honor, and by her side sat her counselor and friend, and the biographer of her husband, the Hon. I. N. Arnold. The petitioner, her son, Robert T. Lincoln, took a seat near her and obliquely to her left. Beside him sat the Hon. Leonard Swett and B. F. Ayer, counsel for the petitioner, while in front of them and on the west side of the room were seated the jurors who were to pass upon one of the most important and regretful cases ever presented to a court.

The news of the case soon flashed through the building and the streets, and when the first witness was called the room was densely packed with the wondering and sympathizing populace.

DR. WILLIS DANFORTH

was the first witness called: He knew Mrs. Lincoln, and in November 1873, visited her professionally. He treated her several weeks for fever and nervous derangement of the head, and observed at the time indications of mental disturbance. She had strange imaginings; thought that someone was at work at her head, and that an Indian was removing the bones from her face and pulling wires out of her eyes. He visited her again in September, 1874, when she was suffering from debility of the nervous system. She complained that someone was taking steel springs from her head, and would not let her rest; that she was going to die within a few days, and that she had been admonished to that effect by her husband. She imagined that she heard raps on a table conveying the time of her death, and would sit and ask questions and repeat the supposed answer the table would give. He expressed a doubt of the reliability of her answers, and she would make what she termed a final test by putting the question in a goblet on the table. The goblet was found to be cracked, and that circumstance she regarded as a corroboration of the raps. Her derangement was not dependent on the condition of her body, or arising from physical disease. He called upon her a week ago at the Grand Pacific Hotel, when she spoke of her stay in Florida, of the pleasant time she had there, of the scenery, and the manners and customs of the Southern people. She appeared at the time to be in excellent health, and her former hallucinations appeared to have passed away. She said her reason for returning from Florida was that she was not well. She startled him somewhat by saying an attempt had been made to poison her on her journey back. She had been very thirsty, and at a wayside station not far from Jacksonville she took a cup of coffee in which, she discovered poison. She said she drank it, and took a second cup, that the overdose of poison might cause her to vomit. He did not see any traces of her having taken any poison, and was of opinion that she was insane. On general topics, her conversation was rational.

SAMUEL M. TURNER,

manager of the Grand Pacific Hotel, was the next witness: Mrs. Lincoln arrived at his hotel March 15. The 1st of April she visited him at the hotel office, and had a shawl wrapped about her head. She asked him to go into the reception-room with her, as she had something to say to him. She said something was wrong about the house, as she heard strange sounds in the rooms. He went with her, and, when about to leave her, she said she was afraid to be left alone. He left her in charge of some female help. And told her he would return in a few minutes. He had scarcely reached the office when a messenger told him that Mrs. Lincoln was at the elevator and wanted to see him. She said there had been a strange man in the corridor, and that he was going to molest her. He went up in the elevator and walked with her through the house, and did not see any strange man; she was greatly excited, and desired to go to some of the lady-boarders' rooms that she might be safe. He showed her to Mrs. Dodge's room, who at the time was at dinner, promising that he would return soon. He was again summoned by her, when her appearance was wild and her fears were repeated. He believed her deranged. No one had called to see her since her arrival except her son. He did not regard it as safe to leave her alone.

MRS. ALLEN,

housekeeper at the hotel, testified that Mrs. Lincoln seemed to suffer from nervous excitement. She imagined that a small window in her room boded ill, and used to say that the window disturbed her. She walked her room most of the night. Witness had slept with her two nights at her request. Last Wednesday Mrs. Lincoln was very much excited. She mixed several kinds of medicine together and took the mixture. She had a large closet filled with unopened packages she had purchased. She considered her insane, and that she ought to be placed somewhere for treatment and care.

MAGGIE GAVIN,

employed at the hotel, testified that she had had the care of Mrs. Lincoln's room, and heard her complain frequently that people were speaking to her through the wall. She was most anxious about her son, and sometimes called her attention to voices she heard through the floor. She complained that a man had taken her pocketbook, but witness found it in the bureau drawer. She at times called witness to the window, and, pointing to the smoke from an adjacent chimney, would declare that the city was burning down. Lately Mrs. Lincoln bought several new trunks and a number of packages of goods, which she never opened. Upon one occasion Mrs. Lincoln left her room and went to her son's room, saying she was afraid to remain there, having on her night-dress. Witness considered her of unsound mind.

JOHN FITZHENRY,

second waiter at the Grand Pacific, testified that April 1 he went to Mrs. Lincoln's room, at her request. He found her carelessly dressed and excited. She asked him to call the tallest man in the dining room to her and she exclaimed several times, "I am afraid! I am afraid!" Mr. Turner, to whom she alluded, subsequently saw her.

CHARLES DODGE,

cashier of the hotel, corroborated Fitzhenry's statement as to her excited and nervous condition, and added that she said some one, a stranger, had been in her room, and that she was afraid of being molested.

MR. SEATON,

Agent of the United States Express Company, testified that one day in April he sent eleven trunks to Milwaukee for Mrs. Lincoln. She told him she was going to spend her summer in Wisconsin. Her manner was very strange.

DR. ISHAM

testified that on the 12th of March he received a telegram from Mrs. Lincoln, from Jacksonville, Fla., as follows: "My belief is my son is sick. Telegraph. I start for Chicago tomorrow." Her son was perfectly well at the time, and witness so telegraphed her. Mr. Lincoln also telegraphed to her, telling her to remain in Florida until perfectly well. He received a second telegram after a lapse of an hour and a half. It read, "My dearly beloved son, Robert T. Lincoln; rouse yourself, and live for your mother. You are all I have; from this hour all I have is yours. I pray every night that you may be spared to your mother."

ROBERT T. LINCOLN,

the petitioner, then took the witness stand. His face indicated the unpleasantness of the duty he was about to perform and his eyes were expressive of the grief he felt. Mrs. Lincoln at first looked on calmly, but during the recital of the incidents of the family history and reference to the death of his father and brother, she gave way to tears and buried her face in her hands.

He testified that he did not know why his mother thought he was sick, unless she had read some newspaper paragraph to that effect. He had not been sick in ten years. The action he had taken was sad to contemplate, but he had done it in the interest of his mother. He did not want any money from her. He had money in trust for her. He met her in the car upon her arrival from the South, and upon meeting her she was startled. She had the appearance of good health, and did not even seem fatigued by the trip. He asked her to come to his house, but she declined, and went to the hotel. He went with her and took supper. She told him that at the first breakfast she took after leaving Jacksonville an attempt was made to poison her. He occupied a room adjoining hers that night. She slept well that night, but subsequently was restless, and would come to his door in her night-dress and rap. Twice in one night she aroused him, and asked to sleep in his room. He admitted her, gave her his bed, and he slept on the lounge. He got Dr. Isham to attend her. About April 1 she ceased tapping at his door, he having told her that if she persisted he would leave the hotel. He went to her room April 1, and found her but slightly dressed. She left the room in that condition under some pretext, and the next he knew of her she was going down in the elevator to the office. He had the elevator stopped, and tried to induce her to return to her room. She regarded his interference as impertinent, and declined to leave the elevator, but he put his arms about her and gently forced her. She screamed, "You are going to murder me." After a while she said that the man who took her pocketbook had promised to return it at a certain hour. He said the man was a wandering Jew she had met in Florida. She then took a seat near the wall, and professed to be repeating what the man was saying to her through he wall. She had, since the fire, kept her trunks and property in the Fidelity Safe Deposit Company's building. He called on her the last week in April, and she told him that all Chicago was going to be burned, and that she was going to send her trunks to some country town. She said Milwaukee was too near Oshkosh, where there had been a terrible fire the night before. She told him that his home was going to be the only one saved, and he suggested to her to leave her trunks with him. The following Sunday she showed him securities for $57,000 which she carried in her pocket. She had spent large sums of money recently. She had bought $600 worth of lace curtains; three watches, costing $450; $700 worth of other jewelry; $200 worth of soaps and perfumeries, and a whole piece of silk. He had no doubt she was insane. He had had a conference with her cousin and Mayor Stuart, of Springfield, and Judge Davis, of the Supreme Court, all of whom advised him to take the course he had taken. He did not regard it as safe to allow her to remain longer unrestrained. She had long been a source of great anxiety. He had had a man watching her for the last three weeks, whose sole duty it had been to look after her when she went out on the street. She had no home, and did not visit his house because of a misunderstanding with his wife. She had always been kind to him. She had been of unsound mind since the death of her husband, and had been irresponsible for the last ten years. He regarded her as eccentric and unmanageable. There was no cause for her recent purchases, as her trunks were filled with dresses she never wore. She never wore jewelry.

MR. ALBERTSON,

salesman for Matson & Co., jewelers, was the next witness. He knew Mrs. Lincoln. She had come to the store and made expensive and reckless purchases, and acted in a queer way generally.

J. B. STONE,

salesman with Allen & Mackey, testified that he sold her $300 worth of lace curtains. He did not think she knew what she was doing at the time, but he sold her the goods as a matter of business, without passing upon her sanity or insanity.

DR. N. S. DAVIS

testified that Mrs. Lincoln had no symptoms of epilepsy, but he did not regard her safe to be left alone. He had visited her professionally years ago, but saw nothing in her to indicate unsoundness of mind. She was eccentric and suffered from nervousness.

W. H.WOOSTER,

doing business on Wabash avenue, said he knew Mrs. Lincoln. She had called to purchase watches and spectacles of him. She contracted a bill of $300, but the goods were taken to her son before delivering them, and he ordered them returned.

J. S. TOWNSEND,

of a jewelry firm, and E. T. Moulton, of a dry-goods house, testified to having similar dealings with Mrs. Lincoln, and they regarded her as insane.

T. C. MATTOCK,

under The Tribune Building, testified to a long list of dealings with Mrs. Lincoln, and to selling her several trunks. He regarded her as insane, and her manners were eccentric and excited.

DR. JOHNSON

testified that he knew Mrs. Lincoln, and that from the evidence heard was satisfied that she was deranged. He did not regard her as in condition to be left alone, and thought she ought to be put in a private asylum.

DR. SMITH

had listened to the evidence, and seeing that her actions had been without proper motives, was of opinion that her mind was not sound. On cross-examination he stated that, if she was not of sound mind, he attributed it to the events in her recent history.

Robert T. Lincoln was recalled, and testified that insanity was not hereditary in her family, and that she was 56 years of age.

Mr. Swett then spoke to the jury of the sadness of the case and the necessity of Mrs. Lincoln being cared for, after which the jury retired.

DURING THE ABSENCE OF THE JURY,

Robert T. Lincoln approached his mother and extended his hand. She grasped it fondly, remarking with a degree of emphasis, "Robert, I did not think you would do this." His response was stifled by the spring of tears, and the conversation ended. She was next approached by Mr. Swett, who tried to persuade her that it was for her good that the action had been taken. She could not be persuaded to believe what was said, however, but replied with promptness that she would try to endure her persecutions.

THE VERDICT.

The jury had been absent but a few minutes, when it returned with the following verdict:

> We, the undersigned, jurors in the case of Mary Lincoln, alleged to be insane, having heard the evidence in the case, are satisfied that the said Mary Lincoln is insane, and is a fit person to be sent to a State Hospital for the Insane; that she is a resident of the State of Illinois and County of Cook; that her age is 56 years; that the disease is of unknown duration, and is not with her hereditary; that she is not subject to epilepsy; that she does not manifest homicidal or suicidal tendencies, and that she is not a pauper.

The verdict was received by Mrs. Lincoln without any visible emotions. She was stolid and unmoved, and did not allow its reading to interrupt the conversation in which she was engaged with Mr. Arnold.

Immediately after the verdict was announced the courtroom was deserted. Mr. Swett obtained an order of the Court for her delivery to the proper officer, who served the necessary papers upon her and furnished her with duplicates.

A CONSULTATION

of her friends was then had, when it was agreed that she should be committed to the care of the Bellevue Place, Batavia, Ill., superintended by Dr. R. J. Patterson.

Subsequently she was placed in a carriage and taken to the Grand Pacific Hotel to remain over night under proper guards. This morning she will be taken by the authorities to Batavia.

About 11:30 o'clock last night it was found necessary to send for an officer to watch over Mrs. Lincoln, whose lunatic symptoms became quite violent. Station-Keeper Rickey, at Police Headquarters, sent to the Armory, and a policeman was detailed to attend to the unfortunate lady.

Chicago Tribune, Thursday, May 20, 1875, 1

"A SAD REVELATION"
Chicago Times, May 20, 1875

Mrs. Mary Lincoln, the Widow of the Late President, Adjudged Insane.

———

At Last the Strange Freaks of the Past Ten Years Are Understood.

———

And the Unfriendly Criticism Will Change to Heartfelt Commiseration.

———

The Poor Lady a Victim to Many Strange and Startling Hallucinations.

———

Walls Had Voices, Indian Troubled Her Scalp, and She Had a Mania for Shopping.

———

A Sorrowful Spectacle in Court.

———

The conduct of the widow of the lamented Abraham Lincoln has been criticized by many people since the death of her husband. Some have accused her of serious indiscretion, while some have pitied her and pronounced her actions the result of mental weakness. She has certainly been credited with some extraordinary freaks of conduct within the past ten years, as was averred yesterday, by a score of her friends and acquaintances. Her eccentricities have frequently been the subject of comment, and her methods have been anxiously studied by members of her family, as well as by life-long friends of President Lincoln, who have ever been interested in the welfare of his relict; and it has become a matter of serious consideration with them as to its cause. Gradually the terrible truth has dawned upon their minds that her reason has become partially dethroned. Those who have known her intimately knew her to be of a very excitable nature, and since the assassination of her husband they have observed peculiar traits in her character which they never noticed before. The first thing that attracted the attention of the public was

THE VOLUNTARY DISPLAY BY HER OF
HER MATCHLESS WARDROBE,

for the purpose of gain. This was criticized by the people as being an act unworthy the widow of our nation's martyr, and cries of shame were suppressed within many a patriot's bosom. The action on her part years ago, and soon after the death of Mr. Lincoln, will be viewed in an entirely different light now by the people who read THE TIMES this morning an account of the terrible misfortune which has overtaken her and her family. All her former actions are now explained, with the motive which prompted them, and the public will pity the poor woman who has lived alone, almost entirely apart from her near relatives and friends for so long a time, universal sympathy will take the place of censure, for her actions will be understood now.

A WOMAN OF WEAK NATURE.

Mrs. Lincoln has ever been considered a woman of strong nature, and, being so closely connected with a man of noble purposes and sound judgment, the contrast was the more striking. It has been mistrusted by her near friends and relatives that she has been the victim of mental aberration, and they have studiously avoided making the discovery public, but have striven to conceal the fact, in the hope that she would eventually recover. In this, however, they have been sadly disappointed, and yesterday disclosed the secret to the people of the nation, who will this morning again mourn the cowardly assassination of the beloved president.

At 2 o'clock

YESTERDAY AFTERNOON,

a large concourse of people assembled in the county courtroom. Among them were observed some of the most prominent citizens of Chicago—lawyers, judges, merchants, and capitalists; men who are seldom seen in places of this kind, to the neglect of their business, unless something of more than usual importance is to occur. An air of mystery pervaded the place, and nobody had anything to say except in whispers and in confidence. All appeared to be waiting for an event which was anticipated, though exactly what that event was to be, was seemingly known only to a few. The reporters were eyed uneasily, and they were as much in the dark as anyone. The judges and lawyers passed silently and solemnly about the room, from one to another, and held whispered consultations, as though arrangements were being made for a funeral or a critical operation which would involve the life or death of a human being. A double row of chairs were placed against the west end of the courtroom, and twelve solid men took seats in them. It was evident a jury trial of no little moment was about to take place.

At length the solemn arrangements were completed, the door was opened, the crowd parted from left to right, and in walked no less a personage than

MRS. ABRAHAM LINCOLN,

accompanied by Mr. S. M. Turner, of the Grand Pacific hotel, and one or two others. She was assigned a chair at the end of one of the tables, near the outer railing, and facing the court. She was attired in the deepest mourning, and wore a long veil of black crepe, thrown over her left shoulder and to one side of her face, which looked pale and perplexed. Her son, Robert Lincoln, entered almost immediately, in company with Hon. Isaac N. Arnold, who was retained, at the request of Mrs. Lincoln, as her counsel. Robert advanced and shook the hand of his mother cordially, after which he presented his father's old friend, Mr. Arnold. The latter took a seat to the right and in near proximity to her, while her son occupied a chair at her left hand.

All being in readiness, the bailiff announced that the trial on hand was for the purpose of testing the sanity of Mrs. Mary Lincoln, and by the direction of the court proceeded to call the roll of

THE JURORS.

All answered to their names twice, as follows: Dr. S. C. Blake, Hon. C. B. Farwell, C. M. Henderson, S. M. Moore, L. J. Gage, H. C. Durand, S. B. Parkhurst, Wm. Stewart, D. R. Cameron, J. A. Mason, J. McGregor Adams, and Thomas Cogswell.

Hon. I. N. Arnold announced himself attorney for the defense, and B. F. Ayer conducted the examination of witnesses. Hon. Leonard Swett was also present, and took part in the proceedings. The testimony of the witnesses was unanimously to the effect that Mrs. Lincoln had been subject to actions such as no person of sound mind would ever exhibit. Some of the testimony was of the most startling nature, and served to show a great degree of forbearance and patience on the part of her son and her friends. From the nature of the portion of

THE EVIDENCE,

Mrs. Lincoln is believed to have been for a number of years a confirmed Spiritualist, and a part of her faith seems to have been that the departed spirit of her dead husband was constantly hovering near her. Directing her movements and counseling with her upon every subject of possible interest to her. It appears that she even went so far as to make preparations for her death, which she firmly believed would occur on the 6th of September last. She seems to have had no appreciation of money, in one sense, though she was declared by all the witnesses to be fond of driving what she considered "a good bargain." She has evinced

A MANIA FOR SHOPPING,

and has accumulated a large amount of valuable goods, which, however, did not appear to have been selected with a view of benefiting herself. She would purchase the most expensive and absurd articles of toilet and household goods, such as she might never anticipate deriving any benefit from. Her insanity has assumed a variety of shapes, and while she has invested thousands of dollars of her income in frivolous and fantastic ornaments, she has not exhibited any startling manifestations of them in the way of personal decoration. In the closet of her room, at the Grand Pacific, it is reported there are hundreds of packages intact, as they came from the stores, that have never been opened.

THIS COLLECTION

embraces a great variety of articles—remnants of silk, dress patterns, jewelry, lace curtains, etc., too numerous to mention. She is said to have $57,000 in government securities, which, until a short time ago, were deposited for safekeeping in the Fidelity Savings bank. Here another phase of her aberration is illustrated. She has labored under the hallucination that the city of Chicago was going to be subjected to another conflagration, and several times she has imagined that it was already on fire. With this fear upon her, she went to the bank and drew out her bonds, together with some dozen trunks of clothing which were also deposited there. The former she carried about with her for some time in the pocket of her dress, and the latter

SHE SENT TO MILWAUKEE,

to await her orders. They are still in the hands of the American Express company at that place. The bonds are also believed to be still in her possession. According to the testimony of her son, Robert, she sold one of the $1,000 bonds a short time ago in order to obtain ready money. She draws, besides her own revenues, a pension of $3,000 annually from the government for her support.

Another feature of her derangement was exhibited in a constant fear which seemed to possess her that she was about to be subjected to personal injury, and that

HER LIFE WAS IN DANGER;

that she was being poisoned by rebels, and fears of every description; that an Indian spirit was at times working upon her head, raising her scalp and taking wires from her head, steel springs from her jaws, and loosening the bones of her face.

During the trial the poor lady sat quietly in her chair, looking at the witnesses who were swearing away her liberty, with a steadfast gaze, intermingled with a certain wildness of expression in her keen dark eyes which contrasted painfully with her pallid features. Occasionally, as a witness was giving his testimony, she would turn her head toward her counsel, and seem to protest against the assertions being made, and several times her voice was heard in low but vehement denunciation of the proceedings. Particularly was this the case during the testimony of Robert. Almost perfect silence reigned in the courtroom, and the audience listened, with breathless interest.

The first witness called was

DR. WILLIS DANFORTH,

who testified substantially as follows: He had been called to attend Mrs. Lincoln first while she was residing upon Wabash avenue; had treated her for nervous derangement and fever in her head; had noticed peculiar symptoms in the patient, and he thought indications of derangement; she seemed possessed with the idea that someone was working on her head, taking wires out of her eyes (particularly the left one), at times taking bones out of her cheeks and face, and detaching steel springs from her jawbones; she imagined the fiend at work in this manner to be an Indian spirit; this was the prominent hallucination to which she was subject; at other times she imagined her scalp was being lifted by the same invisible power and being placed back again, the spirit in the meantime accompanying the ghastly work with hideous yells; she did not often experience pains, but at times was sensitive of a cutting sensation; this continued for some time. Witness first attended the patient in 1873; he attributed the disturbances in her head to ailments of her body, and the disturbances of her mental system; he at length discontinued his visits, the patient having improved in health, and did not see her again for several weeks; saw her again in March 1874; continued to visit her up to September, most of the time daily; he still noticed the disturbances in her head, and a general indisposition and debility appeared to pervade her system—the same condition of affairs which he had noticed in his first visits, cutting, scraping, and removing bones from her face and wires from her eyes; noticed no other vagaries at that time, except that she thought she was going to die at one time, and that she had been admonished by her husband of the time she was to pass away; she fixed the time on the 6th of September last; the last interview the witness had with the patient was at the Grand Pacific, when she returned from Florida this spring; she told him she had been very sick on her trip home; had a hallucination that she had been poisoned with coffee; she said she drank two cups, and believed by this means she received an overdose, and vomited it up. This witness believed Mrs. Lincoln to be insane, and a fit subject for an asylum.

MR. S. M. TURNER

manager at the Grand Pacific Hotel, was next called and sworn, and testified that he was acquainted with the patient; she came to the hotel on the 15th of March last; she appeared perfectly well at the time; she expressed great anxiety as to her son's health; witness never noticed anything peculiar about her except one day; she had meals sent up to her room; she always did this; had made this arrangement when she first came to the house; she had requested that some of the servants be allowed to sleep in the room with her, as she was nervous and excitable; her request was granted; on the morning of April 1 the bell from her room rang violently; a colored boy was sent up, but she met him at her door and returned with him to the office; she appeared with a shawl over her head and carelessly dressed; she requested witness to go into the reception room with her, as she had something important to communicate to him; he went with her, and she remarked that there was something strange going on; that the whole South side was ablaze, and was being burned up; she requested witness to return with her to her room, when he arrived at the door, she requested him to come in, and to sit down, which he did; she said she had received strange communications from a man who talked through the wall to her; he had told her that a man by the name of Shoemaker had sent a card to her, and requested her to meet him in room 137; she desired witness to go with her to the room; witness told her that there was no such room in the house; she insisted upon going to the room, and witness accompanied her; there was nobody there; she then wished to go to No. 127, 107, and lastly to room 27, which was a parlor; still she did not find the person who was looking for [her]; she went back to her own room, but could not get over the hallucination; she did not want witness to leave her alone, as she was afraid; he left a servant with her and returned to the office, promising to return again in 15 minutes; he had not been gone five minutes when she again appeared at the office; she appeared nervous and excited, and insisted upon his going to the reception room again with her; she wanted to see Mr. Shoemaker who she said had sent her his card; she said something was wrong; she believed the hotel was going to burn down; she wanted to go to some lady's room, where she would be safe; witness took her to the room of Mrs. Gen. Dodge, but that lady was at breakfast in the ladies' ordinary; Mrs. Lincoln was afraid to stay alone; and witness escorted her back again to her own room and left a servant with her; witness went up the third time to pacify her; that was the last time he heard from her that day; the next day he heard she was much better; her appearance was at times very strange; she was in the habit of going out shopping once or twice a day; sometimes she walked and sometimes she would ride; it was seldom any friends called to see her; the prevailing impression in the house was that it was not safe for her to remain there alone.

Question by Arnold—Did Mrs. Lincoln look as though she had any fever? Was she flushed?

A. No her face was white as it is today. There was more an expression of fear than anything else about her—a fear of personal violence.

MRS. HARRINGTON.

The next witness sworn was Mrs. Harrington, housekeeper at the Grand Pacific. She testified that she had known Mrs. Lincoln since early in the spring; had never seen her except when she was sent for; her manner was nervous and excitable; she was not like ladies in general; first, the small window in the washroom disturbed her very much; she had one of the servants in the room with her; she expressed a constant anxiety about her son; she feared the malaria and its effect upon him; she had one of the chambermaids stay with her in her room two or three weeks; then she wanted witness to stay with her and occupy same bed with her; witness did so; she was very strange; she would take medication from several bottles left with her by Dr. Isham, mix it all together, and take it; the 1st of April she went to the office after Mr. Turner; she had been wild and nervous ever since she had been there; witness did not know of any purchases in particular which Mrs. Lincoln had made, but her closet was piled full of packages, which were unopened, just as they came from the stores; her manner never seemed rational; she was full of strange actions; witness never had much conversation with her; considered it unsafe for her to be alone at the hotel.

Mrs. Lincoln here asked whether it was allowable for witnesses to express an opinion as to the sanity of the subject. The court decided that it was, provided they confined their opinions to their own observations.

MARY GAVIN,

the servant who occupied the room with Mrs. Lincoln, being sworn, testified that the patient was always imagining that she heard noise through the walls and the floors, and that all was not well with her son; at one time she thought she heard voices through the walls and the floor all day, and she would stand in a particular place and hold conversation with an imaginary person; she thought her pocketbook had been stolen from her, and the voice told her it would be returned to her at 3 o'clock that afternoon; then again she thought some foe was about to take her life; that it was not safe for her to remain in the hotel, and she was afraid to go to her own room as the city was burning up; she was out shopping at least once a day and sometimes twice; there was a large number of packages in the closet; witness did not know what they contained; had stayed with her four weeks; Mrs. Lincoln frequently called her up during the night; did not want to be alone at all; she went across the hall to her son's room one night; witness thought she was not in her right mind; she was restless during the fore part of the night, but slept toward morning; she kept the gas burning all night.

JOHN BESSINGER

being sworn, testified that he was second waiter in the Grand Pacific hotel; he was sent for by Mrs. Lincoln one morning; went upstairs and saw her standing in her door; she said she wanted to see the tallest man in the dining room; said she would go down on the elevator, and said, "I'm afraid! I'm afraid!" She went down to the dining room door, and witness went in and called Mr. Dodge.

MR. DODGE

cashier at the Grand Pacific, stated that a lady came to the door of the dining room one morning, and said she wanted to see the largest man in the room; he went to her; she wanted him to go up the elevator with her to her room; when she got to the elevator she wanted to see Mr. Turner; she wanted somebody to go with her to her room, as she was afraid; her manner appeared very much excited.

MR. SEATON,

agent for the American Express company, testified that the patient called on the 28th of April at the office, and wanted somebody to go to the Grand Pacific hotel and get some trunks which she wanted to send up to Milwaukee; she asked if there could not be some arrangement made by which she could have them stored there until she had settled upon some place in Wisconsin where she would spend the summer; witness told her she could; he noticed nothing remarkable in her behavior; he got into the carriage with her and they drove to the hotel; noticed a number of parcels and packages in the carriage; then she began to act strangely and appeared excited; witness thought the trunks were at Milwaukee yet; there were 11 trunks.

EDWARD ISHAM

testified that he was a law partner with Robert Lincoln; had been with him about two years; about the 12th of last March he received a telegram from Mrs. Lincoln from Jacksonville, Fla., as follows:

To Edward Isham, 554 Wabash avenue: I am persuaded that my son is ill. Telegraph me without delay. I leave for Chicago as soon as I receive your telegram.

Witness went to Robert's house and the two went to the telegraph office and telegraphed to her that she had a wrong impression; that her son was well; witness received several more telegrams of a similar nature form her, one of which, although addressed to him, read as though addressed to her son: "My dearly beloved son; rouse yourself and live for my sake. From this moment all I have is yours. Live for your mother. Deliver without fail." Tracing dispatches were sent by Robert and witness and manager of the telegraph office to managers of the telegraph offices at Jacksonville, and to intermediate points between that city and Chicago, so that Robert was kept advised of her whereabouts from the time she started for home until her arrival in this city; another dispatch was received by witness, which read as follows:

I start for Chicago tonight. You shall have money as soon as I arrive.

ROBERT LINCOLN

Being sworn, corroborated the statements of the preceding witness; had no idea what caused the excitement in Florida unless it was mental aberration; did not know that she had seen a paragraph in one of the papers; witness never needed any money of her; on the contrary he had some of her money; she sent a letter to him for money, and he sent her $375; he met her at the depot when she came home; she seemed somewhat startled at seeing him; witness gathered his hands full of her bags and requested her to come with him to the carriage; she had been on the road 72 hours, and was very tired; he wanted her to go to his house, but she refused, saying she was going to the Grand Pacific; she acted strangely; she said some rebel had poisoned her the morning after she started; also requested witness to occupy a room at the Grand Pacific as her guest, which offer he accepted, his wife being absent from the city; every night she came to his door in her night dress and knocked; witness would get up and go to the door and tell her to go back; witness told her after a while that if she did not stop such proceedings he should leave the hotel; one night she came to his room and he let her in; she wanted to sleep in his room the rest of the night; he allowed her to sleep in his bed and he laid down upon the sofa; one morning witness came up to the hotel to see his mother, being somewhat anxious about her; he met her in the hall, and she was determined to go down in the elevator; she was carelessly dressed; he told her he wished to borrow some money from her, as an excuse to detain her in her room; she said she wanted to see Mr. Turner first, and then she would see him; witness turned about, and when he looked for her again she was going down in the elevator; he went to the door and called the elevator back again; he tried to persuade her to return to her room, but she refused; witness then compelled her to return by force; she was afraid witness was going to kill her then, and screamed for help; she did not want Maggie Gavin to leave her; she said she expected her pocketbook back at 3 o'clock; witness asked where it was, and she said the man who had been talking to her through the wall had got it, and would bring it back at 3 o'clock; witness told her she ought to know she was out of her head.

Mr. Albertson, salesman with Matson & Co., jewelers; James P. Stone, with Allen & Mackey, carpet and lace curtain dealers; Mr. Dropp, with Mayo; T. C. Matley, with Haskel Bros., trunks; Mr. Morton, dry goods; testified to Mrs. Lincoln having made heavy purchases of them, and Drs. N. S. Davis, Isham, Johnson, and Smith testified as to their opinions regarding her mental aberration.

Hon. Leonard Swett then made a short address to the jury, in which he explained the nature of the case, and the motives which prompted the action.

Following is the verdict of the jury:

We, the undersigned, jurors in the case of Mary Lincoln, alleged to be insane, having heard the evidence in the case, are satisfied that the said Mary Lincoln is insane, and is a fit person to be sent to a State Hospital for the Insane; that she is a resident of the state of Illinois and the county of Cook; that her age is 56 years; that the disease is of unknown duration, that the cause is unknown; that the disease is not hereditary; that she is not subject to epilepsy; that she does not manifest homicidal or suicidal tendencies, and that she is not a pauper.

The afflicted woman was removed to her room at the Grand Pacific, where she was placed under the charge of Dr. Patterson. This morning she will be taken to Batavia, at which place Dr. Patterson has a private institution located for the treatment of this unfortunate class, and where she will receive every attention that filial affection can suggest.

Chicago Times, Thursday, May 20, 1875, 2[*]

"MRS. LINCOLN"
Chicago Inter Ocean, May 20, 1875

The Widow of the Martyred President Adjudged Insane in the County Court.

———

One of the Saddest Spectacles Ever Witnessed in a Courtroom in This City.

———

Eminent Medical Men Pronounce Her to Be of Unsound Mind and Incapable of Self-Care.

———

The Dread Affliction Owes Its Origin to the Assassination of the Lamented President.

———

She Will be Removed Today to a Private Asylum at Batavia, Ill.

———

A case of sad interest to the nation at large suddenly broke in upon the monotonous routine of the County Court yesterday. It was the trial of the question of the insanity of Mrs. Lincoln, the widow of Abraham Lincoln, President. Besides the lawyers and persons summoned as witnesses, there were very few in the courtroom when the venerable lady, her son, and her friends entered. But the report of the nature of the trial soon spread through the County Buildings, and the courtroom soon became crowded.

MRS. LINCOLN,

gentle looking and modestly attired, was regarded with pity by all present, and not infrequently during the proceedings, particularly during her son's recital of her

---

[*] This was the only Chicago newspaper to label Mary Lincoln a Spiritualist and directly connect her beliefs to her insanity.

eccentricities, many as well as the witnesses were effected. The proceedings were instituted by her son, Mr. Robert T. Lincoln, through feelings of concern for his mother's safety. Still Mrs. Lincoln did not exhibit any annoyance with him for his action until the verdict was returned. She was perfectly cognizant of what had taken place, but displayed no emotion. But when Mr. Lincoln approached her after the verdict, and taking her hand spoke affectionately, the lady sadly, sorrowfully, and

REPROACHFULLY EXCLAIMED:

"O Robert, to think that my son would ever have done this!" Mr. Lincoln turned aside and concealed his grief. The calamity dates from the assassination of President Lincoln, and developed itself in different vagaries; at one time in extreme solicitousness for her son's health, at another in imagining that spirits conversed with her; again in apprehending personal violence, and in unnecessary and extravagant expenditures.

THE JURY.

The following gentlemen sat as jurors: Dr. S. C. Blake, C. B. Farwell, C. M. Henderson, S. M. Moore, L. J. Gage, H. C. Durand, S. B. Parkhurst, William Stewart, D. R. Cameron, J. A. Mason, J. McGregor Adams, and Thomas Coggswell.

Judge Wallace presided.

The proceedings were based on a petition filed by Robert T. Lincoln, setting forth that Mary Lincoln, his mother, has property and effects, consisting of negotiable securities and other personal property not exceeding $75,000; that she is *non compos mentis* and incapable of managing her estate; and praying for the issuance of an order for a warrant and venire to test the

QUESTION OF HER SANITY.

The petition was accompanied with a certificate from Dr. Ralph N. Isham to the effect that he had examined Mrs. Lincoln, and was of the opinion that she was insane, and a fit subject for hospital treatment.

Hon. Leonard Swett and Benjamin F. Ayer supported the petition, and Isaac N. Arnold appeared for Mrs. Lincoln. Mr. Ayer opened the trial by a brief statement to the jury saying that the friends of Mrs. Lincoln had to their intense grief discovered that she was suffering from a severe mental malady. They feared that some harm might befall her unless she is placed under some restraint. They do not intend that she shall be sent to a State Asylum but to a private asylum where she will be cared for properly.

DR. WILLIS DANFORTH

Was then called as a witness. He testified that he is acquainted with Mrs. Lincoln; called to see her Nov. 24, 1873, at her residence on Wabash avenue and Twenty-second street; treated her some weeks for fever and nervous derangement of the head; observed at that time indications of mental disturbances; she had strange imaginings; thought that someone was at work at her head, thought it was an Indian removing the bones of her face and pulling wires out of her eyes. These were the prominent hallucinations she suffered from; visited Mrs. Lincoln again on Sept. 16, 1874. She was suffering from debility of the nervous system. She complained that someone was taking steel springs from her head, and would not let her rest. She believed that she was going to die within a few days, and she had been admonished to that effect by her husband. She imagined that she heard raps on a table conveying the time of her death to her. She sat by the table and asked questions and repeated the supposed answer the table returned, although no one heard any sounds. When witnessed expressed a doubt as to the reliability of the information given, Mrs. Lincoln made what she termed a final test, by putting the question in a glass goblet which was on the table. The goblet was found to be cracked, and that circumstance she regarded as a corroboration of the table raps. These were derangements not dependent on the condition of her body, not delirium arising from physical disease. A week ago called on Mrs. Lincoln at the Grand Pacific Hotel. She spoke of her stay in Florida, the pleasant time she had there, of the scenery, and manners and customs of the Southern people. She spoke rationally and appeared to be in excellent health, and the hallucinations formerly noticeable seemed to have passed away. She said that her reason for returning from Florida was that her son was not well. Suddenly she startled witness somewhat by saying that an attempt had been

MADE TO POISON HER

on her journey from the South. She said that she had been very thirsty, and, at a wayside station not far from Jacksonville, she obtained a cup of coffee; discovered there was poison in the coffee, and drank another cup, so that the overdose of poison might cause her to retch. Witness did not see any traces that she suffered from mineral poison. His professional opinion was that Mrs. Lincoln is insane.

To Mr. Arnold—On general topics her conversation was rational.

SAMUEL M. TURNER,

manager of the Grand Pacific Hotel, was the next witness. He testified that Mrs. Lincoln arrived at the Grand Pacific from the South on March 15. On April 3 she visited him at the hotel office. She had her shawl wrapped about her head. She asked him to go to the reception room, as she had a communication to make. She said that something was wrong going on upstairs, and she heard strange sounds in her rooms. Accompanied her to the rooms. As witness was leaving she declared she was afraid to be alone. Left her in care of one of female help, and told her he would return in fifteen minutes. Had scarcely been in the office five minutes when a messenger informed him that Mrs. Lincoln was at the elevator and wanted to see him immediately. She declared that there had been a strange man in the corridor, and he was going to molest her. Went up in the elevator with her; walked through the corridors; did not see any strange man, and no one had seen him. Endeavored to calm her fears; she was excited. She desired to go to some lady-boarder's rooms that "she might be safe." Showed her to Mrs. Dodge's room. Mrs. Dodge being at dinner, requested Mrs. Lincoln to wait for Mrs. Dodge, and in the meantime witness would return to the office and get off some passengers. Had not left her above a few minutes, when witness was summoned to see her again. Her appearance was wild. She repeated her fears. From all the circumstances witness believed she was very much

DERANGED MENTALLY.

Since her return from the South no one called to see her except her son. The general impression among the guests of the hotel and others is that it is not safe to leave her alone.

To Mr. Arnold—Mrs. Lincoln was not feverish on that day; she did not appear so. She feared personal violence.

MRS. ALLEN,

housekeeper at the Grand Pacific Hotel, testified that Mrs. Lincoln seemed to suffer from excitement nervously. She imagined that a small window in her bedroom boded ill, and used to say that associations connected with the window disturbed her. She used to walk her room most of the night. At her request witness slept with her two nights.

Last Wednesday Mrs. Lincoln was very much excited—agitated, restless and nervous. She mixed several kinds of medicines together. The closet in her room—a large closet—was full of packages of goods purchased by her; the packages are unopened—remain as they were sent from different stores. Consider her to be insane; felt she should be placed somewhere to receive all necessary attention and care.

MAGGIE GAVIN,

employed in the hotel for the past seventeen months, testified that she had the care of Mrs. Lincoln's room. Heard her complain frequently that people were speaking to her through the wall; she was most anxious about her son, and sometimes called witness attention to voices she heard speaking through the floor of the bedroom. Complained that a man had taken her pocketbook, but witness found it in her bureau drawer. She used to call witness to the window and, pointing to smoke issuing from a chimney, she used to say that the city was burning down. Lately she bought several new trunks and parcels; could not tell what the parcels contained; never opened them. Slept in her room at night for four weeks. She was very restless; walked the rooms. One night she left the room, saying she was afraid to be there, and crossed the corridor to her son's room; she had only her night-dress on. Considered Mrs. Lincoln was not in her right mind.

To Mr. Arnold—Never remember that she slept well at night; she generally slept in the morning. She used to keep the gas burning full blaze all night.

JOHN FITZHENRY,

second waiter at the Grand Pacific, testified that on April 1 he went to see Mrs. Lincoln at her request. She was carelessly dressed, and was excited. She asked witness to call the tallest man in the dining room to her, and she exclaimed several times, "I am afraid; I am afraid." Mr. Dodge, the cashier, spoke to her, and subsequently Mr. Turner, to whom she alluded, saw her.

CHARLES DODGE,

cashier of the hotel, corroborated Fitzhenry's statement as to her excited and highly nervous condition, and added that she said some one had been in her room, a stranger, and she was afraid that he would molest her.

MR. SEATON,

agent of the United States Express Company, testified that on April 28 he sent eleven trunks by express to Milwaukee for Mrs. Lincoln. She told him she was going to spend the summer in Wisconsin. Her manner was strange.

DR. ISHAM

testified that on the March 12 he received a telegram from Mrs. Lincoln, at Jacksonville, Fla., as follows: "My belief is my son is ill; telegraph. I start for Chicago tomorrow." Mr. Lincoln was perfectly well, and the telegram rather startled witness then. Wired her to that effect, and Mr. Lincoln sent a telegram telling her to remain in Florida until she was perfectly well. Received another telegram one hour and a half after the receipt of the first. It read: "My dearly beloved son, Robert T. Lincoln—Rouse yourself and live for your mother; you are all I have; from this hour all I have is yours. I pray every night that you may be spared to your mother."

ROBERT T. LINCOLN,

the petitioner, then took the witness stand. His face was pale; his eyes bore evidence that he had been weeping, and his whole manner was such as to affect all present. His mother looked upon him benignly, and never betrayed the emotions which must have filled her breast during the recital of the unfortunate and regretful scenes they were parties to. He testified that there was no reason his mother should think he was sick unless that she had seen some newspaper paragraph. He had not been sick in ten years. He did not want any money from his mother. He owed her money, that is, he had some in his hands in trust for her. Mother arrived from the South on March 15. When witness entered the car in which she was she appeared startled. She looked well and not fatigued after her journey of seventy-two hours. Asked her to come to witness' home. She declined, and went to Grand Pacific. Had supper together, and after it sat talking. She told him that at the first breakfast she had after leaving Jacksonville, an attempt was made to poison her. Occupied a room adjoining hers that night. She slept well that night, but subsequently was restless. Several nights she tapped at witness' bedroom door; she would be in her night gown. Twice in one night she roused him up. One night she aroused him, and asked that she might sleep in his room. He gave his mother his bed, and he slept on the lounge.

The witness gave vent to his feelings in tears, and the scene was

MOST TOUCHING.

He continued: Then I got Dr. Isham to attend her. On April 1 she ceased tapping at witness' room door, for witness told her she must not do it or he would leave the hotel. On that day he went to her room. She was not properly dressed. She left the room under some pretext, and the next thing he knew she was in the elevator going down to the office. Called back the elevator and endeavored to induce her to return to her room. She regarded witness' interference as impertinent; declined to leave the elevator. Just then the bell rang several times. She was not in a condition of dress to be seen, and witness gently forced her out of the elevator by putting his arm around her waist. Maggie Gavin assisted him, and they together got into her room. She screamed, "You are going to murder me," and would not let Maggie Gavin leave the room to do her work. After a while she said that the man who took her pocketbook promised to return it at 3 o'clock. Asked her who the man was. She replied he was

THE WANDERING JEW;

had seen him in Florida. Then she sat near the wall and for an hour professed to be repeating what this man was telling her through he wall. During the afternoon she slept. Since the fire she has kept her trunks and property in the Fidelity Safe Deposit Company's building. In the beginning of the last week in April he called on her. She said that all Chicago was going to be burned, and intended to send her trunks to some country town—to Milwaukee. Told her that Milwaukee was too near Oshkosh, where there had been a terrible fire the night before. She said that witness' house, of all Chicago, would be saved, and witness then suggested that was the best place to send the trunks. On the Sunday following she showed witness securities for $57,000 which she carried in her pocket. She has spent large sums of money lately; bought $600 worth of lace curtains; three watches costing $450; $700 worth of jewelry; $200 worth of Lubin's soaps and perfumeries, and a whole piece of silk. Witness had no doubt that

SHE IS INSANE.

Had had a conference with her cousin, and Major Stuart, of Springfield, and Judge Davis, of the Supreme Court, as to the best thing to be done for her. They advised the present course.

Q: Do you regard it safe to allow your mother to remain as she is, unrestrained?

A: She has long been a source of much anxiety to me. (Again Mr. Lincoln was affected to tears.) I do not think it would be safe or proper. Have had a man watching her for the last three weeks, whose sole duty was to watch her when she went on the street. She knew nothing about it. She has no home, and does not visit witness' house because of a misunderstanding with his wife. Has always been exceedingly kind to witness. She has been of unsound mind since the death of father; has been irresponsible for past ten years. Regarded her as eccentric and unmanageable, never heeding witness' advice. Had no reason to make these purchases, for her trunks are filled with dresses and valuables of which she makes no use. She wears no jewelry and dresses in deep black.

MR. ALBERTSON,

salesman for Matson & Co., jewelers, testified that Mrs. Lincoln made expensive purchases and behaved in a eccentric manner.

J. B. STONE,

salesman with Allen & Mackey's dry goods house, testified that he sold her $300 worth of lace curtains. On cross-examination by Mr. Arnold, witness said he suspected strongly that Mrs. Lincoln was not a judge of her actions, that she was not in her right mind. Still he sold her the goods, for his business was to sell, and not to determine questions of sanity or insanity. It was stated that Allen & Mackey will take back the laces and refund the money.

DR. N. S. DAVIS

testified that Mrs. Lincoln had no symptoms of epilepsy, but he did not regard her safe to be left alone. Had visited her professionally at the Clifton House, never saw anything that could be denominated an unsoundness of mind; she was of eccentric and undue nervous impressibility.

W. H. WOOSTER,

doing business on Wabash avenue, testified: Mrs. Lincoln purchased two watches. She wanted two ladies' and gents' watches, offered $300. She wanted spectacles. The watches were taken to Robert Lincoln, who ordered them to be returned.

J. S. TOWNSEND,

With Mayo, jeweler, testified: Mrs. Lincoln priced watches and spectacles. The bill came to $400. She was nervous and tried to beat him down in the price.

T. C. MATLOCK

testified that she was in his store April 20, and bought a trunk; a few days later bought a satchel; next day got another. Went there again and bought another trunk. Her manner was excited.

E. G. MOULTON

testified that she bought $80 worth of dry goods from him. He thought she was crazy.

DR. JOHNSON

testified that, in his opinion, Mrs. Lincoln is deranged, and not safe to be left alone; ought to be sent to a private asylum.

DR. SMITH

declared that her mind is unsound. Her actions being without proper motives indicate that.

Mr. Lincoln stated that insanity was not hereditary. His mother was 56 years of age.

This closed the evidence, and after a brief address by the Hon. Leonard Swett the jury retired. They were ten minutes in consultation, and brought in the following

VERDICT:

State of Illinois, County of Cook, as

We the undersigned jurors in the case of Mary Lincoln, alleged to be insane, having heard the evidence in the case, are satisfied that the said Mary Lincoln is insane, and is a fit person to be sent to a State Hospital for the Insane; that she is a resident of the State of Illinois and County of Cook; that her age is 56 years; that the disease is of unknown duration, and is not with her hereditary; that she is not subject to epilepsy; that she does not manifest homicidal or suicidal tendencies, and that she is not a pauper.

THE WARRANT.

Mr. Swett then made application to the court for the issuance of a warrant. The request was granted, and court officer Hanchett served the warrant on Mrs. Lincoln. She regarded it with unconcern, and soon after left the court in company with Messrs. Arnold and Swett. The three entered a carriage and drove to the Grand Pacific Hotel, where she remained last night under the surveillance of a sheriff's deputy. This forenoon she will be conveyed to the private insane asylum at Batavia, superintended by Dr. R. J. Patterson and known as Bellevue Place.

Chicago Inter Ocean, Thursday, May 20, 1875, 1.[*]
Testimony of all physicians and of Robert Lincoln
also reprinted in "A Mind Diseased," *Illinois State
Journal,* June 22, 1875, 2.

"MRS. LINCOLN: THE WIDOW OF THE LATE PRESIDENT LINCOLN ADJUDGED INSANE"
Chicago Evening Journal, May 20, 1875

She is to be Taken to a Private Asylum for Treatment.
———

Her Hallucinations.
———

Yesterday afternoon, in the County Court, Mrs. Mary Lincoln, widow of the late President Lincoln, was adjudged insane. For many years her actions have given much uneasiness to her family and friends, as she exhibited unmistakable symptoms of a disordered mind. It finally became necessary that she should be sent to an asylum for treatment, and that was the result of the inquiry yesterday. Mr. B. F. Ayer and Hon. Leonard Swett conducted the case and Hon. Isaac N. Arnold appeared for Mrs. Lincoln. The jury was as follows: Dr. S. C. Blake, Hon. C. B. Farwell, C. M.

---

[*] This is the only Chicago newspaper to explicitly report rebuttal questions or cross-examination of witnesses by Mary's attorney, Isaac Arnold.

Henderson, S. M. Moore, L. J. Gage, H. C. Durand, S. B. Parkhurst, William Stewart, D. R. Cameron, J. A. Mason, J. McGregor Adams, and Thomas Coggswell.

Dr. Willis Danforth, Mr. S. M. Turner, Mrs. Harrington and Mary Gavin, of the Pacific Hotel, where Mrs. Lincoln has been staying, her son, Mr. Robert Lincoln, and other witnesses testified to the

STRANGE CONDUCT

of Mrs. Lincoln. She had a mania for shopping, buying unnecessary articles; thought persons spoke to her through walls; that her life was in danger; and was subject to other hallucinations. The jury returned a verdict of insanity, and her friends determined to send her to the private asylum of Dr. Patterson, in Batavia, Kane County, for treatment.

In the evening Mrs. Lincoln was taken to the Grand Pacific Hotel to the room which she has occupied for some time past. She was in one of her sane moods. She seemed to fully realize what had taken place, but she could not rid herself of the feeling that the action of her son was unfilial, and the decree of the court unjust. When rational, a condition which she is in a large part of the time, no one would have any occasion to suspect the soundness of her intellect. At these times her deprecations of her treatment coming apparently from a person of sound judgment, were very hard to bear. The early part of the evening she spent in harmless complaints, and in packing and unpacking her trunks and valise for her expected journey. The rich laces and other finery which she had recently purchased were carefully laid away in the trunks, while the almost equally costly silks were jammed into satchels. The nurse who attended her allowed her to continue, as she did not show any symptoms of a violent nature. Later in the evening her son and another gentleman spent a few moments with her. Then occurred the only scene of the evening of any importance. Her son knowing that she had somewhere in her possession a large number of

GOVERNMENT BONDS,

besought her to tell where she had hidden them. This she refused to do. She was told that an officer would have to be sent for to make a search if she would not give them up quietly and immediately. Seeing no way of escape, she forthwith cut the lining of the dress which she was in the habit of wearing every day and took out a number of United States bonds amounting to the large sum of $57,000. It seems that she had been in the habit of wearing them about her person, a fact which many wondered at as having not been the cause of personal injury to her from some person who might have discovered the secret.

The report of a morning paper that there were symptoms of violence so pronounced that an officer had to be called, were entirely unfounded. She was perfectly quiet in disposition until 10:30 o'clock when she retired and rested quietly until late this morning when she arose and ate heartily. She was entirely rational and quiet. At about half past 9 o'clock her faithful son called upon her and remained for some time. During the night Officer Garson and in the morning Officer Parker were on duty in the corridor to keep order.

Chicago Evening Journal, Thursday, May 20, 1875, 4.* Reprinted in part as "A Mind Diseased," *Illinois State Journal,* May 22, 1875, 2.

"MRS. LINCOLN: THE WIFE OF THE MARTYRED PRESIDENT DECLARED INSANE"

St. Louis Globe-Democrat, May 20, 1875

Strange Hallucinations of the Demented Lady.

———

Special Dispatch to the Globe-Democrat

CHICAGO, May 19,—Mary Lincoln, widow of the martyr president, was adjudged insane by the Cook County Court this afternoon. The strictest secrecy had been maintained respecting the affair, and very few persons besides those directly interested were in attendance. The proceedings were at the instance of her son, Robert Lincoln. The unfortunate lady appeared in court neatly attired in the deepest mourning, and requested Isaac N. Arnold, one of Mr. Lincoln's foreign ministers, to act as her attorney. A jury was chosen from among the most intelligent citizens, Congressman Farwell being one. The testimony left no room to doubt

THE LADY'S INSANITY.

Her family physicians expressed their opinion as positive, and were corroborated by employees of the hotel at which Mrs. Lincoln has boarded, and several others. The mania had assumed several phases, the chief of which was a desire to purchase an extravagant wardrobe, for which she had no use. Her closet was literally so filled with unopened packages of silks, laces and like articles of dress, that it was impossible to close the doors. She also labored under the hallucination that Chicago was about to be burned again, and drew fifty-seven thousand dollars' worth of bonds she had deposited at a bank, and carried them about her person for safety. She also lived in constant terror of personal injury from the rebels and other imaginary enemies. An army of jewelers, dry goods men and other tradesmen appeared in

---

* The *Chicago Evening Journal* also printed supportive paragraphs about Mary Lincoln's trial and mental troubles on pages 1 and 2, declaring her illness caused by her husband's assassination, that the public should now understand some of Mary's strange behaviors, that Robert Lincoln acted "obviously" for his mother's good, and hoping for a positive outcome to her treatment.

court to testify to her oddities. A trunk maker swore to her having purchased of him a large number of trunks and valises which she could not possibly use.

ROBERT LINCOLN

thought it unsafe to permit her further freedom. The jury, after a very short deliberation, found her insane, and a fit subject for an asylum. Mrs. Lincoln is not fifty-six years of age. Her mind has doubtless been diseased for several years. Since her residence in Chicago, which covers a period of eight years, her conduct has always been considered remarkable. She will be sent to a private asylum at Batavia, Ill., tomorrow morning.

St. Louis Globe-Democrat, May 20, 1875, 1.
Reprinted in *Illinois State Journal,* May 21, 1875, 2.

Chapter 3

Trial of 1875
Correspondence

After the trial, Robert received letters of support from his mother's cousins and from David Davis. One of the most interesting, and most important, letters of the entire insanity period was written to David Davis by Leonard Swett a few days after the proceedings, in which Swett details to Davis everything he personally witnessed before, during, and after the trial.

ELIZABETH J. TODD GRIMSLEY BROWN
TO ROBERT LINCOLN
May 19, 1875

My dear Bob,

   If I had received your telegraph of the 18th before night I should have gone up on the night train, but my going today would be of no service to you. You received cousin John's answer to your communication so of course did not expect us this morning, but I assure you dear Bob I have a heavy heart for you and your poor Mother this day. I have not seen cousin John for several days but hear through the family that a majority of consulting physicians think the case urgent enough to request an asylum. Can your mother be induced to go to a private asylum? And could I influence her in such a decision, or must it be compulsory? After I found I could not go last night, and submitted to what I could not prevent, I came to the conclusion that it was *Providence* that prevented. That perhaps strangers could accomplish that in which relatives might fail. Neither you, cousin John or myself could have *induced* your mother to have gone voluntarily before a jury and our presence perhaps would have rendered her violent. I felt dreadfully at the idea of her being alone, at such a time, and I also felt as if it proved me ungrateful to have accepted her hospitalities and kindnesses at a time when it was so pleasant for me, and now to leave her alone when she needed a friend. I have held myself in readiness to go to her, when you thought she needed me, but still thought you would send next week perhaps for me. Please notify me at once dear Bob, of the result of today's proceedings. I shall wait for news very anxiously. Let me know if I can still do anything for you or her. And if you desire me to come telegraph me care J. T. Grimsley and I will come.

Yours affectionately,

E. J. Brown

JOHN TODD STUART TO LEONARD SWETT
May 21, 1875

Sir: I received yours of the 16th inst. and would have answered sooner but for a telegram I received from Robert informing me that the inquisition would take place the next day. I then thought I would postpone an answer until after it was held. I could not be at Chicago on that day because my wife's health is very precarious and also we had on that day a joint meeting of the Penitentiary and State House boards in relation to some stone cut by the Penitentiary for the State House. My reputation as a commissioner was so much involved that I dare not leave moreover I did not believe that my presence there was necessary especially as I had given Robert a letter which he was authorized to use at his discretion showing that he had my full support in the contemplated proceedings.

I have been very familiar with the facts you detail for some weeks past. They left on my mind no doubt of the insanity of Mrs. Lincoln and indeed I have had no doubt of it for the last ten years and so far as I am advised all her relatives here concur in that opinion. I advised Robert when he first consulted me to delay the proceedings not because I had any doubt of her insanity but on Robert's account that he should have such facts and surroundings that when he did institute proceedings he should be fully sustained and justified by his friends and the public and in this he has been very successful. I am glad it is over and so well done.

Your friend,

John T. Stuart

JOHN TODD STUART TO ROBERT LINCOLN
May 21, 1875

My dear cousin: I received your telegram of Tuesday addressing me that the inquisition would be held the next day and requesting my presence. I answered that I could not come. The condition of my wife was one reason and another reason was that the State House and Penitentiary Boards were holding on that day a joint meeting in relation to some stone cut for the new State House which was alleged to be improper to be used. My reputation was too much involved in the question for me to leave moreover I did not think I could be of any service.

I am very glad that it is over and so far as I am able to judge from the newspapers everything was done that the melancholy occasion required of you. The presence of Mssrs. Swett and Arnold was especially fortunate and the character of the jury not less so.

In my consultations with you from the beginning I had no doubt of the insanity of your mother and the necessity of legal proceedings but counseled delay that when you did schedule proceedings that it should be done under such circumstances that your friends and the public should sustain and justify you. In this you have been fully successful. You have the sympathy of all in the sad affair.

Yours affectionately,

John T. Stuart

Folder 26, Box 2, Mary Todd Lincoln Insanity File

DAVID DAVIS TO ROBERT LINCOLN

May 23, 1875

Dear Robert,

It is a source of deep thankfulness that the matter passed off so well. The terrible strain on you will be removed and you can go to work. Some good comes out of almost everything and the necessity of confining your mother in an asylum will go very far toward removing the unfavorable impressions created by her conduct since your father's death. I knew Mr. Swett was the right person when I suggested him to you at Springfield. He has more resources than most men, indeed I know no one that has more. Apart from this, he had a strong attachment to your father.

In great haste,

Your friend

David Davis

Folder 15, Box 2, Mary Todd Lincoln Insanity File

LEONARD SWETT TO DAVID DAVIS

Chicago, Ill., May 24, 1875

Dear sir:

I propose through the hasty though diffuse mode of dictation to give you the circumstances attendant upon the commission of Mrs. Lincoln to the insane asylum.

On Saturday, a week ago yesterday, I received a note from Mr. B. F. Ayer, whose office is in the same building with mine asking me to come there upon business of some urgency and importance. I there learned that in a few hours there was to be a consultation of physicians upon Mrs. Lincoln's case, and agreed to attend it.

At two o'clock I met there Drs. Johnson, Davis, Jewell, Patterson, Isham and Smith, and upon a full statement of her condition, Mrs. Lincoln was pronounced insane by all the physicians and her confinement recommended. Although there was no doubt of the fact of the insanity, Robert was so careful to keep within the truth that the physicians doubted whether we would be able to make out a case sufficiently strong to satisfy the general public, and perhaps not strong enough to secure a verdict. Upon this subject I never had any doubt because of my conviction in regard to her real condition, and because I did not doubt when the case was put together it would appear stronger than when described in the manner it was.

Thinking the matter over Sunday, I advised Robert to write the letter to you, Mr. Stuart and all the physicians, asking from the physicians their written opinion as to her real condition, irrespective of the degree of evidence we might be able to obtain in regard to it, and yourself and Mr. Stuart, as to a proper course of action, provided the physicians were willing, in writing, to pronounce her insane.

Having done this we intended to let the matter rest until replies came in from all sources. But the next day she was worse, and certain facts developed, which induced us to act without advice.

Up to about the time of writing you, although she had been buying expensive lace curtains, perfumery and watches, she paid for very little, and arrangements having been made with the traders to return the goods, there was not much danger of serious loss. On Monday last Pinkerton's man reported that she was being visited in her room by persons regarded by us as suspicious. She was also known at that time to have about a thousand dollars in money which must have come through sale of some of her bonds. She was also contemplating leaving town for parts unknown.

Under these circumstances I advised Robert, in consideration of the danger of injury to herself, the loss of her bonds through sharpers,[*] the certainty in my mind of her condition, to take the responsibility and act upon it. In the event of his doing this I told him I would take charge of the question of her arrest and production in court and generally of the custody of her person.

This determined on[,] I took a cab and went personally to see all the witnesses upon whom we relied to make a case. As expected, I found the case very much stronger than represented, and such as admitted of no doubt.

The matter of her custody was a worse question, and to my mind presented more real terrors than anything I have ever undertaken. To have advanced on a battery instead would, it seems to me, have been real relief.

---

[*] Con men.

The writ having been issued, I took two reliable courageous young officers and went to the Pacific Hotel. The jury had been summoned for two o'clock, and at this time it was about one. I had in the morning tried Arnold to get him to go with me, but he thought it unwise. Ben Ayer went to the hotel but waited outside. I finally got Sam Turner to enter the room with me, following a bundle boy who was bringing her eight pairs of lace curtains bought that day.

As I entered the room she seemed cheerful and glad to see me, apologized for her undressed appearance, and seemed in no way different from what she has always been. I said, "Never mind your hair, Mrs. Lincoln, sit down here, I have got some bad news for you." She seemed startled, as a person ordinarily would, by such an announcement, and sat down. About this time Turner left and I was thereafter alone.

"Mrs. Lincoln," said I, "Your friends have with great unanimity come to the conclusion that the troubles you have been called to pass through have been too much and have produced mental disease."

"You mean to say I am crazy, then, do you?"

"Yes," said I, "I regret to say that is what your friends all think."

"I am much obliged to you," said she, "but I am abundantly able to take care of myself, and I don't need any aid from any such friends. Where is my son Robert," said she, "I want him to come here."

I told her that she would see him in the court.

"The court," says she, "what court do you mean; who says I am insane?"

"Judge Davis says so," said I, "and your cousin, John T. Stuart; Robert says so; and as I do not want to throw the responsibility of this upon others, I say so."

I then pulled from my pocket the letters from four or five of the physicians named, and submitted them to her as opinions establishing her insanity.

"I haven't seen these physicians," said she, "they do not come to see me, they know nothing about me, what does this mean?"

I then explained to her that when a person was believed to be insane that an affidavit had to be filed in the County Court, whereupon a writ issued and the sheriff taking the writ ordinarily went and arrested the party and took him or her to court. In this case I told her Robert had made the affidavit, and two officers had come along with me having the writ, but I could not submit to having her seized by officers and forcibly taken to court, and therefore I had come in lieu of an officer, and requested her to go along with me.

She flatly refused and grew pretty wild. I then explained to her that nothing in her case remained but to go with me or have me turn her over to the officers and let them take her. I told her there were two carriages downstairs—one of them was mine and the other belonged to the officers, and unless she yielded to me I either had to seize her forcibly myself or turn her over to the officers, who might handcuff her if necessary, and certainly would take her to court, "How much better," says I, "you put on your bonnet and go along with me as you ordinarily would."

The contest on this point lasted from twenty minutes past one until half past two. It was accompanied with no violence or unladylike expression, but with bitterness and sarcasm such as wounded me; it seems to me worse than bullets would.

After the subject became serious she said,

"And you are attending to insane people, are you, Mr. Swett, allow me to suggest that you go home and take care of your wife, I have heard some stories on that subject about her—and you my husband's friend, you would take me and lock me up in an asylum, would you?" and then she threw up her hands, and the tears streaming down her cheeks, prayed to the Lord to release her and drive me away.

Finally contemplating going, she said, "See my dress Mr. Swett, it is all muddy from shopping, I must change my dress and certainly you would not humiliate me and compel me to undress myself in your presence?"

I replied that I regretted that she would throw the necessity upon me, that there was no necessity for a change in her dress, and that whatever might come it might as well be understood that I was not going to leave her, that she must go with me.

"And why won't you leave me alone a moment?" she said.

"Because if I do, Mrs. Lincoln, I am afraid you will jump out of the window."

Finally she stepped in a closet at the side of the room, some eight or ten feet square, and changed her dress; and at last she went.

"Will you take my arm, Mrs. Lincoln?" I said as we stepped out the door.

"No, I thank you," said she, "I can walk yet."

As we got to the elevator for which we had to wait for a moment, she asked me if we had any accidents over at the Palmer House, and then commenced to chat glibly about foreign matters. Thus we reached the carriage.

The street not being graded there was a steep step down and I offered to help her. "No," said she, "Mr. Swett, I ride with you from compulsion, but I beg you not to touch me."

Reaching the courtroom, as I opened the door she saw men standing inside and shrank back. I said, "Come right along, Mrs. Lincoln, Robert is in here and I will sit by the side of you." Thus assured she came in quietly and without speaking.

Giving her a seat, I immediately went to Robert, who hesitated.

I told him she had denounced him bitterly for the course he was taking in the proceedings. Said I, "we must act as though we were her friends, come sit beside her and do everything as though she was sane."

He came, and she received him kindly, and then turning to Mrs. Lincoln I said "you are entitled to counsel; your old friend Mr. Arnold, is here, he was your husband's friend and maybe you would rather have him and Robert sit by you than have any stranger brought in here." "Yes," she said, she would, whereupon, in a moment I had Mr. Arnold be by her side.

I then stepped over to Mr. Ayer at the other side, and telling him I was too much used up to do anything more, asked him to take charge of the case.

This remark was scarcely made, when Mr. Arnold came over, saying that believing Mrs. Lincoln insane, he doubted the propriety of his defending her.

"That means," said I, "that you will put into her head, that she can get some mischievous lawyer to make us trouble; go and defend her, and do your duty." Thereupon immediately the proceedings commenced.

The trial lasted some three hours in which the evidence of insanity was so overwhelming, and so conclusive that we did not put in [the] whole case, no one entertained the slightest doubts.

As an argument at the end, I simply stated to the jury that Mrs. Lincoln in the opinion of her most intimate friends, had been insane ever since the assassination, that the weight of her woes had been too great for her, and as the recent developments were made, yourself, John T. Stuart, and the physicians who had been consulted whereupon the present action had been taken, that I had no doubt it was proper, and all Mrs. Lincoln's friends so far as we knew approved the course, then asked them without delay to render their verdict. They stepped aside and in a moment did so.

Robert then came to me and said I must get her bonds away. Believing that to be indisposable, I said to her in the courtroom "Mrs. Lincoln you have $56,000 of money and bonds on your person, and one of the unpleasant necessities of this case is, that you must surrender them." I said that I could get an order of court or have the sheriff take them forcibly from her, but I hoped she would not impose that necessity on me, and asked if she would not give it properly to Robert. "No," she said Robert never could have anything that belonged to her.

I then said, "Here is Mr. Arnold, won't you surrender them to him?" she then told me she could not, because they were upon her underthings, and "certainly," said she "you would not be indelicate to me in the presence of these people. Please," said she "take me to my room, it is so hot here;" I replied "Yes Mrs. Lincoln, I would be glad to take you to your room, and nothing remains but these bonds. Now if you will promise me after you get there that you will give them to Mr. Arnold, we will go there." She made the promise and we at once started.

Going through the tunnel she said "Mr. Arnold I have always been very careful about my money matters, there is no danger that any thing will happen to them, and as I am very much fatigued and need rest, suppose you come down tomorrow and we will talk that matter over." He made no reply, neither did I.

As soon as we entered the room at her hotel, as I shut the door, I said "Mrs. Lincoln, you promised as a lady at the court, if I would not permit those sheriffs to be rude to you, that you would give your bonds to Mr. Arnold as soon as we came to the room, now I am compelled to exact the performance of that promise. We ought to give a receipt" said I, "and I will go down stairs, to get some paper." As soon as I could get the paper I returned and wrote the receipt. "Let me read the receipt" I said, "Mrs. Lincoln." "Received of Mary Lincoln $50,000."

"Fifty six thousand dollars" she spoke immediately.

"I beg your pardon" said I, and wrote a new receipt. Having read that over to her, I said, "Now, Mrs. Lincoln, the receipt is all right, but we haven't got any bonds." She rose up, the tears streaming from her eyes, and said "And you are not satisfied with locking me up in an insane asylum, but now you are going to rob me of all I have on earth. My husband is dead, and my children are dead and these bonds I have saved for my necessities in my old age; now you are going to rob me of them."

And to her it was such, and although I tried to explain, it had no effect, and when she did yield, although she yielded peaceably, she yielded as to force. Stepping to the side of the room she pulled up her outer skirt, and wearied and worn out, she called Mr. Arnold to come and help her to tear out from her pocket she had made there $56,000 in Government bonds.

I then arranged for her care during the night, and left.

The next morning Robert told me she was mild and had yielded everything to him, and we thought it best for me not to go to her room again, unless my presence was necessary. She was in care of one woman and two men whose instructions were in no event to let her go out. So Robert and I went for a special car, and to do other things necessary for her departure that evening.

Coming around to Robert's office about two o'clock in the day we met a messenger in haste, stating that Robert's mother had escaped. Arriving at the hotel as soon as possible, we found her absence was only momentary and she had returned. This with the subsequent facts about the poisoning determined us to stand guard personally until she should go.

It is perfectly frightful to think how near she came to poisoning herself. Notwithstanding the instructions to the people guarding her, by plausible stories she worked her way through there to the street, and going to a drug store in the Pacific Hotel, said she wanted two ounces of laudanum and camphor as an application, said her shoulder was paining her badly. Fortunately the druggist knew her situation; he said he would have it ready for her in ten minutes; whereupon she left immediately, saying she would be back at the time. From there she went to another drug store, ordering the same prescription, but some body followed her, notifying the new druggist of the facts; from there she went to a third place with the same result. From there she came to the first drug store, received her prescription which had been put up without the laudanum, and immediately swallowed it.

While Robert and I remained with her after this and until she departed, she seemed cheerful and kind, apologized for many things she had said to me the day before, and urged upon me at the train to visit her, which I promised to do. Going over with me to the depot she took my arm, and in every regard was kind and uncomplaining.

From the beginning to the end of this ordeal, which was painful beyond parallel, she conducted herself like a lady in every regard. She believed she was sane. She believed that I, who ought to be her friend, was conspiring with Robert and you, to lock her up and rob her of her money. Everything she did and said coincided with the condition of sanity, assuming these facts to have been true, excepting there was a conscious weakness in her, and a yielding to me which would not be found in a sane person. In the court room she never spoke, and from beginning to end, was as ladylike and as much above criticism as possible to be found in any person however well bred or cultivated.

Yours truly,
Leonard Swett

Folder A-73, Box 5, David Davis Family Papers

Chapter 4

Trial of 1875
Newspaper Editorials

Newspapers around the country, but especially in her hometown of Chicago, not only reported on Mary Lincoln's insanity trial but also offered their editorial comments on it. The majority feeling was that Mary had been insane for a long time and deserved nothing but sympathy and understanding, while her son Robert had done his brave and manly duty in having his mother committed.

EDITORIAL

Chicago Tribune, May 20, 1875

The proceedings in the County Court yesterday in the case of Mrs. Lincoln will have a painful interest. Nothing but an imperative sense of duty and of filial devotion could have compelled the institution of the inquiry. It has been generally known in the circle of the lady's acquaintances and personal friends that something of this kind would eventually be necessary. The terrible event of which she was an eyewitness has at last completed the dethronement of perfect reason. The long years of painful brooding over the dreadful homicide of her husband have gradually produced the necessity of the proceedings taken yesterday. To the Court, the gentlemen comprising the jury, the physicians, witnesses, relatives, and friends, the action taken was distressing in the extreme, but its necessity made them unanimous. Judge Davis, of the Supreme Court, the executor of the estate, and the Hon. John T. Stuart, of Springfield, Mrs. Lincoln's cousin, also approve of what has been done. As will be seen from the evidence, Mrs. Lincoln's mind has been for ten years the prey to growing madness, and this fact, now made public, will cast a new light on many of her past actions, which were harshly criticized by those who did not know her, and which, while understood by her personal friends, could not be explained by them, since to have done so would have been to have exposed her mental condition, which it was then hoped might improve.

Chicago Tribune, Thursday, May 20, 1875, 4

Chicago Times, May 20, 1875

It will pain our readers to learn that Mrs. Lincoln, the widow of our martyred president, has been adjudged insane, and sent to a private lunatic asylum. The symptoms of her mental derangement have of late been painfully apparent to those around her, and, within the past few days, although her relatives and friends have striven to avoid it, it has been manifest that it would be necessary to place her under surveillance. However repugnant such a step might be, justice to the unfortunate lady and those related to her imperatively demanded that it be taken. Mrs. Lincoln and her family will have the sincere sympathy of the entire country in this emergency. It is to be hoped that her malady will give way under skillful medical treatment, and that she will soon be restored to the full possession of her mental faculties.

Chicago Times, Thursday, May 20, 1875, 4

EDITORIAL
Chicago Inter Ocean, May 20, 1875

The County Courtroom was yesterday the scene of one of the saddest trials that has ever appeared on the docket of any court in this or any other country. A writ *de lunatico inquirendo* was issued against Mrs. Mary Lincoln, wife of Abraham Lincoln, the nation's martyred President, upon petition of her son, Robert T. Lincoln. The testimony of the witnesses examined was conclusive as to her insanity, and the jury adjudged her a fit subject for a hospital for the insane. Among the witnesses were her son, her physician, several friends, and others who from their association with her were qualified to speak. It has long been known that Mrs. Lincoln was subject to hallucinations, indicating mental derangement, the exciting causes being the assassination of President Lincoln and the subsequent death of her idolized son, "Little Tad." Latterly these eccentricities have assumed a more pronounced form, as will appear from a perusal of the evidence published elsewhere, and it became the sorrowful duty of her son to institute proceedings to determine the facts as to her sanity. She will be removed to a private hospital at Batavia, Ill., where it is to be hoped she will fully recover.

Chicago Inter Ocean, Thursday morning,
May 20, 1875, 4

"THE CASE OF MRS. LINCOLN"
Chicago Tribune, May 21, 1875

We refer to this case with no purpose grieving the friends of the lady or of pandering to curiosity, but simply to explain that in all the painful proceedings Mrs. Lincoln has been treated in the kindest and gentlest manner by her own personal friends, and that from the beginning to the end she maintained her dignity and character as a lady. For several years after the assassination of her husband, Mrs. Lincoln was pursued by a mental picture of the dreadful scene. She could not shake it off. She courted solitude, denied herself to all visitors and friends, and became a victim to hysteria, accompanied by various apprehensions, of which destitution, poverty, and absolute want were the most violent. A gentleman of this city, one of the warmest personal friends of her husband, succeeded in obtaining an interview, and then free access to her at all times. During a period of more than a year, during which he visited her mainly at her special request, she never failed to begin the interview with a minute detail of the events of that fateful Friday on which her husband was murdered. This same story was repeated at every interview, and almost in the exact words each time. It had engrossed her mind to the exclusion of all other things past and present, except the gloomy apprehension that she was reduced to want. At last, he proposed that she leave the hotel, and buy a house, furnish it, and receive friends, and have some cares to divert her mind. She at last consented, and he states that during the few months in which the house was purchased, and she was engaged in furnishing it, and thus had active employment, she was comparatively happy, and had shaken off the terror and wretchedness which had previously afflicted her. But when this business was completed, when there was nothing more to be done, her home again became a sort of prison, and she relapsed into all the old gloom, despondency, and terror. Acting under these combined influences, she did many things which were surprising, if not painful, to her friends. She had an aversion for companionship and acquaintance: she closed all means of social approach; she lived within the seclusion of her rooms, suffering and enduring the ever present horror of the one terrible event. At times she would grow restless, and suddenly change her residence; but wherever she went the relief was temporary, the relapse inevitable. Under this intense strain, her mind gradually became unbalanced, and year after year she has required more and more the vigilant care of her friends.

Her condition, and what was to be done for her, have been long and careful considered, and her mental weakness and eccentricities during the last few months became so alarming that some preventative action became necessary. She had among other things become possessed of the idea that Chicago was on fire, and she had withdrawn the bonds and other securities in which her funds were invested from the vaults of the Fidelity Deposit Company, and carried them on her person, feeling thus prepared for instant flight. There was reason to apprehend that in her restless, troubled state of mind she might receive personal injury, and at last, when longer delay would really be cruelty and neglect of duty, her son was compelled to the painful proceeding which, under the laws of this State, must precede any detention or restraint for insanity. All the old personal friends of Mr. Lincoln were consulted.

The Hon. Isaac N. Arnold was appointed her counsel. The Hon. Leonard Swett assumed the even more delicate task of representing the sheriff and executing the process of the court. It is needless to say that the duty of arresting her, of conveying her to the court room, of communicating to her the character and necessity for the proceedings, and the proposed disposal of her person under restraint, was performed in the most delicate manner, requiring, however, persistent firmness, great patience, and personal kindness. Her peculiar condition of mind was evidenced by many ingenious pretexts to postpone, evade, or delay action; but these being met with kindness and candor, she yielded to her friends, and submitted to the decree of the judicial inquiry.

We refrain from publishing the details of her arrest by Mr. Swett, and the subsequent arrangements for her departure to the place of detention. It is sufficient to say that throughout the trying scenes she was keenly sensitive, was fully conscious of her position, and skillful in her means to evade the execution of the judgment; but there was no violence, no denunciation, no reproaches. Throughout the whole business she displayed the amiability of a cultivated lady.

We close this brief explanation of the causes leading to this proceeding, and of the circumstances attending it, by repeating that it had long been foreseen by her intimates; that it was postponed as long as affectionate regard could do so with safety to herself, and that the result will satisfactorily explain to all many things in the past which were as painful and distressing to her friends and the friends of her husband as they were surprising to those uninformed of the peculiar circumstances.

Chicago Tribune, May 21, 1875, 4

"PRESIDENT LINCOLN'S WIDOW"
New-York Tribune, May 22, 1875

The sympathy of the nation which has been too grudgingly given to the widow of Abraham Lincoln, will certainly no longer be withheld now that a court of justice has declared her bereft of reason. It has long been known to those nearest to her that her mind never entirely recovered from the shock of the President's assassination. It would have been a brain of extraordinary force which could have withstood that night of horrors. Her husband, to whom, in spite of all gossip to the contrary, she was devotedly attached, was shot down at her side in perfect health and strength. Her dress was stained with his blood. She passed the long hours of his agony at his bedside, refusing to believe the sentence of the surgeons, and in the morning, when all was over, she confronted a loss such as has been experienced by few women. For the next few weeks it was doubtful whether she would ever emerge from the shadow of death in which she lay. But everything she did or said in that delirium of despair was wickedly and shamefully used against her afterward.

It was the duty of the country, out of regard for its own honor and dignity, to provide for her future. This Congress for years refused to do. Not a cent was raised for the purpose by public subscription. When at last Mr. Sumner forced a bill through Congress giving her the pitiful pension of $3,000, it only passed after malicious and scurrilous opposition, in the course of which her enemies quoted every utterance and act which had proceeded, after her troubles, from her disordered brain. She was entitled to the gentlest and most tender consideration from every decent man. But she was attacked by Congressmen and vilified by a portion of the press, as if she had been an able-bodied politician, courting votes and criticism. There is no doubt that this treatment had its effect in preventing her recovery from the great shock which had shattered her life. The death of her young boy, whom she idolized, filled up the measure of her sorrows, and finished the wreck of her intellectual faculties. As long as it was possible, her son, the worthy inheritor of his father's character, bore with a touching patience and devotion the consequences of this misfortune. But it became evident at last that to prevent worse disasters the unfortunate lady must be put under restraint, and the proceedings in court were taken, with which our readers are familiar. The attempt upon her own life the next day was a terrible confirmation of the justice of the decree of the Court. We are sure that the long delayed sympathies of the country will attend this deeply afflicted widow to the retreat which has been provided for her, where a cure for her malady may be found which was impossible as long as she remained in contact with the world. We deem it not intrusive to say, also, that the only surviving son of Mr. Lincoln deserves in this calamity the respect and consideration of every one. He has borne himself always with irreproachable dignity and decorum. He has asked nothing from the country which was so deeply indebted to his father. He has gained an enviable position in his profession and in society by his own merit and industry. He is not a man to give way to misfortune, however sorely tried. But he ought not to be left to meet this last affliction without the assurance of the respect and goodwill which his character, no less than his name, deserves.

New-York Tribune, Saturday, May 22, 1875, 6[*]

"MRS. LINCOLN'S INSANITY"
Chicago Times, May 23, 1875

The saddest story of the week has been the disclosure to the public of Mrs. Lincoln's mental aberration. Long known to her immediate friends, the unhappy fact was hardly surmised by the people who often passed harsh judgment upon

---

[*] This article, though unsigned at publication, was written by John Hay, President Lincoln's former secretary and Robert Lincoln's friend.

her eccentric actions, as, from time to time, during the last decade, rumors of them furnished gossip for the social circle. The report of the legal steps reluctantly taken to adjudge her insane, the testimony conclusively showing a disordered mind, the finding of the jury, the attempt to end forever the troubles gathering more darkly about a life already far spent, the final removal to a private asylum for the insane, have made a story of melancholy interest, on which it is not pleasant to linger. It is gratifying, however, to know that at a time when her own faculties were playing her false, the friends of her brighter days did not wholly desert her, and that, trying as was the position of the only one of her name left to counsel and protect her, he discharged his delicate and unhappy task with filial thoughtfulness. That she is happily housed, safe from danger, and in the care of physicians who, if it lies within the skill of the medicines, may successfully minister to a mind diseased, is due to the consummate tact, courage, and discretion of a gentleman who has nobly discharged a duty to the memory of the illustrious man who was his friend long before the nation called him to the highest trust within its gift.

We do not advert to the case now to prolong a morbid interest in its melancholy developments, nor specially to commend the firm yet delicate friendship which was shown in the conduct of its legal aspect. We wish only to instance it for the lesson it contains; a lesson inculcating as powerfully as any may the duty which rests upon all men and women to speak their brother and their sister fair in life, as Antonio begged that he be spoken in death. The murdered husband of the unhappy woman now an inmate of the insane asylum, gave utterance to no sentiment more widely quoted, more generally remembered, than that spoken from his own gentle heart in the phrase, "with charity for all, with malice toward none." Scarcely had the grave closed over his bleeding remains than the country, noticing something peculiar and eccentric in the conduct of the widow, forgot that she had suffered as few women are called upon to suffer, forgot the charity which her husband had begged for all, most ineffectually for her, and sneered, jested, laughed at her waywardness, without doing her the justice to inquire as to its cause. The party to which her husband belonged had no kindly shield to throw over her infirmities; they would have withheld a pension if the more chivalrous opposition had not urged the measure as one no less just than graceful; they professed to believe that as the wife of the head and front of the union cause she was in sympathy with the rebellion, and, after she had left the White House, spoke of her as one of those rebels of the Todd family. As time passed on, and she behaved yet more oddly, the sneer deepened, the jest broadened, the smile grew more satirical, and the words heard in her defense were few and feeble. Yet all the while she was mad. By no code, human or divine, was she responsible for her conduct; and they who laughed and jested at her might as well have laughed and jested at the sick fancies of a daft Ophelia. Who is there now to breathe one unkind word of the woman whom the law consigns to the restraints of a madhouse?

The world needs such a lesson to give it pause. It handles too lightly the reputation of its people. Gossip has too wide and thoughtless a range; slander too free a course. Over how many a fair and spotless character may Hero's epitaph be written, "Done to death by slanderous tongues." And over the grave the very tongues that gave the fatal stab lament the deadly work as that of some heedless talebearer. The world needs to think how easily as a soap bubble in the summer sun a good name may be blasted, and how impossible to restore its rounded beauty. It needs a lesson in charity of thought and kindliness of speech that shall bring enforcement. It needs that healthier moral tone which would lead to the rebuke of idle gossip.

The lesson in Mrs. Lincoln's case should be taken to heart. The safest rule is never to pass judgment upon the testimony offered by appearance which may be explained, or suspicions which reflection will suggest are unreasonable. The better way is to pass no judgment at all. From on the tomb of Abraham Lincoln at Springfield, as from out the cell of Abraham Lincoln's widow at Batavia, comes to the whole world the lesson of, "charity for all, malice toward none."

Chicago Times, May 23, 1875

The final newspaper editorial, from a Democrat Chicago newspaper, is especially interesting in its accusations against her conduct since entering the White House, yet offers simultaneous sympathy for her mental plight. This article also ends with a summary of Mary Lincoln's suicide attempt the day after her insanity trial, which is the focus of the next chapter.

"INSANITY OF MRS. ABRAHAM LINCOLN"
Pomeroy's Democrat, May 29, 1875

The courts and physicians of Chicago, after a sad trial, on the petition of her son, Robert Lincoln, have declared the widow of the murdered President to be hopelessly insane. There is no doubt but she has been thus afflicted at least from the time of her husband's elevation to office as is evidenced by her late purchase of jewelry, laces, etc., for which she had no use. For the credit of history we are glad that this legal finding has been made. It is a mercy to the woman that she is insane, for now the mantle of charity will fall upon and cover the acts and defects of a life which we know brought grief to her husband, great sadness to her children, disgust to the people of this country and food for gossip for all.

From the day her husband was nominated to the Presidency she was eccentric, if nothing more. Her head seemed to be turned. In Washington she was beset by flatterers, continually telling her of her beauty, influence over her husband, and all such balderdash. General Dan. Sickles owes his promotion not to gallant conduct or honest worth so much as to the importuning of the woman who conceived a passion for him, and who must have been as insane then as now. Numerous are the incidents of her life hardly fit to publish, but well known in that society which seems to suck scandal from loose tongues, but which incidents now pass to the account of insanity, not hereditary, but resulting from an elevation she was in nature, mind and education not prepared for.

Her taking away from the White House ninety-three dry goods boxes filled with plunder belonging to the Government;[*] her racing over the country in the effort to dispose of her superfluous finery[†] and those articles of service and gew-gaw, presented to her by loyal Republicans or renegade Democrats, anxious for Presidential favors, or for permits to rob the suffering, the dead and the dying were the acts of a woman, to whom the disease of insanity well becomes.

During the years gone by with their drippings of blood, we have occasionally criticized her and her actions. But we have no criticism now. The veil is lifted, and we behold the wife and widow of Abraham Lincoln not the bad, selfish woman the world came to think her to be, but an unfortunate human being, who grew giddy at her elevation, and whose mind toppled and fell into ruin created by the party her husband so disastrously led.

When Mrs. Lincoln was brought into Court week before last, her appearance was that of a woman suffering greatly from nervous excitement. Her son Robert accompanied her, a face so grief-marked as to sadden the hearts of all who beheld it. The testimony of several persons was taken, together with that of Robert Lincoln, which was, in substance, as follows:

> The action he had taken was sad to contemplate, but he had done it in the interest of his mother. He met her in the car upon her arrival from the south, and upon meeting her she was startled. She had the appearance of good health, and did not even seem fatigued by the trip. He asked her to come to his house, but she declined, and went to the hotel. He went with her and took supper. She told him that at the first breakfast she took after leaving Jacksonville an attempt was made to poison her. He occupied a room adjoining hers that night. She slept well that night, but subsequently was restless, and would come to his door in her night-dress and rap. About April 1st she ceased tapping at his door, he having told her that if she persisted he would leave the hotel. He went to her room April 1st, and found her but slightly dressed. She left the room in that condition under some pretext, and the next he knew of her she was going down in the elevator to the office. He had the elevator stopped, and tried to induce her to return to her room. She regarded his interference as impertinent, and declined to leave the elevator, but he put his

---

[*] Accusations that she looted the White House on her departure in May 1865 were untrue. The numerous trunks she left with contained her own possessions.

[†] Old Clothes Scandal in 1867.

arms about her and gently forced her. She screamed, "You are going to murder me." She had, since the fire, kept her trunks and property in the Fidelity Safe Deposit Company's buildings. He called on her the last week in April, and she told him that all Chicago was going to be burned, and that she was going to send her trunks to some country town. She said Milwaukee was too near Oshkosh, where there had been a terrible fire the night before. She told him that his home was going to be the only one saved, and he suggested to her to leave her trunks with him. The following Sunday she showed him securities for $57,000 which she carried in her pocket. She had spent large sums of money recently. She had bought $600 worth of lace curtains; three watches, costing $450; $700 worth of other jewelry; $200 worth of soaps and perfumeries, and a whole piece of silk. He had no doubt she was insane. He had had a conference with her cousin and Mayor Stuart, of Springfield, and Judge Davis, of the Supreme Court, all of whom advised him to take the course he had taken. He did not regard it as safe to allow her to remain longer unrestrained. She had long been a source of great anxiety. She had always been kind to him. She had been of unsound mind since the death of her husband, and had been irresponsible for the last ten years. He regarded her as eccentric and unmanageable. There was no cause for her recent purchases, as her trunks were filled with dresses she never wore. She never wore jewelry.[*]

After the finding of the court, Mrs. Lincoln managed to elude her watchers and hastened to a drug store and asked for two ounces of laudanum and a like quantity of camphor, saying she wished to bathe her shoulder, as she was troubled with neuralgia. The druggist suspected her intentions, and hoping that her friends would soon be after her, asked ten minutes time to put up the order. She hastened to two other drug stores for laudanum, but was followed, and the poison was not given her. Then she returned to the store she had first visited, to find put up for her a two-ounce vial of dark-colored liquid. She took it, went to her room and swallowed it all at once. Finding that it did not produce the sleep she expected, she returned to the drug store for another ounce of laudanum. After some delay and strategy, she was given a vial filled with burnt sugar and water, which she quickly swallowed. Finding that this did not work as she expected, she gave up the attempt on her life, and with a few friends went quietly and cheerfully to the depot and thence by cars to the Insane Asylum at Batavia, where she is now cared for. The attempt at suicide was not till after she had been informed that she was really insane when she broke completely down and began again to relate the circumstances of her husband's death, the horrible picture and work of that Good Friday night having never been out of her mind.

Pomeroy's Democrat [Chicago, Illinois],
May 29, 1875, 2

---

[*] Robert Lincoln's testimony here is an edited version of the article printed in the May 20 edition of the *Chicago Tribune.*

Chapter 5

Suicide Attempt

Perhaps the most astonishing moment of the insanity case occurred in its aftermath. The morning after the verdict, Mary Lincoln evaded the guards outside her hotel room, went to three local pharmacies to obtain lethal drugs, and tried to commit suicide. Luckily, an astute pharmacist knew who she was and foiled her plan.

Mary's preeminent biographer, Jean Baker, believes that there was no suicide attempt; that the story was planted in the newspapers by Robert Lincoln as an "exculpation of filial treachery."[1] The multiplicity of sources, as well as the variations in each story (which would not exist if all were based on one planted story), plus Leonard Swett's personal letter of the next day, prove that the suicide attempt did indeed take place.[2]

"INSANITY'S FREAKS"
Chicago Times, May 21, 1875

Displayed Yesterday in the Strange Actions of
Unhappy Mrs. Lincoln.

———

Two of the Them Were Determined Attempts to
Commit Suicide.

———

But Both Were Happily Frustrated by the
Ingenuity of a Druggist.

———

How She Was Prevailed Upon to Submit to
Treatment in an Asylum.

———

And How She Regards the Action of Her Friends in
Depriving Her of Her Liberty.

———

Departure Last Evening for Her New Home in Batavia.

THE LAST ACT

There was no strategy used in taking Mrs. Lincoln to the insane asylum; neither was there any force required to bring her into court on Wednesday. To Hon. Leonard Swett is ascribed the credit of effecting a quiet and unceremonious proceeding from beginning to end. When Robert T. Lincoln first decided to deprive his mother of her liberty temporarily, he cast about for a suitable person to conduct the case for him. He had relatives living in the southern part of the state, but when he called upon them to assist him in the delicate operation, they declined from sensitiveness. Judge Davis, an old-time friend of the president and of the family, was appealed to, but he, too, shrank from the delicate task. So one after another of those who were looked to to undertake the unpleasant duty, either from motives of friendship or respect, declined the task, and finally Mr. Swett, who had known the unfortunate lady and her husband well and intimately in brighter days, resolved to undertake it. So it was arranged that Robert should absent himself from his mother, and leave her entire management to Mr. Swett. The latter then drove to the Grand Pacific, and arrived just in time to see Mrs. Lincoln come in, followed by a driver with an armful of packages, which he was about taking to her room. Mr. Swett followed, and as the hackman entered the door, the follower pushed his way in also.

He was met by Mrs. Lincoln, who bade him a hearty welcome. He told her he was glad to see her, but that he was the harbinger of bad news. The poor lady looked at him imploringly, as she exclaimed, "My son! Is Robert dead?"

Mr. Swett answered that Robert was not dead, but that he was well. "But," said he, "you are insane." He thought it the better course to pursue, to come out bold-faced in the matter, tell her the truth, treat her like a lady, gently yet firmly, and rely upon her better instincts prompting her to acquiesce with her friends in the arrangements.

Said she, "Is it possible that you, Mr. Swett, a friend to my poor husband, should seek to place me in an insane asylum?"

"Yes," said Mr. Swett, "I want to put you in an insane asylum."

"I cannot believe it; you are no friend of mine, if you desire to deprive me of my liberty," said the unhappy lady.

Mr. Swett employed all his facilities to persuade her that it was all for the best. He reassured and argued with her; told her that he was afraid to trust her alone any longer. She asked him what he was afraid she would do. "That you will jump from the window," said he. In due course of time he had so far succeeded in the movement that she consented to go anywhere with him that he might dictate. "But," said she, "I have been out shopping, and I have come home with my dress all muddy. You certainly would not like me to go into court looking as I do now? And you would not subject me to the humiliation of changing my clothing while you are in the room?"

Mr. Swett was determined not to leave the room under any circumstances, and the ruse of the lady did not avail. He told her he should not leave the room. She again asked what he was afraid of, and he told her he believed she would jump out of the window, or do any other rash thing that might suggest itself. "What shall I do?" he told her there was a closet into which she might go and change her dress. Thither she went, and in a short time returned to the room, apparently satisfied with her toilet, but she did not manifest any haste to be gone. She was quite angry with Mr. Swett. He told her his own carriage was at the door of the hotel, and waiting for her. He said his wife would have accompanied him, but she feared it might be an indelicacy for her to do so.

Finally, with much persuasion, he succeeded in getting her into his carriage, and she was driven over to the county courtroom, where her son, Mr. Arnold, and others of her friends were awaiting her arrival. In passing out of the hotel from her room to the carriage Mr. Swett gallantly offered his arm, which she indignantly refused, saying she was "able to walk alone yet, if she was crazy." She also refused any assistance in getting into the carriage from the sidewalk.

After the trial, Mrs. Lincoln was deeply offended with Robert, as well as Mr. Swett. She said there was a breach between herself and son which would never be closed; that he was no longer her son who would thus treat the mother who bore him and loved him. It was a sad spectacle; one which the beholder may wish never to see repeated.

In conversation with Mr. Swett, yesterday, the patient appeared to be more reconciled to her fate. In speaking of her insanity, she said to Mr. Swett, "It may be so; and what if it is so, what wonder is it? Haven't I had enough cause to derange any woman's brain? Did I not see my husband assassinated before my eyes? Have I not been homeless for years, and have I not buried all my children, with the exception of Robert? Do you wonder that I am deranged?"

Mr. Swett replied. "It is only a wonder, my dear madam, that your brain has stood it so long. I sympathize with you deeply, but we all believe it to be best that you should be placed in some safe position, where you will receive proper care and treatment. I want you to see it in that light yourself, and become reconciled to the wishes of your friends, who wish you nothing but good. I want you to feel that we are your friends—that I am your friend."

She said: "You are no friend to me, if you want to put me in an insane asylum."

Later in the day, however, she became more reconciled, and her manner betokened that she freely forgave both Robert and Mr. Swett for the part they had acted. She even clung to the latter as a protector, and by her wishes he accompanied her to the depot last evening in his private carriage, with her son. As the day wore away she became almost cheerful. She knew where she was going to, and the treatment she would be subjected to, and her only anxiety appeared to be as to when she would be released. She questioned Mr. Swett closely in regard to this matter, and asked him who should decide. He told her he would probably be the one to decide himself. "Then," said she, "when will you let me come out?" He told her she should be set at liberty as soon as she was well enough to take care of herself.

Yesterday, the $56,000 in '81 bonds which she had in her possession were obtained from her, according to a promise made to Mr. Swett in the courtroom Wednesday. That day she made the excuse for not yielding them up there, that she could not conveniently get at them, but that she would give them to Mr. Swett on the following day at the hotel. Also, a large quantity of the goods and valuables which she had purchased were yesterday taken back by the parties from whom the purchases were made. She had in her possession over 40 pairs of lace curtains, besides jewelry in great abundance—all purchases made by her since she has been at the Grand Pacific. A number of the articles were secreted by her in the washroom adjoining her sleeping compartment.

A strong Irishwoman was placed to watch her movements in the room with her, with strict orders not to allow her to leave the room under any pretext whatsoever. One of Pinkerton's preventive policemen was also stationed at the door outside, with instructions to watch her movements closely. Yet, notwithstanding all this precaution, the wily prisoner managed to escape, and went below. She was missed shortly after her departure, but whither she had gone the servant girl knew not. The latter was in an agony of fear and suspense until her return, a quarter or a half hour later. However, she eluded all questions, and gave evasive answers to all inquiries made as to her whereabouts.

She met Mr. Swett and Robert pleasantly, and appeared quite affable. Mr. Swett took the servant to task about the escape of Mrs. Lincoln, and she confessed that the unfortunate lady had outwitted her, although she had tried to do her duty.

Where Mrs. Lincoln went and what she did will be found below.

The patient was to leave for the Bellevue hospital, at Batavia, on the 5:15 express of the Northwestern road, and by that time everything was in readiness. It was arranged that Mr. Swett should take her to the depot in his carriage, and at the appointed time Mrs. Lincoln, her son, and Mr. Swett proceeded to the train. She was allowed to take all the baggage she wished with her, and she accordingly took some five trunks along; besides these nearly a dozen more are to be sent in a few days. Her son told her she should not be deprived of any comfort which money could buy while out there. She said she liked the country and would enjoy staying there, provided she could have carriages and luxuries.

Mr. Swett left her in charge of Robert at the train, and returned home. Her son, Hon. I. N. Arnold, and Dr. Patterson, who is at the head of the Bellevue asylum, accompanied her to Batavia. At her parting with Mr. Swett, she shook him warmly by the hand, and, still clasping it, made him promise that he would soon visit her. He told her that himself and wife would be out to see her in about ten days at farthest. She said: "Don't wait ten days; come next week."

The car in which the party took transportation was the elegant special car of the directors of the road, proffered by them as a mark of courtesy to Mrs. Lincoln. It is complete in all its appointments, including cooking and sleeping conveniences.

Mrs. Lincoln is a woman of refinement and education. It is said that she speaks and reads French with fluency, is well versed in topics of literature, and has read a great deal in her life. Her talk and conversation betoken her a lady, and one of no ordinary culture. It is sad to think that she has fallen victim to the dread malady, insanity.

————

AN ATTEMPT AT SUICIDE

It was not until a late hour in the afternoon that Mr. Swett and Mr. Lincoln learned the melancholy truth that during the brief time above alluded to, in which she had contrived to elude her guards, the unhappy lady had made a determined but ineffectual effort to commit suicide. The plan she laid and carried out, as she for a time supposed, was contrived with that remarkable degree of cunning which people in her condition of mind so frequently exhibit, and it is almost miraculous that she did not succeed. The determination displayed, too, shows that she had firmly resolved never to be taken to the asylum, and had she not fortunately met with those who knew her and were acquainted with her misfortunes and felt moved by a kindly respect for them, it is almost certain that she would have carried her determination into effect.

Of course every precaution had been taken to guard against any attempt of this kind, both by her son and by Mr. Swett, who has managed this most unpleasant manner with most commendable care and consideration. No one could have been more circumspect than they, the one actuated by motives of filial affection and the other from a strong sense of duty owed to the unhappy widow of his old-time friend and law partner, and both knowing well that almost any wild frenzy might seize upon her disordered mind at any moment, and impel her to end her unhappy life. They thought they had planned well, and that every opportunity for such a thing, should it unhappily suggest itself, was cut off, and placed even beyond the bounds of a possibility.

But the calculations of some minds, shrewd and cunning though they may be, are sometimes outwitted by that keener shrewdness and cunning which shattered intellects are often gifted, and so it was in this case. So near as can be learned she found it an easy matter to convince the girl who had been stationed in her room to prevent any effort on her part to jump out of the window that it was necessary for her to step out into the hall for a moment. The good-natured servant consented, probably after some remonstrance, and once outside she seems to have found it quite as easy to pass the stalwart darky and Pinkerton's man, both of whom had been instructed not to allow her to pass them on any pretense, though in no case to lay hands on her or offer her any violence. She hurried by them and down the staircase toward the east front of the hotel to the drug store of Squair & Co., where she ordered two ounces of laudanum and a like quantity of camphor. The clerk looked at her doubtingly when she made this demand, but she assured him that she was troubled with neuralgia in her shoulder, and the pain was often so severe that she was impelled to seek relief by bathing it in the compound she had ordered. Still the clerk hesitated, and finally consulted the proprietor, who suspected the real object for which the mixture was desired, and concluding wisely that a little strategy was better than an absolute refusal, he told her that it should be prepared for her, but that it would take about ten minutes to put it up, hoping in this brief space of time to find means of again placing her in the control of her friends. But this did not suit her, probably for the reason that she suspected the real object of the excuse, or else that she would be discovered before it could be prepared.

Without saying another word to indicate her intention, she stepped out to the sidewalk, called a carriage from the number always waiting there, and, stepping quickly inside, drove to the store of Rogers & Smith, scarcely a block away, at the corner of Clark and Adams streets. The druggist to whom she had first applied suspected her object and hurried after her, as did Pinkerton's man, who was thoroughly alarmed at the predicament in which his orders and the lady's conduct were placing him. She reached the store and gave her order for the same deadly compound, but the druggist and policeman arrived in time to prevent her receiving it, even though the compounder of drugs had been disposed to give it to her. She was again met with some excuse and again she turned to her carriage and drove to William Dale's establishment, two blocks farther away down Clark Street, toward the Sherman house. The druggist and policeman followed, and again she failed to procure the deadly fluid.

By this time it seemed to occur to her that her prescription must have been compounded at the first place to which she had applied, so she again entered her carriage and drove back to Squair's store at the Pacific hotel. Arrived there she renewed her demand, and seeing no other way out of the difficulty, a four-ounce vial was filled with a colored but harmless fluid and given her. She grasped it eagerly and started for her room, but had scarcely passed beyond the door when she placed the vial to her lips and drained it of its contents. She then went quietly to her room and with the utmost composure awaited what she supposed was the inevitable approach of death.

But in this she was disappointed, and she was not slow to discover it. After waiting about 15 or 20 minutes without feeling any unpleasant effects from the draught, she essayed to repeat the effort and again slipped from her room and passed down to the drug store. She told Mr. Squair that the lotion seemed too weak to afford her any relief, and asked for another ounce of laudanum to strengthen it. In order that there might be no mistake about it, she stepped behind the prescription case to see that it was properly prepared, thus putting the druggist to his wits' ends to find a new way to deceive her. Mr. Robert Lincoln, for whom he had sent the moment he first saw her in his store, had not arrived, and there was no one at hand into whose care she could be given. The only thing to be done was to keep her waiting as long as possible, in the hope that relief of some kind would come. So he informed her that all the laudanum he had was kept in the cellar, and to that place he withdrew to prepare another compound of burnt sugar and water. An ounce vial was filled with this, labeled, "Laudanum—poison," and given her, and, as in the former case, she stepped out on the sidewalk and drank the fluid, after which she hurried to her room. Shortly afterward her son arrived, and finally, finding all her efforts futile, she quietly submitted to surrounding circumstances, and when the hour for her departure arrived she accepted the kindly attentions of the friends who came to escort her to the depot so pleasantly that not one of the party suspected the terrible determination she had had in her mind until it was told them after her departure.

Chicago Times, May 21, 1875, 5. This story widely reprinted in whole or part, including the *Illinois State Journal, Boston Globe,* and the *New-York Tribune.*

"MRS. LINCOLN ATTEMPT AT SUICIDE"
Chicago Tribune, May 21, 1875

Between 2 and 3 o'clock yesterday afternoon Mrs. Lincoln went into the drug store of Frank Squair, pharmacist, in the Grand Pacific Hotel, and wanted him to give her some laudanum and camphor, saying that she needed it for neuralgia in the arm. Knowing her mental condition, he pretended he had none ready, and that it would take half an hour to put it up. She said she would call in again for it, and then walked out into the street. Mr. Squair, supposing that she was going to some other drug store, put on his hat and followed her. She went directly across the street to Rogers & Smith's, at the corner of Adams and Clark. Just as she was telling Mr. Smith that she wanted some laudanum, Mr. Squair beckoned to Smith, and, when he came up, told him who it was that he was talking to, and that he must not give her any laudanum. Mr. Smith then said to her he could not sell her any without a doctor's order, and she left and went down the street to Dale's, where she asked for laudanum and camphor separately. Mr. Squair got in ahead of her, and was consequently able to prevent her getting anything there.

Then, seeing that she was about returning to the Pacific, he hurried back to his own place, and put up a mixture of one drachm of liquid burnt sugar and ten drops of tincture of camphor, in a 5-ounce bottle filled with water and labeled "Laudanum and Camphor." She took it and went outdoors, and as soon as she got on the sidewalk she drank the contents. About ten minutes afterwards she returned to the drug store, saying that her arm troubled [her] very much and she wanted some more laudanum to add to the mixture. Mr. Squair asked her if she had used it, and she said no, that she wanted it stronger. She went behind the counter and began watching him. He told her the laudanum was kept in the basement, so he went down there and made up a mixture of an ounce of liquid burnt sugar, labeled it "Laudanum Poison,"—cautioned her to be careful, and gave it to her. She took it out and drank it. In the meantime he had sent for her son, who came and took charge of her.

Chicago Tribune, May 21, 1875, 8

"MRS. LINCOLN: AN ATTEMPT TO COMMIT SUICIDE YESTERDAY"
Chicago Post and Mail, May 21, 1875

Mrs. Lincoln, yesterday, attempted to commit suicide by swallowing what she supposed was a two-ounce draught of laudanum, but which was in reality some burnt sugar and water, happily substituted for the deadly liquid by a druggist's clerk, who suspected her intention. She accidentally escaped from her room at the Grand Pacific, and, while out, applied for the drug at three different places, on the pretense that she needed it for a lotion. The attempt has emphasized the knowledge that great precautions are needed, and the distressed lady will be placed under more complete care. She left last night for Dr. Patterson's asylum at Batavia.

Chicago Post and Mail, May 21, 1875, 4

[MRS. LINCOLN TAKEN TO PRIVATE HOSPITAL]
Chicago Inter Ocean, May 21, 1875

Mrs. Lincoln was yesterday taken to the private hospital for the insane at Batavia, Ill. She yesterday purchased what she supposed to be a bottle of laudanum, and swallowed the contents, with the evident intent of committing suicide. The mixture, however, was of a harmless nature and her design was thwarted.

Chicago Inter Ocean, Friday morning,
May 21, 1875, 4

CRIME: MRS. LINCOLN MAKES PERSISTENT
EFFORT TO COMMIT SUICIDE
Illinois State Journal, May 21, 1875

CHICAGO, May 20—The *Times* has information that Mrs. Lincoln today, attempted to commit suicide by poisoning. After being removed from the courtroom, where she was adjudged insane yesterday, she was put under the strictest surveillance, it being feared that she might do injury to herself. Today she escaped from her room and hurried to the drug store of Frank Squair, under the Grand Pacific Hotel. She ordered a compound of camphor and laudanum, ostensibly for neuralgia. The clerk informed her it would take about ten minutes to make it, whereupon she took a carriage and drove to two other drug stores. She was followed by Mr. Squair, who, in each case, prevented the druggists from giving her the compound. She finally returned to the first place and procured a mixture which she supposed was what she wanted; but which was harmless. She drank this as she left the store. As it had no effect, she tried to leave her room again to obtain a larger dose, but was prevented. She was removed to a private hospital at Batavia, Ill., this afternoon, where she will have every attention.

Illinois State Journal, Friday morning,
May 21, 1875, 1

"MRS. LINCOLN: HER ATTEMPT AT SUICIDE"
Illinois State Journal, May 24, 1875

Her Efforts to Procure Laudanum Foiled—
Departure for Batavia

————

From the Chicago Inter Ocean, May 21

The sorrow which was generally experienced yesterday when it was known that Mrs. Lincoln, the widow of Abraham Lincoln, had been adjudged insane, came near being extremely intensified by the positive attempt which the unfortunate lady made to poison herself. Although she had been eccentric in her manner and the victim of extraordinary vagaries, a burning love for her son, Mr. Robert Lincoln, was at all times cognizable * * * *

Mrs. Lincoln's

QUIET DEMEANOR

during the Inquisition was noticeable, and her indifference to the testimony of the doctors and others. But, as though she fully comprehended the nature of the proceeding and the part her beloved son was acting therein, the look of sorrow and silent reproach she cast on him when testifying was more than he could bear, and his feelings found vent in tears. The verdict, which she fully understood, seemed to dispel all hope in this world, all confidence in him in whom her affections were centered. When Mr. Lincoln approached, and taking his mother's hand, spoke affectionately to her, she said: "Oh, that my son would have done this; you have struck my heart." She then withdrew her hand from his.

These circumstances tend to show the gloomy and despairing state of Mrs. Lincoln's mind on Wednesday evening. She returned to her rooms at the Grand Pacific Hotel, ate a sparing supper and retired at an early hour. A woman employed at the hotel occupied a bed in the room, and she states that Mrs. Lincoln slept well for a few hours, but towards morning she was even

MORE RESTLESS

than she had been heretofore. A detective officer occupied a chair in the corridor in case she should become violent, and beyond the power of the woman to restrain. There was no occasion for his interference, and Mrs. Lincoln seemed to be growing calm. During the forenoon yesterday she was quiet in her manner, and busied herself for a journey with her son, as she said. The Hon. Leonard Swett visited her and questioned her about the government securities she was known to have had in her possession on last Sunday. She refused to give them up, and Mr. Swett felt called upon to threaten her that he would call an officer, whereupon Mrs. Lincoln went to the closet and, taking out a dress, ripped up a portion of it and took out $57,000 worth of securities. She would not, however, give them to Mr. Swett, but handed them to Mr. Arnold, her special legal friend. Subsequently Mrs. Lincoln appeared to have recovered from her agitation, and the officer in the corridor retired. As soon as the lady became aware of that fact she put on her bonnet, and despite the entreaties of the woman in care of her, and beyond her power to restrain, she left her room and went out of the hotel to the drug store kept by Frank Squair in the hotel building. The druggist recognized Mrs. Lincoln immediately, and suspected her mission. She asked for a three-ounce

BOTTLE OF LAUDANUM

and camphor, and stated that she required it as she was suffering from neuralgia in the arm. Mr. Squair told her it would take half an hour to get it ready and Mrs. Lincoln left, promising to return. As she went out Mr. Squair followed her. She went into the drug store of Rogers & Smith, corner of Adams and Clark streets, and asked for fifty cents' worth of laudanum. Mr. Squair admonished Mr. Smith not to give her the drug under any circumstances; that she was insane. Mr. Smith told Mrs. Lincoln that his stock had run out, but he might have some next week. She then left, and Mr. Squair, anticipating her intention, reached Dale's drug store, on Clark street, before she entered. He informed Mr. Dale of the condition of the visitor he would soon have. Mrs. Lincoln asked for an ounce and a half of laudanum and an ounce and a half of camphor, in separate bottles, which she would mix herself. Mr.

Dale told her he did not sell laudanum by retail, and Mrs. Lincoln left and retraced her steps to Squair's store. The active druggist was in the store to wait on her, and proceeded to make up

THE PRESCRIPTION

for her, but instead of the death-dealing poisons, he put up a three-ounce mixture consisting of one dram of burnt sugar, two drops of camphor, and the remainder aqua pura. He labeled the bottle laudanum and camphor. Mrs. Lincoln took the bottle, and as soon as she reached the sidewalk, drew the cork and swallowed the contents. She then repaired to her room. The hotel managers, becoming aware of these facts, dispatched a messenger for Mr. Lincoln. After an interval of ten minutes Mrs. Lincoln again visited Squair's drug store. She stated that the pain in her arm had become unbearable and she required

SOME MORE LAUDANUM.

She went into the laboratory to watch the druggist putting up the prescription. But Mr. Squair told her he must go down to the cellar for the drug. When he returned the bottle contained the same harmless mixture as the first. The woe-begone, heart-stricken, despairing lady clasped the bottle and heaved a sigh, as though she comprehended the act she imagined and intended to accomplish. When outside the store she drank the contents of the bottle, and, as before, returned to her room. Soon after she was seized with nausea, but it was not distressing and she soon recovered. Mr. Lincoln just then reached the hotel, and remained with his mother until 5 p.m., when they started for Batavia.

It was fortunate that the lady first visited Mr. Squair's store, for through his activity the nation was spared an additional sorrow, and a life was saved which may yet in the fullness of her god-given reason appreciate the kindly action of her son and her friends.

THE DEPARTURE FOR BATAVIA
From the Chicago Times, May 21

The patient was to leave for the Bellevue hospital, at Batavia, on the 5:15 express of the Northwestern road, and by that time everything was in readiness. It was arranged that Mr. Swett should take her to the depot in his carriage, and at the appointed time Mrs. Lincoln, her son, and Mr. Swett proceeded to the train. She was allowed to take all the baggage she wished with her, and she accordingly took some five trunks along; besides these nearly a dozen more are to be sent in a few days. Her son told her she should not be deprived of any comfort which money could buy while out there. She said she liked the country and would enjoy staying there, provided she could have carriages and luxuries.

Mr. Swett left her in charge of Robert at the train, and returned home. Her son, Hon. I. N. Arnold, and Dr. Patterson, who is at the head of the Bellevue asylum, accompanied her to Batavia. At her parting with Mr. Swett, she shook him warmly by the hand, and, still clasping it, made him promise that he would soon visit her. He told her that himself and wife would be out to see her in about ten days at farthest. She said: "Don't wait ten days; come next week."

The car in which the party took transportation was the elegant special car of the directors of the road, proffered by them as a mark of courtesy to Mrs. Lincoln. It is complete in all its appointments, including cooking and sleeping conveniences.

Mrs. Lincoln is a woman of refinement and education. It is said that she speaks and reads French with fluency, is well versed in topics of literature, and has read a great deal in her life. Her talk and conversation betoken her a lady, and one of no ordinary culture. It is sad to think that she has fallen victim to the dread malady, insanity.

Illinois State Journal, Monday, May 24, 1875, 3

LEONARD SWETT TO DAVID DAVIS
Chicago, Ill., May 24, 1875

(excerpt)

. . . . Coming around to Robert's office about two o'clock in the day we met a messenger in haste, stating that Robert's mother had escaped. Arriving at the hotel as soon as possible, we found her absence was only momentary and she had returned. This with the subsequent facts about the poisoning determined us to stand guard personally until she should go.

It is perfectly frightful to think how near she came to poisoning herself. Notwithstanding the instructions to the people guarding her, by plausible stories she worked her way through there to the street, and going to a drug store in the Pacific Hotel, said she wanted two ounces of laudanum and camphor as an application, said her shoulder was paining her badly. Fortunately the druggist knew her situation; he said he would have it ready for her in ten minutes; whereupon she left immediately, saying she would be back at the time. From there she went to another drug store, ordering the same prescription, but some body followed her, notifying the new druggist of the facts; from there she went to a third place with the same result. From there she came to the first drug store, received her prescription which had been put up without the laudanum, and immediately swallowed it. . . .

Folder A-73, Box 5, David Davis Family Papers

On May 20, 1875, Mary Lincoln, accompanied by her son, traveled ninety miles to Batavia, Illinois, to begin residence at her new home, Bellevue Place sanitarium. Bellevue Place was a three-story limestone structure set on twenty acres of secluded and manicured grounds. The interior of the building was bright, spacious, and cozy, intending to create a homelike and relaxing atmosphere. The inmates all were high-class female patients who were typically nervous invalids, many suffering depression, whose families wanted better care and more privacy than state asylums offered. Bellevue was equipped for twenty-five to thirty patients, but only twenty were there when Mary Lincoln arrived in mid-1875. Mary had her own private suite of two rooms on the second floor, including a private bath, and her own personal attendant.[1]

Dr. Richard J. Patterson, proprietor of the sanitarium, was one of the most respected psychiatrists in the Midwest. He practiced the modern techniques of "moral therapy," which included, "rest, diet, baths, fresh air, occupation (typically gardening), diversion, change of scene, no more medicine than . . . absolutely necessary, and the least restraint possible."[2] He allowed all the patients freedom to walk the grounds and even leave the grounds while attended by a nurse, and had carriages and sleighs available for rides.

Bellevue Place was a highly esteemed sanitarium that boasted a high "cure" rate of its patients. Robert Lincoln later told his aunt that he considered it "a blessing" that his mother was there under such good care.

DAILY PATIENT PROGRESS REPORTS
Bellevue Place Sanitarium, Batavia, Ill., May 1875

> 20—Mrs. Mary Lincoln admitted today—from Chicago—age 56—widow of Ex-President Lincoln—declared insane by Cook County Court May 19, 1875. Case is one of mental impairment which probably dates back to the murder of President Lincoln—more pronounced since the death of her son, but especially aggravated during the last two months.

21—Mrs. Lincoln slept well last night—today her pulse is 100 but she has no fever.

22—Mrs. Lincoln has seemed cheerful and is apparently contented—she took a long walk this morning—sleeps well at night.

23—Mrs. Lincoln out riding today—seems well and contented—quite talkative.

24—Mrs. Lincoln as usual—went to ride today—sleeping well.

25—Mrs. Lincoln rather depressed—went out to drive as usual.

26—Mr. Lincoln came to see his mother—she was comparatively cheerful—went out in the evening for a drive to Geneva.

27—Mrs. Lincoln as usual—went to ride in evening.

29—Mrs. Lincoln out walking today—she did not wish to ride.

30—Mrs. Lincoln out riding today—very melancholy.

31—Mrs. Lincoln as usual—did not ride today.

Ross, "Mary Todd Lincoln"

ROBERT LINCOLN TO SALLY ORNE

Chicago, Ill., June 1, 1875

My dear Madam:

Your letter written immediately after you received the news of the proceedings which I was unhappily compelled to take, should have received an earlier reply and I must beg you to excuse my apparent neglect.

If you have since seen any detailed account of the occurrences which forced me to place my mother under care, I think, indeed I know, you could not but have approved my action. Six physicians in council informed me that by longer delay I was making myself morally responsible for some very probable tragedy, which might occur at any moment. Some of my eastern friends have criticized the public proceedings in Court which seemed to them unnecessary. Against this there was no help, for we have a statute in this state which imposes a very heavy penalty on any one depriving an insane person of his liberty, without verdict of a jury.

My mother is, I think, under as good care and as happily situated as is possible under the circumstances. She is in the private part of the house of Dr. Patterson and her associates are the members of his family only. With them she walks and drives whenever she likes and takes her meals with them or in her own rooms as she chooses, and she tells me she likes them all very much. The expression of surprise at my action which was telegraphed East, and which you doubtless saw, was the first and last expression of the kind she has uttered and we are on the best of terms. Indeed my consolation in this sad affair is in thinking that she herself is happier in every way, in her freedom from care and excitement, than she has been in ten years. So far as I can see she does not realize her situation at all. It is of course my care that she should have everything for her comfort and pleasure that can be obtained.

I can tell you nothing as to the probability of her restoration. It must be the work of some turn if it occurs. Her physician who is of high repute is not yet able to give an opinion.

The responsibility that has been and is now on me is one that I would gladly share if it was possible to do so, but being alone as I am, I can only do my duty as it is given me to see it, trusting that I am guided for the best.

Very sincerely yours,
Robert T. Lincoln

Box 2, Folder 5, Mary Todd Lincoln Insanity File

DAILY PATIENT PROGRESS REPORTS
Bellevue Place Sanitarium, Batavia, Ill., June 1875

1—Mrs. Lincoln not out today.
2—Mr. Lincoln came to see his mother today. She did not go outdoors at all today. She seems pleasant at all times but quite restless and uneasy.
4—Mrs. Lincoln has not been riding today—she keeps to her room quite closely and refuses to ride.
5—Mrs. Lincoln out walking today.

Ross, "Mary Todd Lincoln"

ROBERT LINCOLN TO JOHN HAY
Chicago, Ill., June 6, 1875

My dear John,

I do not usually see the Tribune here but some person sent me the paper of May 22nd (I think) and I want to thank you for your article.[*] It is nearly impossible for anyone to realize the distress and anxiety of my mind for the two months before that time. I knew that on the next day after my action the whole country would be flooded with criticisms, kind or unkind as might happen, but all based on a short press dispatch, which could not sufficiently give the facts. Yet I could not wait any longer when six of our most eminent physicians assembled in council, after hearing the statements in writing of most of the witnesses who afterwards testified at the Inquisition, gave me to understand that by longer delay, I was rendering myself responsible for a probable tragedy of some kind.

---

[*] "President Lincoln's Widow," *New York Tribune,* May 22, 1875, 6; see also chapter 4.

I suppose you saw some of our Chicago papers. The accounts were factually accurate, except that they left an impression that my mother was angered at me. This really lasted for a moment only. She has since been extremely cordial with me (I see her every week) and while she will not in words admit that she is not sane, still her entire acquiescence in absolutely everything, while it arises in part from the plain enfeebled condition of her mind, makes me think that she is aware of the necessity of what has been done.

In the catastrophe, the value of Mr. Swett's earnestness, tact and resources have placed me in debt to him to an extent I can never repay. He alone was right in his judgment as to the means of getting my mother into Court, while all the rest of us, including Judge Davis and Mr. Stuart, thought his plan not worth trying. He took upon himself a most painful task and by his marvelous fairness and kindness accomplished it and saved me from the commission of a terrible blunder. But I could talk all night about Swett.

I am of course in receipt of a great many letters, some of which are worthy of and receive attention, but most of them are impertinent. I see in all of them, however, the impression that my mother is in close confinement. The writers using the word "asylum," with a notion of straightjackets, cells and brutal keepers. This idea is probably in the heads of the majority of people and Mr. Swett and I think it would be well if a short article could be started on its travels containing a statement of the actual situation. The article to be in the form of a letter from your Chicago Correspondent but as to that we would defer to your better judgment. We think it better to be started in your paper for several reasons. One is on account of the broad field you cover. A negative reason is the sensational character of our local papers. I will take the liberty of assuming that I can count on you for this and will put some hints on a separate sheet. I know that some of your people can better put these in a form which will attach a proper amount of attention. . . .

With our kindest regards to Mrs. Hay,

Sincerely yours,

Robert T. Lincoln

P.S. June 8

I have held this to show Swett the enclosure. He thinks it about the thing and sufficiently short to ensure being scissored—

On second thought, we think it would appear best in a personal column, but do you decide as to that.

It will be a "triumph of journalism" for there isn't a lie in it, but you must not tell the personal column man so, or he wouldn't touch it with a pair of tongs.

R.T.L.

John Hay Papers

DAILY PATIENT PROGRESS REPORTS

Bellevue Place Sanitarium, Batavia, Ill., June 1875

> 7—Mrs. Lincoln keeps her room today.
>
> 8—Mrs. Lincoln the same as she has been—will not ride.
>
> 9—Mrs. Lincoln same.
>
> 10—Mrs. Lincoln same—tries to pack a trunk of things to send back to her son:—but fails to complete it.
>
> 11—Mrs. L same.
>
> 12—Mrs. L same will not ride or walk out.
>
> 13—Mrs. L same.
>
> 14—Mrs. Lincoln complains some of neuralgia and gives this as a reason for not riding out.

Ross, "Mary Todd Lincoln"

EDITORIAL (ANONYMOUSLY AUTHORED BY JOHN HAY)
New-York Tribune, June 14, 1875

The action taken by Mr. Robert T. Lincoln in regard to his mother's mental disorder was founded upon consultation with members of her family, with the most intimate friends of the late President, and with six of the leading physicians of Chicago, who after full examination of the case assured him that by any further delay he would render himself responsible for a probable tragedy. Mrs. Lincoln is receiving treatment under the care of Dr. R. J. Patterson, at his residence, Bellevue-place, situated at Batavia, one of the most beautiful villages in Northern Illinois, about 37 miles from Chicago. Dr. Patterson is a gentleman of high repute for his skill in mental disorders, but devotes his attention entirely to ladies, of whom there are about a dozen under his charge. Mrs. Lincoln (with her attendant, a young lady formerly a school teacher, selected for this position on account of her kindness and intelligence) occupies two very pleasant rooms in the part of the house reserved for the private residence of the Doctor and his family, and has no reason to be aware that any other patients are in the house. She takes her meals in her rooms or at the Doctor's private table as she chooses, drives and walks out when and where she pleases, but when out is always accompanied by either Mrs. or Miss Patterson or her special attendant, for all of whom she expresses a great liking. Such has been the influence of the quiet and pleasant surroundings that nothing whatever has occurred to render necessary anything more than a prudent supervision, and this is given by pleasant companionship, without any appearance of restraint. At present her derangement exhibits itself mainly in a general mental feebleness and incapacity, and it is not yet possible to give an opinion as to her restoration.

New-York Tribune, Monday, June 14, 1875, 6

ROBERT LINCOLN TO JUDGE M. R. M. WALLACE

June 14, 1875

In the County Court
Of June Term A.D. 1875

To the Honorable Judge M. R. M. Wallace
Judge of the County Court

I the undersigned, Robert T. Lincoln, appointed on the 14th day of June, A.D. 1875, Conservator of Mrs. Mary Lincoln, who was on the 19th day of May, A.D. 1875, in this Court declared to be insane, respectfully respond that on the day after the rendering of the verdict, Mrs. Lincoln was placed under the care of Dr. R. J. Patterson at Batavia, Illinois, where she now is.

The undersigned restored to various merchants in the City of Chicago, such articles of merchandise lately purchased by Mrs. Lincoln, and useless to her as he was able to identify. In three cases, the articles returned had been paid for by Mrs. Lincoln and in three cases the money paid was refunded to the undersigned, and he charges himself with the same in the preliminary account herein set forth.

The preliminary account begins with the amount which the undersigned was indebted to Mrs. Lincoln at the time of her arrival from Florida, on March 16th, 1875, and extends to the date of the appointment of the undersigned as Conservator, by this court.

Preliminary Account

The undersigned charges himself as follows:

March 16	Amount due Mrs. Lincoln by him at that date	$625.00
April 1	Cash taken from her for safekeeping	$157.35
April 1	Amount falling due this date under an obligation of the undersigned mentioned in Inventory[*]	$125.00
May 1	Amount falling due this date under same obligation	$125.00
May 4	Cash refunded Haskell Bros. for a satchel	$7.00
May 20	Cash from Mrs. Lincoln	$7.00
May 25	Cash from Mssrs. Hollister Johnson for goods returned	$336.83
May 29	Cash from Mssrs. Allen & Mackey for goods returned	$213.00

[*] See page 80.

June 1	Amount due this date under obligation above mentioned	$125.00
	Total receipts prior to June 14th, 1875	$1,721.18

Out of this amount the undersigned prays to be allowed the amount of the following disbursements made by him during the same period on account of Mrs. Lincoln:

April 10	Paid Dr. Patterson for coming to Chicago to consult with Dr. Isham on April 1st	$10.00
May 19	Paid sundry expenses in proceedings of Inquisition	$25.00
May 21	Paid as gratuities to various persons at Pacific Hotel attending Mrs. Lincoln for two months and aiding in her removal	$20.00
May 22	Paid Dr. Patterson on account of maintenance	$100.00
May 27	Paid A. Pinkerton for services and expenses of special attendant for three weeks	$151.00
May 29	Paid for bedding for Mrs. Lincoln's use at Batavia	$52.00
May 29	Paid Fidelity Safety Deposit for storage of 3 trunks to Sept. 27, 1875	$3.30
May 29	Paid American Express Co. for bringing trunks from Milwaukee	$17.00
June 2	Paid A. J. Wright for carriages on May 19 & 20	$8.00
June 2	Paid Dr. H. A. Johnson for consultation and attendance as witness	$15.00
June 8	Paid expressing trunk to Fidelity Safe Deposit	$1.00
June 8	Paid Mrs. Lincoln's account at Pacific Hotel	$11.50
June 8	Paid Pacific Hotel for board of special attendant for three weeks	$64.00
June 9	Paid notice of application in *Inter Ocean*	$1.00

Total disbursement to June 14, 1875	$479.40[*]
Balance carried to Inventory as cash on hand	$1,241.78
	$1,721.18

---

[*] The figures here actually total $478.80; the discrepancy of $0.60 cannot be accounted for.—Ed.

Respectfully submitted
Robert T. Lincoln
Conservator of Mrs. Mary Lincoln

LB 1:1:120–22

ROBERT LINCOLN TO JUDGE M. R. M. WALLACE
June 14, 1875

In the County Court
Of June Term A.D. 1875

To the Honorable Judge M. R. M. Wallace
Judge of the County Court

The undersigned respectfully submits the following Inventory of the Estate of Mrs. Mary Lincoln, who was on the nineteenth day of May, A.D. 1875, declared to be insane.

Money on hand

Cash on hand June 14th, 1875, being the balance shown by a preliminary account this day filed	$1,246.76

Bonds and securities—all good

United States Registered Bond payable after December 31, 1880 (6%)	
No. 10244 for	$1,000.00
United States Registered Bonds payable after June 30, 1881 (6%)	
Nos. 5574, 5629, and 5738 for $500 each	$1,500.00
Nos. 20605, 30020, 30021, and 30022 for $1,000 each	$4,000.00
Nos. 80941 and 10797 for $5,000 each	$10,000.00
No 10348 for	$10,000.00
	$26,500.00

No. 1572 for	$500.00
Nos. 6672, 9474, 9475, 9476, and 9477 for $1,000 each	$5,000.00
Nos. 5700 and 3944 for $5,000 each	$10,000.00
No. 5250 for	$10,000.00

United States Registered Bonds 5/20s of 1867:

Letter B

Nos. 25781, 25782, 25783, and 25784 for $1,000 each	$4,000.00

United States Registered Stock of Funded Loan of 1881 (15%)

Letter A

Nos. 8474 and 8700 for $1,000 each	$2,000.00
Total United States Bonds	$58,000.00

An obligation of Robert T. Lincoln, dated April 6, 1874, providing for the payment of the sum of $10,500 in monthly installments of $125 each, on which three is now unpaid*	$8,875.00
Two gold checks of United States Treasury for the Nov. instant (quarterly) on the 5% bonds not yet cashed, each for $12.50 gold	$25.00

Annuity

Mrs. Lincoln is entitled under an act of Congress appointed July 14, 1870 to a pension at the rate of $3,000 per annum [to be paid in] Chicago on the fourth day of March, June, September, and December. The quarterly payment ($750) which became due on the 4th day of June, A.D. 1875, is not yet collected.

---

* This was for Robert's purchase from his mother of the family home at Eighth and Jackson Streets in Springfield for $500 and his purchase of her Chicago house at 375 West Washington Street for $10,000.

Other personal property

The box containing personal jewelry and nine (9) trunks containing wearing apparel and other articles for safekeeping in the Fidelity Safety Deposit at Chicago, having been locked and the keys retained by Mrs. Lincoln.*

Real estate—none

Chicago June 14, 1875
Robert T. Lincoln
Conservator of Mrs. Mary Lincoln

LB 1:1:124–26

DAILY PATIENT PROGRESS REPORTS
Bellevue Place Sanitarium, Batavia, Ill., June 1875

> 17—Mr. Robert Lincoln came to see his mother—he thought her not quite
> so cordial in her manner toward him as at previous visits. He insisted on
> taking her trunk back with him—and she finally got it packed and he took
> it—she did not care to ride.

Ross, "Mary Todd Lincoln"

**ROBERT LINCOLN TO THE COMMISSIONER
OF PENSIONS, WASHINGTON, D.C.**
Chicago, Ill., June 18, 1875

Sir:

Unfortunate circumstances, of which you are doubtless unofficially informed, have compelled the appointment of myself as Conservator of the estate of my mother Mrs. Mary Lincoln, under the laws of the State. I have duly qualified and enclosed to you a certified copy of the "Letters of Conservatorship" issued to me.

Mrs. Lincoln, under a special act approved July 14th 1870, receives a Pension of $3,000 per annum (certified No. 146718) under which there is now undrawn the

---

* Robert Lincoln's final and "perfect" submittal of his mother's inventory, dated August 10, 1875 (Folder 33, Box 2, Mary Todd Lincoln Insanity File), is exactly the same as this of June 14, except that it estimates the value of Mary's "other personal property" at $5,000; it also includes a "lot of lace curtains and curtain material" of estimated value at $549.83.

Quarterly Installment In June 4th 1875 and I write to request that you will cause such directions to be given that I may receive the payment now and also the later installments, until the occasion of my appointment shall cease, of which you will be properly advised.

I shall of course supply with pleasure with any requirement of your office.

Asking the favor of a reply,

I have the honor to be

Very respectfully, your obedient servant

Robert T. Lincoln

LB 1:1:114–15

ROBERT LINCOLN TO THE SENIOR AUDITOR OF THE TREASURY, WASHINGTON, D.C.

Chicago, Ill., June 19, 1875

Sir:

I request to inform you that my mother Mrs. Mary Lincoln has been adjudged, in conformity with a statute of this State, to be *non compos mentis,* and that I have been duly appointed Conservator of her Estate.

I enclose to you a certified copy of the Letters issued to me.

My mother is the owner of Registered United States Bonds, of which I enclose a schedule. They are sometimes payable to her as "Mrs. Mary Lincoln" and sometimes as "Mrs. Abraham Lincoln."

I have also two gold checks for $10.50 each, for interest due May 1, 1875 on the two bonds at the front of the schedule.

The interest on the Reg[istered] Bonds is payable at Chicago.

I will be obliged if you will give such directions that I may collect the two charges and all interest hereafter falling due, until the necessity of my Conservatorship shall cease, of which you will be promptly informed.

I have the honor to be

Very respectfully your obedient servant

Robert T. Lincoln

LB 1:1:117–18

DAILY PATIENT PROGRESS REPORTS

Bellevue Place Sanitarium, Batavia, Ill., June 1875

19—Mrs. Lincoln's trunk sent home—she unwilling to go out to ride.

20—Mrs. Lincoln same.

21—Mrs. Lincoln same.

22—Mrs. Lincoln went out for a ride today—she went to the dressmaker and ordered a lawn dress—she said that she would like to ride out every morning.

24—Mrs. Lincoln did not go out today—no change.

25—Mrs. Lincoln same.

26—Mrs. Lincoln unwilling to go out today.

27—Mrs. Lincoln as usual today—did not ride or go out though asked to do so.

29—Mr. Robert Lincoln came to see his mother today—she went out riding in the forenoon.

30—Mrs. Lincoln as usual today—very quiet and inclined to stay in bed a good part of the time. Did not ride out today.

Ross, "Mary Todd Lincoln"

ROBERT LINCOLN TO MASON B. LOOMIS

At Bon Ami Camp, Lake Geneva, Wis., undated

Mrs. Lincoln is receiving treatment under care of Dr. R. J. Patterson, at his residence "Bellevue Place," situated at Batavia, one of the most beautiful villages of northern Illinois, about thirty-seven miles from Chicago. Dr. Patterson is a gentleman of high repute for his skill in mental disorders, but devotes his attention entirely to ladies, of whom there are about a dozen under his charge.

Mrs. Lincoln, with her attendant, a young lady formerly a school teacher, selected for this position on account of her kindness and intelligence, occupies two very pleasant rooms in the part of the house reserved for the private residence of the doctor and his family and has no reason to be aware that any other patients are in the house. She takes her meals in her rooms or at the doctor's private table as she chooses, drives and walks out when and where she pleases, but when out is always accompanied by either Mrs. or Miss Patterson or her special attendant, for all of whom she expresses a great liking. Such has been the influence of the quiet and pleasant surroundings that nothing whatever has occurred to render necessary anything more than a prudent supervision, and this is given by pleasant companionship, without any appearance of restraint.

At present her derangement exhibits itself mainly in a general feebleness and incapacity, and it is not yet possible to give an opinion as to her restoration.

Folder 37, Box 2, Mary Todd Lincoln Insanity File

Bellevue Place Sanitarium, Batavia, Ill., July 1875

2—Mrs. Lincoln habitually makes an appointment to ride in the morning—when the time comes she puts it off until night—then delays until next morning and so on.

3—Mrs. Lincoln was up 4 or 5 times during the night last night.

4—Mrs. Lincoln as usual today—lies in bed much of the time—does not complain.

5—Mrs. Lincoln had a fit of crying today—went out for a ride in the afternoon—a good many persons being out driving also She insisted upon coming home as soon as possible.

6—Mrs. Lincoln in her room all day—does not say much of anything.

7—Mrs. Lincoln came down and sat on the front steps for a while this morning—she also made a call on Mrs. Patterson—said "good morning" to J.P. 2 or 3 times in 5 minutes—the rest of the day she stayed in her room—she complains of nothing except perhaps, a slight annoyance from the noise of carpenters now working on the building.

8—Mrs. Rayne a correspondent of the *Chicago Evening Post & Mail* was here today—she was acquainted with some of Mrs. Lincoln's friends and wishing very much to see her sent up her name. Much to our surprise and contrary to her usual custom Mrs. Lincoln consented to see her. She made a short call—Mrs. L seemed glad to hear of her Chicago friends.

Ross, "Mary Todd Lincoln"

Mrs. Rayne's article in the Post and Mail, *published a few days after her visit to Batavia, is one of the most interesting and revealing in the entire story of Mary's time in the asylum because of the detailed descriptions it contains of Batavia and Bellevue Place, of Dr. Patterson and his staff, of the characters and symptoms of all the patients in the sanitarium—but especially of Mary Lincoln's physical, mental, and emotional state at the time.*

"MRS. LINCOLN: A VISIT TO HER BY
'THE POST AND MAIL' CORRESPONDENT"
Chicago Post and Mail, July 13, 1875

How She Passes the Time at Dr. Patterson's Retreat.

———

Some of the Peculiarities of Her Mental Delusions.

Some of the Beauties of Batavia and Vicinity

Together with Notes of Some of Its Leading Enterprises

[Special correspondence of The Post and Mail.]

Batavia, Ill., July 9—You cannot imagine a cooler, shadier, more delightful retreat from the noise and heat of the city, than this beautiful little island town, with its charming surroundings, nestled cosily in the green hollow of the Fox River valley, a lovely undulation of hill and dale threaded by a beautiful river, about whose borders a dense foliage casts lingering shadows. No picture on canvas can rival the landscapes I have seen here. Calm, still pools of water, become graceful bends of the river where hanging branches droop to meet, while placid-faced cows, mildly watching their shadows as they stand half submerged in the tranquil waters, or darker, stiller spots, where a boat lies idly moored with a lazy fisherman extended at ease, intent only on his pipe and rod. Right in the center of the pretty town, one finds such pictures; not one or two, but a constant succession of them, each more attractive than the last. It was through pleasant lingerings in such as that I reached a spot of more than ordinary interest to all visitors to Batavia, albeit of a melancholy nature. I allude to the

BELLEVUE INSANE RETREAT,

the elegant asylum, owned and managed by Dr. R. J. Patterson, which stands at the head of Union avenue, a delightfully shaded spot that has an enclosed area of twenty acres under cultivation. The house is a massive stone mansion, built upon a natural elevation, facing the wide drive, which leads to it, and presenting the appearance of a gentleman's residence, other than a hospital for minds diseased; the grounds are of great natural beauty, and they are cultivated with much care, being laid out in walks and flower beds, which are under constant tribute to the inmates who desire them; evergreens and other shade trees are planted at regular intervals, and a fine greenhouse is nearly completed which will have a capacity for 6,000 plants, and has already nearly a thousand winter roses budded. This will connect by steps and an ornamental porch, with the first hall, so that patients can visit the greenhouse under cover. Pleasant lawn seats, rustic chairs and croquet games for those who wish are added to the comfort for inmates. The house itself,

BELLEVUE PLACE,

as it is familiarly called, is built of Batavia stone, cut from the quarries here, and is four stories in height. I must acknowledge that when I stood on the steps and pulled the bell, there came over me a nervous inclination to run away. The tranquil beauty of the place and everything about it had reassured me, but now cold chills assaulted me, and I anticipated blood-curdling cries, and heart-rending appeals as soon as I entered the unhappy domain. Never was I further astray in calculation. The doctor-manager himself opened the door, and one look at his handsome, genial face restored my moral courage. I offered my credentials and was cordially invited to enter. Dr. Patterson led the way into a dainty office, caparisoned like a lady's boudoir and seated me in a luxurious reclining chair, while he went in search of the lady members of his family. These consisted of Mrs. Patterson, who is matron of the Retreat, and her daughter, Miss Blanche, a fair, delicate girl of much culture. There is also a son, Dr. John Patterson, who is medical assistant and in partnership with his father. After a pleasant chat on topics of the day, I inquired after the health of

MRS. PRESIDENT LINCOLN,

who is an inmate of Bellevue Place since her insanity was decided by the courts of Chicago. The doctor was exceedingly reticent about the unfortunate lady, and while I professionally deprecated his caution, I could not but approve of his delicacy. By degrees I learned that Mrs. Lincoln gave but little trouble, that she rested well, and was quite satisfied with her surroundings. A carriage is always at her disposal, and she frequently drives out, always with the doctor and Mrs. Patterson, or her own attendant, a rather attractive young woman belonging to the retreat. In regard to her riding Mrs. Lincoln is very capricious. She will announce her intention of riding before dinner then postpone the ride until afternoon and again until evening or the next day. She brought with her to the retreat ten large trunks, which have not been examined, but are supposed to contain part of the miscellaneous collection of purchases made during her stay at the Grand Pacific Hotel, in Chicago. Shortly after her arrival here, Mrs. Lincoln ordered a morning dress of black French Cambric, quite elaborately made white basque and pockets, and a black and white striped laun, remarking that "every lady needed cool toilets." She has never worn them, or evinced any disposition to even try them on, but as soon as they were completed ordered samples of black alpacca, from which to select a suit; her mind was diverted from this, as it was only a form of her malady to accumulate material. Her dress is at all times plain, even to shabbiness, and no one could be more indifferent to effects of the toilet. In one of Mrs. Lincoln's trunks, at the retreat, are two very expensive

DOLL-BABIES.

She accounts for their presence by saying she intends to present them to Robert Lincoln's little daughter, of whom she is very fond.

I was anxious to pay my respects to Mrs. Lincoln in person, but as she has positively refused to see any visitors, even declining to leave her room when they are in the house or grounds, I anticipated nothing less than a refusal when I sent up my card. To the doctor's surprise and my own, Mrs. Lincoln sent down word that she would be very happy to see me in her room, and I at once accompanied the doctor thither. She occupies a suite in front of the house on the second floor. The attendant sits in the small room, which contains a single bed. The larger room is

Mrs. Lincoln's sitting and bedroom. It is very plainly furnished, the same as it was prior to her coming; an ordinary three-ply carpet, of pleasant colors, harmoniously blended; a bureau, rocking chair, and lounge, and a plain bedstead, with a very fine bed, about which she is quite particular. Mrs. Lincoln was seated in an expectant attitude by the table as we entered the room; she at once arose, shook hands with me cordially, and begged me to be seated, and began at once to inquire after friends in the city. She was dressed in ordinary black, half-worn, with white ruches edged with black, in the neck and sleeves; her dark hair, fast turning to gray was carelessly coiffed in a knot at the back with coronet braid. She looked worn and ill, and her hands, ringless and uncared for, were never at rest. The "Tender grace of a day that is dead" did not linger about her. I could plainly see in her lusterless eyes, and in the forced composure of her manner, evidences of

A SHATTERED MIND.

She was perfectly ladylike in manner, but rambling and diffuse in her conversation. She alluded rationally, however, to the past, spoke tenderly of Mr. Lincoln, once as, "my husband" and again as "the president." Recalled memories of Noah Brooks, then her husband's assistant secretary, with whom I had an old-time acquaintance, and remarked that he had been for ten years engaged on the *New York Tribune.*[*] Asked me with much earnestness if the murderer of Hon. Sharon Tyndale, of Springfield, had ever been discovered,[†] and then alluded very feelingly to her attachment to Judge Bradwell's family. As I arose to leave she took a handsome bouquet from a crystal vase on her table and asked me to accept it. As she shook hands with me at parting, I thought I could perceive in the diplomatic bow and smile a return of the old society manner, and my heart was full for the woman who sat down, silent and alone in her solitary room, to keep imaginary company with senators and ambassadors in the light of that gracious, kindly smile, long since hidden beneath the coffin lid. It is one of the mercies vouchsafed her, to live life over again with her loved ones—dear little Willie, and rollicking boyish Tad—to sit at the head of

---

[*] Brooks was a reporter for the *Sacramento (California) Daily Union.* He served in Washington as the paper's war correspondent from December 1862 to April 1865. He was never Lincoln's assistant secretary. He was intended to replace John G. Nicolay as the president's private secretary in 1865, but never took office due to Lincoln's assassination. In 1871, Brooks moved to New York and became night editor for the *Tribune,* and in 1874 quit to join the staff of the *New York Times,* where he worked for ten years.

[†] Sharon Tyndale was a former Illinois secretary of state who was found murdered near his home on Adams Street in April 1871, apparently the result of a robbery gone awry. His murderer never was found. "A Double Crime: Robbery and Murder," *Illinois State Register,* April 29, 1871; *History of Sangamon County,* 528–29.

the table and hold familiar converse with them all. It has been urged that this is a development of her life among Spiritualists, but it is the result of scenes

PHOTOGRAPHED ON THE BRAIN,

which only the Angel of Death can erase. Mrs. Lincoln did spend several months at St. Charles, in this state, under an assumed name, and in the company of a society of Spiritualists[*] but it will never be definitely known how much their influence had to do with her eclipse of reason. Nor does anyone seem to know who the *pockmarked man* was who called on her at her hotel, and held long consultations with her, but he is presumed to be a prominent Spiritualist. No encouragement is held out that Mrs. Lincoln will ever become permanently well, but she could not be in a better place for her complete restoration. Here she has no responsibility of thought or action. The noise and panorama of the street cannot bewilder her. The injudiciousness of friends cannot reach her; she is unaware of the slightest restraint, and can read, write, ride, or walk at her pleasure. She orders her meals as she would at home, and is served in her room, or at the family table, as she prefers; her son Robert visits his mother every week, bringing her favorite grandchild with him frequently. Here, at least the poor lady can find—if not the fading pleasures and brief triumphs of life—its perfect peace—the peace that passeth understanding—the rest of nature and God.

Quite a romance could be written about the other twenty inmates of this asylum. They are all ladies of position and culture, placed by their friends under Dr. Patterson's care for improvement and final restoration to mental health. They come from different parts of the state—some from Great Britain—one from Australia. Their insanity arises from different causes, but principally from physical infirmities which drain the brain forces, and leave them powerless to recuperate. The majority are melancholy—some are suicidal—all are quiet—the doctor preferring not to take noisy patients into his well organized family. There are three handsome halls in the house, off which, the sleeping rooms diverge, and one could easily imagine it a cozy hotel. The rooms are nicely furnished, airy, and command splendid views from all points—the building being in the center of a beautiful country, with a stretch of vision ten miles in each direction. The patients themselves seem to second the doctor's efforts in their behalf, with the exception of the few who are

BENT ON SELF-DESTRUCTION,

and will eat only by compulsion. These are the aggravated cases, and require constant watching, not being trusted with pins, needles, scissors, or even a pen. They have different idiosyncrasies, one elderly lady hearing

WHISPERS IN THE AIR,

---

[*] Mrs. Rayne later went to St. Charles to interview Mary's Spiritualist advisor there. See chapter 7.

and imagining that parts of her body are taken from her and replaced by portions of some one else. Another, a young lady from Chicago, imagines that she has committed

THE UNPARDONABLE SIN.

She was a member of a prominent Baptist church, and had the Bible at her finger ends, but no amount of reasoning could produce the least impression upon her. She knew she was lost, and her punishment, she said, was that others would not believe her, so that she was the whited sepulcher of Scripture. Her appearance was pleasing, and she occupied herself with some dainty needlework as she talked. The doctor told me she has lost about forty-seven pounds in three months. The

VICTIM OF HALLUCINATION

of the special senses are the hardest to cure. They hug their delusions with a tenacity that is wonderful. Several elegant and accomplished young ladies are here for epilepsy, the frequent recurrence of which has injured the brain. One belongs to a respectable and influential family traveling in Europe. Each week brings long, loving letters to the sister here, detailing every little occurrence of travel, and often accompanied by tributes of remembrance. A Swiss album and music box, a paper cutter of Sorrento wood, and other loving trifles. One unfortunate girl is an accomplished musician, giving the finest effects of Beethoven, Chopin—or improvising in delightful strains by the hour. Several young wives are here whose husbands come from the city on Saturday to spend the Sabbath with them, showing great patience and devotion in their attention to their irresponsible partners.

Dr. Patterson's twenty years' of practice in this specialty of madness, makes him thoroughly eligible to the situation in which he is installed. As this is his own enterprise, he is wholly responsible for its success, which has long been assured. The perfect order and system of the Retreat; its lovely situation and surroundings, are all conducive to mental and bodily well being; and the kindness bestowed on the patient goes far toward producing a reaction. Many of the patients in this place

ARE NOT MAD.

They are upon what Robert Dale Owen calls debatable land,[*] and across which he, poor fellow, has already passed. They know their weaknesses, and are willing to receive treatment under such favorable conditions, and their disease is classed dementia—insomnia or hysteria—but they can enter here legally upon a court's decision. The Retreat is fitted for 25 or 30 patients, never more. There are a dozen skilled attendants and nurses. One of the doctors is always in attendance. There are no visiting days, nor will the doctors permit curiosity hunters to see his patients; he respects their positions and their dependence too much to allow a crowd of gaping

---

[*] Owen was a well-known reformer and freethinker who began investigating Spiritualism in the 1850s and wrote two well-received books on the subject. Owen, *Debatable Land*.

curious people to inspect them; his experience as Medical Superintendent of the Indiana State Hospital of the Insane, and of the Iowa Insane Asylum, has led him to believe in this mode of treatment. I, too, gladly drop the veil, upon their sacred retiracy.

Chicago Post and Mail, July 13, 1875, 2[*]

DAILY PATIENT PROGRESS REPORTS
Bellevue Place Sanitarium, Batavia, Ill., July 1875

> 9—Mrs. Lincoln did not go out to ride today but came down and sat on the steps awhile in the morning—very pleasant in her manner.
> 10—Mrs. Lincoln same as before. Keeps her room today.
> 11—Mrs. Lincoln sent down word after dinner that she would like to ride, and in about 15 minutes sent word again that she would ride in the morning as she would rather sleep in the afternoon.
> 12—Mrs. Lincoln came down and sat on the doorsteps this morning—though it was hot and sunny—called on Mrs. Patterson twice—slept in afternoon—says very little—did not ride in the morning as she appointed.
> 13—Mrs. Lincoln down this morning to sit on front steps—called on Mrs. Patterson—did not ride today—has promised to give Mrs. Wilmarth's little boy some stockings which she says she bought especially for him. (These stockings she bought in Chicago before she had ever seen Mrs. Wilmarth or her boy.)

Ross, "Mary Todd Lincoln"

"THE CONDITION OF MRS. LINCOLN—
SHE IS NOT IMPROVING—OTHER MATTERS"
Boston Globe, July 14, 1875

[Special dispatch to The Boston Globe]
CHICAGO, July 13—A recent visitor to Mrs. Abraham Lincoln at the private retreat for the insane at Batavia, Ill., reports her condition unchanged. The Superintendent

---

[*] An excerpt of this article was reprinted nationally, probably by the Associated Press: "Mrs. Abraham Lincoln is given up as hopelessly insane. She sits down silent and alone in her solitary room to keep imaginary company with senators and ambassadors in the light of that gracious smile long since hidden beneath the coffin lid. It is one of the mercies vouchsafed her to live life over again with her loved ones—dear little Willie and rollicking, boyish Tad—to sit at the head of the table and hold familiar converse with them all." For example see *Lowell Daily Citizen and News,* August 2, 1875, 3.

evidently did not think the prospects for her ultimate recovery encouraging; she is surrounded by every comfort and is visited every week by her son Robert. She is very quiet and would scarcely be considered insane by a casual observer.

Boston Globe, July 14, 1875, 5

DAILY PATIENT PROGRESS REPORTS
Bellevue Place Sanitarium, Batavia, Ill., July 1875

14—Mrs. Lincoln down stairs today—seems as usual.

15—Mr. Robert Lincoln and daughter came to see Mrs. L—she was very glad to see the little child—after her son went away she had a long talk with Dr. P about going to live with her sister [Elizabeth Edwards]—this sister we understand she might have lived with anytime but has not felt kindly toward her—Mrs. L said, "It is the most natural thing in the world to want to live with my sister—she raised me and I regard her as a sort of mother"—the next moment she complained of her getting so agueish in Jacksonville, Florida and forthwith wanted to get immediately to St. Augustine Fla. To live, etc.

16—Mrs. L down to call on Mrs. Patterson today—as usual.

17—Mrs. Lincoln arguing today—and low-spirited—sleeps almost always in afternoons.

18—Mrs. Lincoln out walking—this morning—more cheerful than yesterday.

19—Mrs. Lincoln moved temporarily to the east side of the house. She admired the new rooms very much and wished to keep them—cheerful and pleasant.

20—Mrs. Lincoln same as yesterday—came down to walk in morning.

21—Mrs. Lincoln came down to call on Mrs. Patterson this morning—only talks in the manner of an ordinary ceremonious call. Does not seem willing to ride though continually making appointments to do so.

22—Mrs. Lincoln came down to the office this morning and made quite a long call. She talked better and with more force of mind than at any time she has been here. Spoke of Mr. [John Lathrop] Motley [former U.S. ambassador to Great Britain] whom she knew very well—talked of her travels—made an agreement to ride in the evening but did not keep it.

Ross, "Mary Todd Lincoln"

New York Observer and Chronicle, July 22, 1875

Mrs. Lincoln, widow of President Lincoln, is represented to be contented in her retreat, but no hopes are indulged of her restoration to a sound mind. She converses intelligently of the past, and appears to be rational on most subjects, but insane on others. Mrs. Lincoln did spend several months at St. Charles, Ill., under an assumed name and in the company of a society of Spiritualists, but it will never be definitely known how much their influence has to do with her eclipse of reason. Her son Robert visits her weekly, and every possible provision is made for her comfort.

New York Observer and Chronicle, July 22, 1875, 230

DAILY PATIENT PROGRESS REPORTS

Bellevue Place Sanitarium, Batavia, Ill., July 1875

- 24—Mrs. Lincoln down stairs on front steps this morning—very pleasant—she talks very little and only on ordinary subjects—seems to be abstracted in her manner.
- 26—Mrs. Lincoln same as yesterday.
- 27—Mrs. Lincoln same as yesterday.
- 28—Mr. Robert Lincoln and daughter came to see Mrs. Lincoln. She was very glad to see them. After they had gone she asked to ride to the Post office to deposit a letter which she had written to a sister in Springfield, at Mr. Lincoln's suggestion—at the P.O. she got out and deposited letter herself—spoke of the ride as a very pleasant one.

Ross, "Mary Todd Lincoln"

Mary Lincoln's July 28 visit to the post office was the first stage in her attempt to secure an early release from Bellevue Place. While she said she wrote to her sister, she actually wrote to multiple old friends and acquaintances seeking their help in a campaign for freedom. Neither Robert Lincoln nor Dr. Patterson had any idea about Mary's unhappiness or her plans.

MARY LINCOLN TO JAMES BRADWELL

Batavia, Ill., July 28, 1875

My dear Friend:

Judge Bradwell

May I request you to come out here just *so* soon as you receive this note. Please bring out your dear wife, Mr. Wm Sturgess,[*] and any other friend. Can you not be *here*, tomorrow on the noon train. Also bring Mr. W. F. Storey,[†] with you. I am sure you will not disappoint me. Drive up to the house. Also telegraph to Genl Farnsworth[‡] to meet you here.

With much love to Mrs. Bradwell, believe me, truly yours,

Mary Lincoln

Please pardon me, if I mention that I will meet the expenses of your trip. M.L.

In the event of Judge B. not receiving this note in time, please come out on at afternoon train. M.L.

Folder 1, Cont. 8, Part 2,
Robert Todd Lincoln Family Papers

DAILY PATIENT PROGRESS REPORTS

Bellevue Place Sanitarium, Batavia, Ill., July 1875

29—General Farnsworth has just been to see Mrs. Lincoln—says she wrote him a note yesterday asking him to come—(this note she must have put in the office yesterday when she claimed to have written only to her sister) Gen. F says she wants her liberty and she wanted him to help her—she makes no complaints—says she feels under some restraint—looks better than when he saw her last—he thinks *she does not talk like a sane woman* but still she would hardly be called insane by those who used to know her—he thinks she has been on the border of insanity for many years—he thinks that if she were free and her property still under the control of Mr. Robert Lincoln she would not do much harm, but would do many outré things—she asked the General to bring his wife to see her which he promised to do.

———

[*] Possibly William Sturges a Chicago banker.

[†] Wilbur F. Storey, editor of the Democrat *Chicago Times,* and former antiwar Copperhead during the Civil War. Storey did not visit Bellevue, but sent reporter Franc B. Wilkie instead.

[‡] General John Franklin Farnsworth, a radical Republican Congressman during part of the Civil War, who was a Chicago lawyer in 1875.

She wrote a letter today purporting to be to her old washerwoman but which evidently contained letters to others—we sent it in care of Mr. Robert Lincoln.

7:30 p.m.—Since writing the above Mr. and Mrs. Bradwell of Chicago have called to see her in answer to a similar invitation to the one sent to Gen. Farnsworth. They made quite a long call—Mrs. B thought that Mrs. Lincoln was not quite right, but that she still ought to be at home and have "tender loving care."

30—Mrs. Lincoln very much afraid that the Dr. would not trust her again because of her deceit in the matter of letter writing—wanted to write to Mrs. Bradwell about her washerwoman who she says has some clothes of hers. She had a long talk with Dr. P in the morning and he told her that she was at liberty to write where she pleased and to whom she pleased—but that she ought to be open about it—he also told her that as Mr. Lincoln was her legal conservator he should think it proper in case he did not know the person written to by Mrs. L to send the letters under cover to him (Mr. Lincoln)—Mrs. Lincoln thought this fair and right.

Ross, "Mary Todd Lincoln"

JAMES BRADWELL TO JOHN TODD STUART

Chicago, Ill., July 30, 1875

Dear Sir,

I saw Mrs. Lincoln at Batavia on yesterday. She desired me to write to you and say that she very much wants to see you, and would like you to visit her as soon as you can as she feels lonesome and that the restraint of the place is unendurable. I believe a visit from you would do her good and I hope you may be able to make it.

Mrs. Lincoln's general health has greatly improved. She spoke of Mrs. Edwards in the kindest terms, and expressed the wish that she might visit her at Batavia and said that she would like to return to Springfield with her and make a visit. I believe such a visit would result in good to Mrs. Lincoln, and do no one any harm. Dr. Patterson said of all the patients he ever had at the retreat, Mrs. Lincoln had given him the least trouble. I am,

Very truly yours,

James B. Bradwell

Folder 5, Cont. 8, Part 2,
Robert Todd Lincoln Family Papers

MYRA BRADWELL TO ELIZABETH EDWARDS

Chicago, Ill., July 30, 1875

Dear Madam:

I have just returned from a visit to your dear sister, Mrs. Lincoln. She desires me to write to you asking you to come up and visit her and expresses a wish to return with you to Springfield. She feels her incarceration most terribly and desires to get out from behind the *grates and bars*.* I cannot feel that it is necessary to keep her thus restrained. Perhaps I do not look at the matter rightly, but let this be my excuse—I love her most tenderly and feel sorry to see one heartache added to her already overburdened soul.

She has always spoken most tenderly of you and I do believe it would do her good to meet you and receive a sister's loving tenderness.

Pardon the liberty I have taken in addressing you and believe me, your sister's friend

Myra Bradwell

> Folder 1, Cont. 8, Part 2,
> Robert Todd Lincoln Family Papers

DAILY PATIENT PROGRESS REPORTS

Bellevue Place Sanitarium, Batavia, Ill., July 1875

31—Mrs. Lincoln did not come down stairs today—otherwise as usual.

> Ross, "Mary Todd Lincoln"

---

* Mary Lincoln's room at Bellevue had no grates and bars, but did have a wire mesh on the windows to prevent suicides.

Chapter 7

August 1875

August was the seminal month of Mary Lincoln's time at Bellevue Place, when her protests about her situation and her desire to leave Batavia—amplified and publicized by the Bradwells—reached their climax, both publicly and privately.

DAILY PATIENT PROGRESS REPORTS
Bellevue Place Sanitarium, Batavia, Ill., August 1875

> 1—Mrs. Lincoln did not come downstairs today—gave her a letter, which came last night from Mrs. Myra Bradwell, who also wrote the Doctor telling him of the letter.
>
> 2—Nothing new in regards to Mrs. Lincoln today.

Ross, "Mary Todd Lincoln"

[MRS. LINCOLN GIVEN UP AS INSANE]
Lowell Daily Citizen and News, Aug. 2, 1875

Mrs. Abraham Lincoln is given up as hopelessly insane. She sits down silent and alone in her solitary room to keep imaginary company with senators and ambassadors in the light of that gracious smile long since hid beneath the coffin lid. It is one of the mercies vouchsafed her to live her life over again with her loved ones—dear little Willie and rollicking, boyish Tad—to sit at the head of the table and hold familiar converse with them all.

Lowell Daily Citizen and News, August 2, 1875, 3.
Excerpt from "Mrs. Lincoln," *Chicago Post and Mail,*
July 13, 1875, 2, nationally reprinted, probably from
the Associated Press

Batavia, Ill., n.d. [Aug. 2, 1875]

My Dear Mrs. Bradwell:

Last evening I received your two most welcome letters. It is impossible to express the delight they afforded me and yet my disappointment is great that you do not propose coming out here until Friday. Your short stay prevented my doing what I had proposed or rather what I had mentioned to you.[*] Please write a letter to Mrs. Robert Anderson of St. Louis, also Mrs. Judge May[†] I most *earnestly* entreat you, my very kind friend to come out on *Friday morning,* fail not, I beg of you.

It does not appear that God is good, to have placed me here. I endeavor to read my Bible and offer up my petitions three times a day. But my afflicted heart fails me and my voice often falters in prayer. I have worshipped my son and no unpleasant word ever passed between us, yet I cannot understand why I should have been brought out here.

I must see some of my friends and your noble, kind hearted husband will see to this, I am sure, immediately. May I trouble you to write a letter to *Mrs.* Henry T. Blow[‡] with a request that it will be forwarded to her in the event of her absence from St. Louis.

Mrs. Bradwell, my dearest friend, I love you very much. Go to my friends, go and see Mrs. Harriet Farlin and her son Mr. Farlin, a partner of a Mr. Wing, real estate agents. Go to Mrs. F., she resides at 505 Michigan Avenue. Write a note when you receive this to Gen'l Farnsworth requesting him to come and see me on tomorrow afternoon at four o'clock.

Pray for me that I may be able to leave such a place as this. Let me see Judge Bradwell. I beg you to come *Friday morning.* I should like to see *Dr. Evarts.*[§] I feel that I must have some further conversation with him. Write me, your heartbroken friend, frequently, *daily.* But come to me. Will you kindly bring me out some samples of black alpaca a best quality without luster and without cotton. Also some samples of heavier black woolen goods.

Mary Lincoln

Folder 5, Cont. 8, Part 2,
Robert Todd Lincoln Family Papers

---

[*] Unknown reference.

[†] Unknown.

[‡] Minerva Grimsley Blow, wife of Henry Taylor Blow, who served as President Lincoln's minister to Venezuela from June 1861 to February 1862, and then as a Republican Congressman from St. Louis, Missouri, from March 1863 to March 1867. Minerva Blow died in June 1875, two months prior to this letter.

[§] Possibly the Reverend Dr. W. W. Evarts, pastor of the First Baptist Church in Chicago.

Bellevue Place Sanitarium, Batavia, Ill., August 1875

3—Mrs. Lincoln this morning asked the Dr. if she might write to Mrs.
Bradwell and Mr. Stuart. He told her she might. He being away at Chicago—Mrs. Lincoln was very anxious to ride—she took a long ride and
talked much as usual until coming home. She wanted to go to the [post]
office to mail some letters. As I had previously told her that any letters
would be sent direct, I told her that I did not think she was treating us
fairly, and offered to take them to the office. She finally gave them to me
and I sent them. She made a call on Mrs. Patterson.

Ross, "Mary Todd Lincoln"

ELIZABETH EDWARDS TO MYRA BRADWELL
Springfield, Ill., Aug. 3, 1875

Dear Madam:

I hasten to reply to your kind note, relative to my unhappy sister. My heart re-
belled at the thought of placing her in an asylum; believing that her sad case merely
required the care of a protector, whose companionship, would be pleasant to her.
Had I been consulted, I would have remonstrated earnestly against the step taken.

The judgment of others must now, I presume, be silently acquiesced in, for a time,
in the hope, that ere long, her physical and mental condition, will be improved, by
rest and medical treatment.

The sorrows that befell her in such rapid succession and *the one, so* tragic, was
enough to shatter the nerves, and infuse the intellect of the bravest mind and heart.
I regret to say that I cannot just now visit Mrs. Lincoln, being prostrated from the
effects of a recent surgical operation. But will at once write to her, and soothe her
burdened heart, if possible, with words of love and sympathy.

It is my opinion, that she should be indulged in a desire to visit her friends as
the surest means of restoring her to health and cheerfulness.

Accept my thanks, for your interest, in my sister, and the suggestions you have
made me.

Yrs truly
Mrs. N. H. Edwards

Folder 1, Cont. 8, Part 2,
Robert Todd Lincoln Family Papers

HENRY T. BLOW TO ROBERT LINCOLN

St. Louis, Mo., Aug. 3, 1875

My dear Mr. Lincoln:

Your unfortunate mother has requested that I should visit her, with the hope no doubt that I could in some way help her in her troubles, as in times past, I did without solicitation.

The more I reflect on the exalted character of your illustrious father and the services which under Divine Providence he rendered his country, the more I feel as one of his friends the obligation to care most tenderly for the character and comfort of those he so much loved while living, and if it should seem to you that under present circumstances, I can in any way benefit your dear mother, I shall be most happy to place myself at your disposal.

I am dear sir

Your affectionate friend

Henry T. Blow

Folder 8, Box 2, Mary Todd Lincoln Insanity File

Robert's response is detailed and fascinating, and has never before been cited, quoted, or published in any accounts of his mother's insanity case.

ROBERT LINCOLN TO HENRY T. BLOW

Chicago, Ill., Aug. 4, 1875

My dear Mr. Blow,

I hope you will not think the length of this letter an unkind return for the exceeding kindness of your letter of yesterday but I think I ought to give you the details of my mother's situation. I could wish no worse punishment for an enemy than the distress her troubles have given me in the last few months, and no one could seek out more earnestly and faithfully than I have done, the proper path to take.

As you may not have seen an account of the Inquisition I send you one letter from the Inter-Ocean of May 21st which is substantially correct, though short. In explanation of the course taken you ought to know that in consequence of the statutes of this state which are highly [penal], no compulsory internment can be given an insane person except under verdict of a jury of the County Court.

I filed the petition with the full approval of Hon. Jno. T. Stuart of Springfield (my mother's cousin), Judge David Davis of the U.S. Supreme Court, and of all the persons whom I consulted. Especially, I called a council of six of the most eminent medical men of this place and their opinions were unanimous that any delay was very hazardous—and that a conservator for her property was not only necessary, but that she should be under personal guardianship. I am her only living child. Since my father's death she has not been on terms with her sisters in Springfield for no reasons except those arising from her abnormal mental condition—but with them she has no communication. About a year ago, she became angry with my wife for some cause arising in the same way and since then would not call at my house. It not being possible therefore to help her under the surveillance of relatives, I thought myself fortunate in finding such a place as Dr. Patterson's at Batavia—where she went with no apparent reluctance. It is in a beautiful village and has every comfort.

There are a dozen or more lady patients staying in the house, all of them quiet and I do not think she has ever seen or heard of them. The rooms are in the private part of the house and the only restraint which is put upon her is that she understands (and acquiesces) that in walking or driving, which she does whenever and wherever she likes, some member of Dr. Patterson's family must be in company. They are cultured and pleasant people and are anxious to make her stay with them agreeable to herself. Of course she has her own bath and maid. Her means are ample for every need and any but extravagant whims and I have instructed the Dr. to let her amuse herself in getting fitted for new dresses and having them made. This is one of her chief vagaries. She never wears or puts on one out of ten dresses she gets. Batavia is nearly forty miles from here and I make it a rule to go there as [nearly once] in ten days as I can get away from work—usually I take my little daughter with me. My own judgment is that the quiet and absence of excitement and responsibility is doing her good. Her conversation is entirely rational. Dr. Patterson thinks she would be as wild [again if] allowed to get into the world again. Dr. Patterson is of the firm opinion, says that he thinks she will have momentary feebleness of brain motion for a year. When I call on her I find it hard to convince myself that she is not as sane as I am. Yet small things show the truth. Her letter to you was mailed by her on the pretense that it was to her sister. If she were sane, she would know that she could write to you freely so far as I am concerned. I have told her she could not write to Spiritualists [herself]—beyond that I now have no interest. They have exercised a most pernicious influence over her mind, there is domestic affections which are extravagant if I may use the word. If my mother were not in such a situation in life that her insane vagaries make national scandals, there might be no harm in letting her do as she chooses, if there was no danger of her harming herself or others, but as she is, living as I believe in more comfort than she has experienced in ten years, I think it would be inexcusable in permitting her to follow her insane vagaries. If she could she would at once put herself beyond the reach of restraint from me, and what would then happen I cannot imagine.

I suppose her letter to you was written with the hope of your aid to free her from the almost nominal restraint she is now under. I think if you saw her you would approve my course. My responsibility is great and I cannot shirk it and I would be very glad to have the benefit of your advice. If you should come to Chicago at any time I should be glad if you could visit my mother. She would be pleased to see you and it might be that your visit would be productive of good to her.

Please excuse the length of this reply. It is called for by your sympathy for my mother's unhappy state and I am very grateful to you.

Very sincerely yours,

Robert T. Lincoln

LB 1:1:127–31

DAILY PATIENT PROGRESS REPORTS
Bellevue Place Sanitarium, Batavia, Ill., August 1875

4—Mrs. Lincoln came down to visit Mrs. Patterson—did not ride today— sleeps a good deal of the afternoon—her conversation is usually of the most commonplace character and there is much repetition—gave her a letter.

5—Mrs. Lincoln came downstairs and made her usual call on Mrs. P—seemed cheerful and pleasant—did not ride today.

Ross, "Mary Todd Lincoln"

MARY LINCOLN TO MYRA BRADWELL
Batavia, Wednesday, n.d. [Aug. 5, 1875?]

My dear Mrs. Bradwell:

Your letter was received on yesterday. You did not state in what manner your Sabbath was passed. I am sure it was in a profitable way. I shall certainly trust to hear from you very soon, and without doubt, you will not forget me. God will not fail to reward you if you do not *fail* to visit the widow of Abraham Lincoln in her solitude. Does not Judge Bradwell's business bring him to the country *this* week and surely you will accompany him. Do not fail in coming to me when you receive this letter. Dear friend, as you love your Heavenly Father, come to me, bring your husband, the best of men. See Mrs. Farlin and Mrs. Davis her daughter. Please write at once to my sister, Mrs. N. W. Edwards to come out here to see me. Explain everything. And if I have used excited words in reference to my son, my God forgive me, and may *you both* forget it. *Come,* come, is the watchword. You will when you receive this. Write to my sister. She is a sweet, intelligent, loving woman. And *Mrs. Blow* is nobleness itself. Write and do not forget my pleading. With kindest love to your husband and children, believe me,

Most affectionately yours,

Mary Lincoln

Say nothing to these people or any one else about the alpaca—you will understand.

Folder 5, Cont. 8, Part 2,
Robert Todd Lincoln Family Papers

DAILY PATIENT PROGRESS REPORTS
Bellevue Place Sanitarium, Batavia, Ill., August 1875

> 6—Mrs. Bradwell of Chicago came to see Mrs. Lincoln today—had a long conversation with Mrs. B in the office—she told the doctor distinctly that she had no doubt that Mrs. Lincoln was insane and had been for some time—but she doubted the propriety of keeping her in an asylum for the insane—stayed with Mrs. Lincoln overnight—Mrs. Lincoln as usual—Mrs. B thought she (Mrs. L) was very much better—she advised her removal to Springfield to her sister's house.

> 7—Mrs. Bradwell went down in town this morning about 10 o'clock—at 1 o'clock p.m. (the senior Doctor being in Chicago) Mrs. B came back attended by a "Mr. Wilkie of Chicago"*—Mrs. Lincoln came down to meet them. After being introduced to Mr. Wilkie she invited them up to her rooms and the three stayed there in conference for two hours. The visitors then returned to the city—Mrs. Bradwell told Mrs. Lincoln that she would come and see her again soon.

Ross, "Mary Todd Lincoln"

ROBERT LINCOLN TO ELIZABETH EDWARDS
Aug. 7, 1875

My dear Aunt,

Dr. Patterson of Batavia today showed me, as I understand by Mrs. Bradwell's request, your letter to Mrs. Bradwell.[†] I do not know of course what Mrs. B has written to you[‡] but she has been allowed very free access to my mother and expresses herself in a very melodramatic way to Dr. Patterson that "her dear girl" is not a fit subject

---

* Franc B. Wilkie, reporter for the *Chicago Times*.

[†] August 3, 1875.

[‡] July 30, 1875.

for "bolted doors and barred windows" but ought to be allowed to be under the care of "some kinder and sentimental friend," and I have no doubt she has written in some such strain to you. As you know, my mother has chosen to establish such relations between herself and you and everyone of her near relations (excepting only Cousin John Stuart and Cousin Lizzie Brown) that I could not in self respect ask your help or sympathy in anything concerning her affairs. There is no need of my rehearsing ten years of our domestic history. If it has caused you one tenth of the grief it has caused me, you will remember it. Rightly or wrongly I consider that I alone must assume the entire and absolute charge of her unfortunate situation and I must deal with it as my condition allows me to do. I am alone held responsible and I cannot help it. If you can and will take any part of the burden from me I will be only too glad and grateful to you for it. I judge from your letter that you consider her insane or of unsound mind—but you do not express yourself as acquiescing in the mode of treatment. You probably saw an account of the Inquisition. I would be ashamed to put on paper an account of many of her insane acts—and I allowed to be introduced in evidence only so much as was necessary to establish the case. That she is insane and entirely incapable of taking care of herself was established beyond question. What was to be done with her? I could not take her to my house without a separation from my wife and children. I tried it after poor Tad's death, and had to break up housekeeping to end the trouble. In 1873, after my wife's return home, my mother became evidently angry (I think you can imagine what her anger means) at my wife for some trifle and they have never met since but when my wife has sent our children to see her, she has driven my servants out of the room by her insulting remarks concerning their mistress and this in the presence of my little girl. I do not write this in any anger, but to you alone to show you one or two reasons why she could not be a guest of my wife. She has always seemed very much attached to my eldest child, a little girl, now nearly six years old. She about a year ago suggested to a lady (who told me of it in some alarm) the idea of running away with the child. Such a freak would be no more astonishing than a good many I could tell you that you have never heard of.

In this situation I consider it a blessing that I could place her under Dr. Patterson's care. There is nothing about his house to indicate an asylum except that outside of the windows there is a white wire netting such as you may see often to keep children from falling out of the window. My mother's rooms (two) are in the private residence part of the house, entirely separated from the large Ell in which are about a dozen lady patients, none others. I do not think she has ever seen or heard of them. She has her own private bath and keeps the key of her own room as she would at a hotel. She goes driving whenever she likes and in short her "prison" is the region known as the "Fox Run Valley" the most beautiful country west of New

York. I wish you could come up and call on her. If you can my wife will be glad to welcome you here and make you in every way as comfortable as our way of living permits and I will escort you to Batavia which is 90 minutes ride from here.

What trouble Mrs. Bradwell may give me with her interference I cannot foretell. I understand she is a high priestess in a gang of Spiritualists and from what I have heard it is to their interest that my mother should be at liberty to control herself and her property. I have done my duty as I best know and Providence must take care of the rest. If you have in your mind any plan by which my mother can be placed under care and under some control which might prevent her from making herself talked of by everybody, I hope you will write it to me. I do not know who is willing to assume such an undertaking, nor do I believe anyone could succeed in it unless backed by the authority of law, as is Dr. Patterson. He is a most excellent and kind hearted man and as she knows his authority, he has absolutely no trouble with her.

My opinion is that the quiet and absence of all chance of excitement have I own been a great deal of good. Dr. Patterson today expressed a fear that Mrs. Bradwell's visits and manner of late would tend to undo the good that has been accomplished. Mrs. Bradwell does not consult me at all.

It is mere guesswork to say what my mother would do, if at liberty to go where she pleases. At my last visit to her (ten days ago) she expressed a desire to visit you. I suggested her writing you first and said, as I say now, that I had no possible objection to her visiting you, if you were willing. I told Dr. P. to forward unopened any letter to you. The same afternoon while driving, she said she had written to you and desired to post the letter herself and was allowed to do so. Instead of a letter to you, she mailed letters to Mrs. Bradwell, Gen. Farnsworth and Hon. Henry T. Blow of Illinois. She has probably told Mrs. Bradwell that I would not let her write to you. My experience for a long time has taught me that she will say anything to accomplish [her goals] and her suggestion of going to you was caused by her knowledge of how much I have deplored her self isolation from you all. I cannot have any confidence in her sincerity in this and I do not believe that if her object was accomplished, she would receive a call from any one of her sisters. Keep this letter and see if I am not correct, when the time comes.

I think she would at once go to Europe and such a thing in her present state of mind would be productive of the most disturbing events to us all.

Do you think it would be right to allow her to do so?

She is now living in as much comfort as she ever does. When here she would receive no callers, until people have long ceased, with two or three exceptions, to call upon her.

I hope you will write freely what you think and I hope especially that you may be able to come here and learn the facts in person rather than from Mrs. Bradwell.

Excuse this long letter but I could not well write fewer words.

Believe me, appreciatively your nephew,

Robert T. Lincoln

LB 1:1:133–39

SALLY ORNE TO ROBERT LINCOLN

Aug. 8, 1875

Dear Sir:

Your letter dated June 1st has just reached me on my return from Saratoga. I thank you very much for it. It is a great comfort to hear from your own self, of the loving care and wise guidance which your dear Mother is under. Not that I ever had one doubt of that—for I know too much of your goodness as a son from her own lips to ever allow the first thought or suggestion to have any influence over me—and I doubt if there ever was more than one or two persons that had, for at Saratoga where there is always a great concourse of people, I never heard the first person say ought but that you had done perfectly right and spoke warmly in your praise also.

I only wish all the States had the same 'Statute.' It is a blessed one. I can readily see how comfortable your dear mother is made by your thoughtful care, and can with you believe her happier than she has been for years.

Dear precious one! How my heart goes out towards her with love and affection!

You may hope for her restoration. The physicians both here and in Europe pronounced my son in law incurable. Still he surprised them all with return to health.

There is a "Great Physician" above all others "Whose arm is not shortened," and to whom we may all look. God give you strength to bear up under this chastening, and crown your days with such happiness that such a son of such a father most justly deserves.

And now, Mr. Lincoln, if there is ever anything I can do for your Mother, remember I am at your service.

With kind regards to yourself and your wife, I remain, with

great respect,

Yours very truly,

Sally B. Orne

Folder 5, Box 2, Mary Todd Lincoln Insanity File

MARY LINCOLN TO JAMES BRADWELL

Aug. 8, 1875

My dear friend

Judge Bradwell:

Knowing well your great nobleness of heart, I can but be *well* assured, that you will soon see that I am released from this place. Mrs. Bradwell will explain every thing. I am sleeping very finely and as I am perfectly sane, I do not desire to become insane.

I pray you to see that justice is done immediately to me, for my mind is entirely clear and my health is perfectly good.

With a high appreciation of yourself and your wife, son, and daughter, whom I love very much,

Believe me,

Very truly,

Your friend

Mary Lincoln

Folder 1, Cont. 8, Part 2,
Robert Todd Lincoln Family Papers

DAILY PATIENT PROGRESS REPORTS

Bellevue Place Sanitarium, Batavia, Ill., August 1875

8—Mrs. Lincoln as usual today—quite cheerful—says she wants very much to go and live with her sister—Mrs. Edwards—she has however not yet answered a letter which her sister wrote her, inviting her to live with her, a week or more ago—she promises to write soon.

9—We wrote to Mrs. Bradwell today protesting against her bringing strangers to see Mrs. Lincoln in the absence of the senior doctor—copied letters—moved Mrs. Lincoln back to her old rooms today—she was very unwilling to have any furniture changed for better—very unwilling to have different bed springs though of the same pattern. After she had gone to bed at night she got [up] and called the doctor and wanted a third mattress on her bed because it was not high enough—seems pleased with her rooms.

Ross, "Mary Todd Lincoln"

DR. PATTERSON TO MYRA BRADWELL

Batavia, Ill., Aug. 9, 1875

Mrs. Myra Bradwell
Chicago, Ill.

Enclosed find letter which I returned.

I saw Mr. Lincoln yesterday, who expressed a wish to see you and said he would call on you soon.

I regret to learn that during my absence on Saturday, you brought an entire stranger to my house, a stranger both to me and to Mrs. Lincoln, proposing a visit to her private room. I can but regard this as a breach of hospitality, and of common courtesy to me.

In Mr. Lincoln's proposed conference with you, I shall feel obliged if you will, before making another visit to Mrs. Lincoln, secure his approval of your visits and ask him to indicate the extent to which, in his view, it is proper to introduce strangers to his mother.

In making future visits, if any should be made other than with authority to remove Mrs. Lincoln, I will thank you to select some other day than Saturday, the day when it is well known I am absent from home.

In your conference with Mr. Lincoln, I will thank you to call his attention to the propriety or otherwise of conveying any letters that Mrs. Lincoln may write, unknown to him or to me.

I understand from Mrs. Lincoln that you propose to again visit her soon.

Respectfully,

R. J. Patterson

Folder 23, Box 2, Mary Todd Lincoln Insanity File

DR. PATTERSON TO ROBERT LINCOLN

Batavia, Ill., Aug. 9, 1875

Dear Sir:

Enclosed find letter to Mrs. Myra Bradwell, which I will thank you to read and drop in a mail box. On Saturday afternoon last, Mrs. Bradwell introduced a "Mr. Wilkie of Chicago," to Mrs. Lincoln, and the three held a private conference in Mrs. Lincoln's room. I know nothing of the nature of the conference or its object. I should be thankful for any advice from you in reference to the matters in my letter to Mrs. Bradwell.

I am happy to say that both mentally and physically Mrs. Lincoln is greatly improved and as she has expressed a desire to live with her sister Mrs. Edwards, I see no reason medically why she may not do so unless her condition should change for the worse.

Yours truly

R. J. Patterson

Folder 23, Box 2, Mary Todd Lincoln Insanity File

ROBERT LINCOLN TO ELIZABETH EDWARDS

Aug. 10, 1875

My dear Aunt,

After I had mailed my long letter to you I learned that Mrs. Bradwell intended to call on me. She did so this afternoon. We had a long talk—the result which was that she thinks my mother is not entirely "right" but that she ought to be at large. The only plan she suggested was her visiting you. I told her I do not object to that and we would await your letter.

I think I said in my letter that I understood that Mrs. B is a Spiritualist. Her language to me today indicates that I was misinformed.

How completely recovered my mother really is is shown by Mrs. B's saying she was to take out to her samples of dress goods she wants to buy. She has with her *seven* trunks of clothing and there are stored here *nine* more. I told Mrs. Bradwell that the experiment of putting her entirely at liberty would be interesting to those who have no responsibility for the results. They can afterwards dismiss the matter with a shrug of the shoulders.

Affectionately your nephew,

Robert T. Lincoln

P.S. Please regard my letters to you as confidential for I write to you as I cannot to some.

LB 1:1:141–42

DAILY PATIENT PROGRESS REPORTS

Bellevue Place Sanitarium, Batavia, Ill., August 1875

10—Mrs. Lincoln as usual—cheerful today—gave her two letters.

11—Mrs. Lincoln came down to the office this morning to mail some letters—has not written to Mrs. Edwards yet, though continually promising to do so. For the last few days has shown a little more capriciousness.

Ross, "Mary Todd Lincoln"

ELIZABETH EDWARDS TO ROBERT LINCOLN

Springfield, Ill., Aug. 11, 1875

My dear Robert,

I received your letter of yesterday, and haste to say, how much I regret, that any act of mine, should have occasioned your annoyance. You may believe, that I was surprised to receive a communication from Mrs. Bradwell, written as she said at your mother's request, desiring me to visit her, and to bring her home with me.

I at once suspected, that her motive was to carry out some plan. Of course courtesy required me to reply to Mrs. B. The contents of that note you have seen. I made a mistake in expressing to her, my views, upon the subject, of the treatment, I supposed would have been most beneficial to your mother. After having all the facts from you, her position, and difficulties in your family, I do not see, that you could have pursued, any other course.

Mr. C Brown called about a week ago, to show me a letter addressed to Mr. Stuart, requesting him to go to Batavia, and to take me, with him. The touching appeal, prompted me to write, and soothe, her if possible. I promised a visit, when my health permitted, with such other assurances, as my sympathetic nature, is ever inclined to indulge. I thought it unnecessary to ask special permission, supposing that letters were opened, and withheld, when objectionable.

The only atonement I can make for improper interference if what I have done, is thus construed, is to assure you, that in the future, you have nothing to fear, from my intrusiveness.

Be assured of my heartfelt sympathy, for truly, your grief is mine also. It is among my many sorrows, one, of the most grievous.

Many thanks for your kind invitation to visit you, and see your mother. It is altogether impracticable owing to feeble health, and entertaining doubts also, of the expediency.

Present my kind regards to your wife, and believe me

Ever your affectionate

Aunt Lizzie

Folder 16, Box 2, Mary Todd Lincoln Insanity File

MYRA BRADWELL TO ELIZABETH EDWARDS

Chicago, Ill., Aug. 11, 1875

Dear Mrs. Edwards:

I came in from Batavia last Saturday afternoon. Stayed with your sister Friday night. Slept with her and saw not one symptom of insanity. She slept as sweetly and as quietly as a kitten. Robert tells me if you will take her, he will bring her down to

Springfield. I do hope you will for she must be at liberty. Do please take her and love her and I am sure you will not have any trouble with her for Dr. Patterson told Mr. Bradwell and myself that he never had a patient that made him so little trouble.

I am so sorry for the dear woman, shut up in that place. When they tell me she is not restrained, I want to ask how they should like it themselves?

I hope to hear from you soon,

Kindly, Myra Bradwell

Folder 5, Cont. 8, Part 2,
Robert Todd Lincoln Family Papers

ELIZABETH EDWARDS TO ROBERT LINCOLN
Springfield, Ill., Aug. 12, 1875

My dear Robert,

I mailed a note to you on yesterday, and have received yours, of same date.

When your poor mother proposed a visit to me, I felt that I must respond in a kind manner; supposing that if the visit, was permitted, she would be in charge of a responsible person, and taken back again, for a continuation of treatment. The peculiarities of her whole life have been so marked and well understood by me, that I have not indulged the faintest hope, of a permanent cure. The painful excitement of the *past years,* only added to the malady, [*letter missing piece here*] . . . apparent to her family for years, before the saddest events, occurred.

I am unwilling to urge any steps, or assume any responsibility, in her case. My present feeble health, causing such nervous prostration, as would render me, a most unfit person, to control an unsound mind.

I am now satisfied, that understanding her propensities, as you do, the course you have decided upon, is the surest and wisest.

With much love,

Your Aunt Lizzie

Folder 16, Box 2, Mary Todd Lincoln Insanity File

MYRA BRADWELL TO ABRAM WAKEMAN
Aug. 12, 1875

Dear sir,

I write you at the request of Mrs. Lincoln. She is at an insane asylum at Batavia Ill. and is very desirous of seeing you—or communicating with you by letter. She is quite well and as I think not insane. She will not be obliged to remain there much longer I hope. It never seemed necessary for her to be sent there, to me at least—yet we must silently acquiesce in the decision for a time at least. I do hope you will write her—or come and visit her.

Yours respectfully,
Myra Bradwell

Folder 9, Box 2, Mary Todd Lincoln Insanity File

DAILY PATIENT PROGRESS REPORTS

Bellevue Place Sanitarium, Batavia, Ill., August 1875

12—Mrs. Lincoln made a visit to the office this morning—she seemed cheerful—she has not yet written to Mrs. Edwards.

13—Mr. Robert Lincoln visited his mother today—he said that in regard to Mrs. Bradwell that she was a pest and a nuisance. He characterized her introduction of Mr. Wilkie on Saturday last, as an outrage. Mr. Wilkie, we have since found to be the editor of the *Chicago Times*. Mrs. L seemed glad to see her son. She also wrote today to Mrs. Edwards and to Mrs. Bradwell.

Ross, "Mary Todd Lincoln"

MARY LINCOLN TO MYRA BRADWELL

Batavia, Ill., Aug. [13] 1875

My dear friend
Mrs. Bradwell:

My son has just left me after making me a short call. He mentions that he wrote on yesterday, to my sister Mrs. N.H. Edwards of Springfield, requesting information of her, whether she would be willing to receive me as a visitor. I showed him, her letter and he considered it a little cool and perhaps general. I rather think he *would* prefer *my* remaining *here* in his heart. *Myra* Bradwell—write to my sister Mrs. E. *at once* the moment you read this letter and beg and pray her as a Christian woman— to write him (R.T.L.) *urgently* requesting a visit from him. A moment since Dr. P. returned from the drive to the depot and came to my door and announced that the Physician and Matron of the Elgin *Asylum,*[*] requested to be shown my room—and I am now expecting them every moment. I submit this to you both. Hoping and praying that the visit of tomorrow will not be *forgotten.* God in his mercy will not forget you. Also bring an exchange if you please, also that small key. Use your own

---

[*] The Northern Illinois Hospital and Asylum for the Insane, established in Elgin [Kane County], Ill. in 1869.

judgment regarding the trunks. *When* we meet and I trust you will remember my desolation—much I shall tell you. It is necessary to see Judge Bradwell also. I wish I could kneel down for *one* hour; my heart faints within me. Write at once a most urgent letter to my sister, tell her to write urgently to R.T.L. My sister Mrs. C.M. Smith[*] has also written me begging me to come to her. Mrs. E. appears to be his specialty, fail me not.

With much love,

I remain truly yours,

Mary Lincoln

Folder 1, Cont. 8, Part 2,

Robert Todd Lincoln Family Papers

ELIZABETH EDWARDS TO ROBERT LINCOLN

Springfield, Ill., Aug. 13, 1875

My dear Robert,

I received this morning, for the first time, a letter from your mother, and writes lovingly, and very urgently upon the subject of her release. I wish she could be persuaded to be calm, and contented for a while longer—if she complained of physical suffering, her detention could be put upon that ground, but she assures me, that her health is perfect, and her mind entirely sane. The enclosed note, to be handed to Mrs. Bradwell, if here, or otherwise mailed to Chicago. As I do not fully understand the rules of the institution at Batavia, I have concluded to send it to you to deliver, if you see proper.

I would prefer that your mother should not see my letters to you wherein I so fully express myself about her mental condition, both now, and in the past.

I am unwilling to excite her by intimating anything unpleasant, when she seems disposed to be amiable.

In haste,

Your aff

Aunt Lizzie

Folder 16, Box 2, Mary Todd Lincoln Insanity File

---

[*] Ann Todd, Mary's younger sister, the wife of Clark Moulton Smith, a Springfield, Ill., merchant.

MARY LINCOLN TO MYRA BRADWELL

Batavia, Ill., Aug. [14] 1875

My dear friend
Mrs. Bradwell:

I enclose this note to you—hoping my good, kind sister—Mrs. E.—will write you just when this is received and enclose this. Come to me Mrs. B. bring your husband also bring those 2 trunks I wrote you about. A long Russian leather trunk and the tall blk trunk marked M.L. *fail me not.* Come to me. I long to see you both. Bring me also the key of the middle sized trunk. I must have you near me again. Write me more plainly than you do. Write again to Henry T. Blow and his wife and on the envelope request that the letter may be directed wherever they are.

Tell Judge B.—your husband—that dependence is placed upon him and he must not forget to come to me. Write to Mr. and Mrs. C.M. Smith of Springfield.

Tell Mrs. S. she must not go to C. come to [*end of letter missing*]

Folder 1, Cont. 8, Part 2,
Robert Todd Lincoln Family Papers

ELIZABETH EDWARDS TO ROBERT LINCOLN

Springfield, Ill., Aug. 14, 1875

My dear Robert,

After writing to you on yesterday, it occurred to me, that if the responsibility of your mother's detention at the institution, would be assumed by Dr. Patterson, the Judge who decided the case, and Mr. Swett who upon her departure for Batavia told her in reply, to several questions among them, who would decide her recovery? that he would do so—we then would be relieved, from the fear, and possibility of incurring her displeasure. The kindly regard she is now professing for those, from whom, she has been so long estranged is certainly a most pleasing, and encouraging indication.

I will be glad to call upon her when I feel able and would prefer not to write to her, until I hear from you, as to the expediency of the plan I take the liberty to suggest.

With sincere love,
Your Aunt Lizzie

Folder 16, Box 2, Mary Todd Lincoln Insanity File

Chicago, Ill., Aug. 14, 1875

Madam:

Your note came here in my absence. On yesterday I received a letter from my aunt Mrs. Edwards, which I gave this morning to Dr. Patterson. I regret beyond measure that my aunt is not able to aid me, as she says that her health is such that she cannot assume the responsibility. I had hoped for a possibility of benefit from my mother's apparent desire to renew her proper relations with her sister. I hope my aunt may be able to come up here soon, as I have invited her to do.

I visited my mother on yesterday and I could not help observing with pain, a renewal in the degree of the same appearances which marked her in May and which I had not noticed in my last few visits. I do not know of any outside cause for this unless it is the constant excitement she has been in since your first visit. I am persuaded that you wish only her good and that you recognize the responsibility which is on me and which I cannot shift or divide. When you asked me a few days ago whether I objected to you visiting her I said I only desired that you would be prudent in your conversation with her and would not carry letters for her. In view of what I have seen and which I regard as a partial destruction of the good accomplished by two months and a half of quiet and freedom from all chance of excitement, I am compelled to request that you visit her less often and not at all with persons with whom I am unacquainted and especially that you do not aid her in corresponding with persons other than her relatives. As to those Dr. Patterson will mail unopened as many letters as she desires to make.

Very respectfully yours,

Robert T. Lincoln

LB 1:1:143–44

DAILY PATIENT PROGRESS REPORTS

Bellevue Place Sanitarium, Batavia, Ill., August 1875

14—Mrs. Lincoln took a ride this morning—she also sent another letter to Mrs. Edwards and one to Hon. John T. Stuart—she was quite cheerful.

15—Nothing different in case of Mrs. Lincoln—asked her if she expected Mrs. Bradwell tomorrow she said, "no certainly not." She had shown a letter from Mrs. B the day previous which made it probable that she was to be here—shown more discontent during the last week.

Ross, "Mary Todd Lincoln"

ROBERT LINCOLN TO MARY LINCOLN

Chicago, Ill., Aug. 15, 1875

My dear Mother,

Dr. Patterson gave me your note yesterday. I am dreadfully disappointed that Aunt Lizzie writes me that she is not well enough to have you visit her just now but I am going to try to arrange it with her for very soon. There is nothing I want so much as to have you with her—for I am sure nothing would do you more good.

Mamie has put something in an envelope which she calls a letter to you and says I must send it—so here it is. I have not read it but I doubt you can read it.

You must trust me that I can and will do everything that is for your good and you must not allow yourself to think otherwise, for in that way you will only retard the recovery I am looking for. Your stay with Dr. Patterson had plainly benefited you and you must not undo all that has been done.

Affectionately yours,

Robert T. Lincoln

Folder 1, Cont. 8, Part 2,
Robert Todd Lincoln Family Papers

DAILY PATIENT PROGRESS REPORTS

Bellevue Place Sanitarium, Batavia, Ill., August 1875

16—This morning Dr. P said to Mrs. Lincoln—"Then you expect Judge Bradwell to see you today," she replied—"Not at all—not at all"—"But" said the doctor—"you showed me a letter from Mrs. Bradwell saying that the judge would be here today"—she replied that "Mrs. Bradwell was a very singular woman and that it was not probable that Judge Bradwell would be here today." She remarked that "Judge Bradwell has an important paper that belonged to her and which she had been trying to get for some time—she desired very much to see him about it." She has made the same remark at various times before. Mrs. Lincoln is frequently untruthful in her statements, and exceedingly deceitful. Her lying and deceit should be put down to insanity.

[17?]—Mrs. Lincoln received letters today from R.T. Lincoln and one mailed at Oxford O[hio]. Author not known. Judge Bradwell and wife think Mrs. L should be allowed to go to her sister and that her health is suffering in consequence of her confinement on 7th Inst. Mrs. Bradwell said she never saw Mrs. L so well. Mrs. Lincoln does not choose to go out much. She could live out of doors if she would. Her doors are never locked only at night. We often urge her to go out but have not thought it best to compel her to go out.

So much discussion about the patient going away, tends to unsettle her mind and make her more discontented and should be stopped. She should be let alone and this I have told Judge Bradwell. She should never have been subjected to this unnecessary excitement. It is now apparent that the frequent visits of Mr. and Mrs. Bradwell and especially the letters of Mrs. B have tended to stir up discontent and thus do harm. Mrs. Lincoln has shown Dr. P some of Mrs. Bradwell's letters.

Ross, "Mary Todd Lincoln"

ABRAM WAKEMAN TO MYRA BRADWELL
Aug. 17, 1875

Dear Madame,

I have yours of the 12th inst. in regard to Mrs. Lincoln. I have very great sympathy for her in her present situation, but I do not see how I can aid her by either writing or visiting her.

If you will indicate anything I can do for her benefit, or what I should say, I shall feel obliged to you.

You refer to her mental condition as if she were not insane. Of course I know nothing of late except what has appeared in the newspapers. But when she came to this city to sell her wardrobe her conduct in reference to me and others was such as to leave a painful impression as to the state of her mind.

I cannot without great difficulty go to Illinois to visit her now, but I do not decline to do so if I can be of any real service to her.

May I ask whether your letter to me is with the approval of her son and friends, and whether it should not be brought to their knowledge? With the kindest wishes for her,

I remain very respectfully,
Abram Wakeman

Folder 29, Box 2, Mary Todd Lincoln Insanity File

ELIZABETH EDWARDS TO ROBERT LINCOLN
Springfield, Ill., Aug. 17, 1875

My dear Robert,

I have just had a call from Mrs. Bradwell, on an errand from your mother. You are the chief person interested in this painful case, and should determine it, as you think for the best. It may be that a refusal, to yield, to her wishes, at this crisis, will greatly increase her disorder. *She* showed me a letter from you to your mother,[*] which satisfies me that you misapprehended my intention, while willing to receive, I shrank from the responsibility, after your statement of her condition.

I now say, that *if you will bring* her down, *feeling perfectly willing,* to make the experiment, I promise to do all in my power, for her comfort and recovery. I would wish her to have a suitable white person, one wholly competent for the situation, brought with her. Further arrangements when I see you.

I write in haste.

Ever affectionately,

Aunt Lizzie

Folder 16, Box 2, Mary Todd Lincoln Insanity File

DR. PATTERSON TO ROBERT LINCOLN
Batavia, Ill., Aug. 17, 1875

R.T. Lincoln

My dear sir,

On yesterday Judge and Mrs. Bradwell spent an hour in private consultation with Mrs. L. They remained in my office about five minutes only—just long enough for the judge to say that "Mrs. L. ought not longer to remain in confinement and that it was injuring her health." I showed them your letter from Mrs. Edwards and they intimated that improper influences had been brought to bear upon Mrs. E. that had caused her to write such a letter. I presume they will continue their mission.

If Mrs. E. shall change her [*illegible*] purpose, shall I remand the patient to her?

Yours truly

R.J. Patterson

Folder 23, Box 2, Mary Todd Lincoln Insanity File

ROBERT LINCOLN TO DR. RICHARD J. PATTERSON
(TELEGRAM)
Farragut and Atlantic Houses, Rye Beach, N.H., n.d. [Aug. 17, 1875]

Contents of letters sent by you show that your patient must not be allowed to leave you now. Cut off absolutely all communication with improper persons. I write today to you and Mrs. Edwards.

Folder 37, Box 2, Mary Todd Lincoln Insanity File

---

[*] August 15, 1875.

DR. R. J. PATTERSON TO JAMES B. BRADWELL

Batavia, Ill., Aug. 18, 1875

My dear sir,

In regard to the case of Mrs. Lincoln allow me to say that I see no good *to her* but harm only in discussing *with her* the question of her removal from this place. It tends to keep her mind in a constant ferment over questions which should never have been discussed with her. Promises never should have been made to her, the fulfillment of which could by possible circumstances pass beyond the control of those who made them.

I am quite willing to believe that the objects of your visits and the numerous letters of Mrs. Bradwell are well meant and not designed to promote unrest and discontent. But I have become fully convinced that such is their tendency and result. My opinion is that for the present at least, these visits should be discontinued. Mrs. Lincoln may be written to assigning reasons for not repeating visits.

I understand that R. T. Lincoln conservator of Mrs. Lincoln, will be absent from home about two weeks. I will suggest that, at least until his return, Mrs. Lincoln should be simply let alone.

I have written the above in no unkind spirit, but from a sense of duty only to my patient.

Mrs. Lincoln has repeatedly said to me that you have in your possession an important paper that belongs to her. She again alluded to it today, saying, "Judge Bradwell has again forgotten to bring my paper." If you have any paper that belongs to her, *that she ought to have* perhaps it may be well to send it to her or to me and thus relieve her seeming anxiety.

Very respectfully,

R.J. Patterson

Folder 1, Cont. 8, Part 2,
Robert Todd Lincoln Family Papers

DAILY PATIENT PROGRESS REPORTS

Bellevue Place Sanitarium, Batavia, Ill., August 1875

18—Mrs. L seems more capricious and little tendency to irritability—she insists upon corn bread every morning—leaves them untouched and calls for rolls—griddle cakes are ordered for every supper which [she] does not eat but calls for rolls.

19—Mrs. L in a perturbed state of mind generally—rode out in carriage. Was asked if in presence of Mrs. Patterson if she had ever since her residence at my house been unkindly treated by her attendant or others—whether the least impropriety had been shown her and she said "no"—"not [at] all." Shows great capriciousness about her food and her washing.

Ross, "Mary Todd Lincoln"

JAMES B. BRADWELL TO DR. R. J. PATTERSON
Chicago, Ill., Aug. 19, 1875

My Dear Sir:

I have received your letter, stating that you can see no good to Mrs. Lincoln, but harm only, in discussing with her the question of her removal from your place, and that promises should never have been made to her, the fulfillment of which could by possible circumstances pass beyond the control of those who made them, etc., etc.

Now sir, who was it but yourself that told Mrs. Lincoln and also myself that she was in a condition to visit her sister, Mrs. Edwards, at Springfield, Ill., and that you had written a letter to her son Robert to that effect? Mrs. Bradwell, to carry out the expressed wish of Mrs. Lincoln, went to Springfield to see Mrs. Edwards to see if she would take her sister, and was assured by her that she would do so if brought by her son, and saw him day before yesterday.

No, Doctor, if you have the good of Mrs. Lincoln at heart, I am sure that you will see that she is taken to her sister. It is in accordance with your letter, I am satisfied, that Mrs. Lincoln does not require to be confined in a house for the insane, and that it would be greatly for her good to be allowed to visit her relatives and friends. She pines for liberty. Some of the best medical men in American say that it is shameful to lock Mrs. Lincoln up behind grates as she has been, and I concur with them. I believe that such confinement is injurious to her in the extreme, and calculated to drive her insane. Are you not going to allow her to visit her relatives to see if it will benefit her, or will you take the responsibility and run the risk of the American people saying hereafter that it was the restraint of your institution that injured Mrs. Lincoln and proved her ruin?

Should you not allow her to visit Mrs. Edwards, and insist on keeping her in close confinement, and I should be satisfied that the good of Mrs. Lincoln required it, as I certainly shall unless there is change in her condition, I, as her legal advisor and friend, will see if a habeas corpus cannot open the door of Mrs. Lincoln's prison house.

I am, etc.

James B. Bradwell

"Mrs. Abraham Lincoln: Correspondence of
Dr. Patterson and Judge Bradwell," Chicago Tribune,
August 31, 1875, 8

DR. PATTERSON TO ROBERT LINCOLN

Batavia, Ill., Aug. 20, 1875

R. T. Lincoln, Esq.

Dear Sir

I learn that Mrs. Bradwell has just returned from Springfield with the promise of Mrs. Edwards that on your return home, you may take Mrs. Lincoln to her house. Mrs. Edwards is to write you to this effect.

On yesterday two ladies from Springfield, Mrs. Edwards Jr. and her sister Mrs. Reman[n],[*] spent an hour very pleasantly with Mrs. Lincoln. They are indignant at Mrs. Bradwell and say that Mrs. Lincoln's relatives are satisfied with what has been done in Mrs. Lincoln's case, and would feel obliged to Mrs. B if she would mind her own business and not meddle with Mrs. L. They say also that Mrs. B. wrote a very mean letter to Mrs. Edwards, and I understood them to intimate that she charged unkind or improper treatment toward Mrs. L. while here.

On yesterday I sent the following letter to Judge Bradwell.

[copy enclosed of Patterson to Bradwell, August 18, 1875, see above]

Folder 23, Box 2, Mary Todd Lincoln Insanity File

"MRS. LINCOLN: SHE IS RECOVERING FROM HER MENTAL MALADY"

Chicago Post and Mail, Aug. 21, 1875

And Will Very Soon Leave the Asylum Forever.

———

A Talk With the Spirit Medium With Whom She Was Once Intimate.

———

[Special correspondence of The Post and Mail.]

St. Charles, Ill., Aug. 20—I am stopping for a day or two in this pretty, sleepy little town, which once promised to be the largest city on the Fox River, but which has long since subsided into a state of Rip Van Winkle tranquility, with a wholesome reverence for the dust of ages. I had breathed this hushed and pensive air, just long enough to make suicide a pleasant contemplation, when I remembered that hereabouts dwelt a

---

[*] Josephine Remann was the wife of Albert Edwards, son of Ninian and Elizabeth Edwards.

and feeling in a ghostly mood I started off across the river to see her. I easily found the place—a pleasant homestead, near the public school, and on ringing the bell, the door was opened by the lady herself, a plain, middle aged woman, with a peculiar Indian type of features. Mrs. Howard claims no Indian blood, however, but is controlled, so she says, by an Indian doctor, deceased some hundreds of years. This woman, possessed by a familiar spirit, and a professed fortune teller, was the friend and confidential advisor of

MRS. ABRAHAM LINCOLN,

when she resided a year or two ago for a few months in St. Charles. She assured me that she did not know of Mrs. Lincoln's presence here, when she visited her under an assumed name and had her enter the clairvoyant state. The lady visitor was announced as Mrs. May, but when the medium became entranced she at once exclaimed in the broken Indian tongue she uses at such times, "This is

ABRAHAM LINCOLN'S SQUAW!"

This was a revelation to all present, and Mrs. Lincoln did not deny it. She said to the medium that she used another name to escape the blame and notice of the people. "They censure me for everything," said the poor, unhappy lady, with tears in her eyes. "Why, when I sold my wardrobe, which I had a perfect right to do, as I hated the sight of gay clothes, I made the people promise they would not tell of it, but see what they did." She assured Mrs. Howard that she was

NEVER ALONE.

Angels surrounded her bed at night, and wherever she went hosts of spirits accompanied her. "Yet," said Mrs. Howard, "she did not believe in spiritualism, nor do I think the communications she received through me ever satisfied her. She seemed to have established a sort of spiritual religion for herself, which comforted her the most."[*]

As soon as Mrs. Lincoln became known she left St. Charles, but the spiritualists regarded her very kindly. It would seem a strange thing that she could have found peace of mind in the incoherent messages of a dead Indian, but she visited the

---

[*] Mary herself wrote of this in 1869, "I am not EITHER a Spiritualist—but I sincerely believe—our loved ones, who have only, *'gone before'* are permitted to watch over those who were dearer to them than life;" and that she knew her husband so watched over her. "I should have lost my reason long ere this—if I had entertained *other* views, than I do, on this subject." Mary Lincoln to Sally Orne, Nov. 20, 1869, Turner and Turner, *Mary Todd Lincoln*, 525–26. See also Mary Lincoln to Charles Sumner, July 4, 1865, ibid, 256.

medium once or twice every day, remaining hours at a time. The parlor is the usual comfortable apartment of well-to-do people, but it is hung with significant

SPIRIT PICTURES

and gay wreaths and bouquets of painted flowers, representing the spirits of children. The family is much respected by neighbors and citizens, and visitors come all the way from Boston and from Omaha to have their fortunes told by Mrs. Howard.

You will be glad to learn—and this is the first public intimation of it—that Mrs. Lincoln is pronounced well enough to leave the Asylum and visit her sister, Mrs. Edwards, of Springfield. It is not likely she will return to Bellevue Place, as there is some feeling evinced in the matter of her incarceration, by friends who

REFUSE TO BELIEVE HER INSANE.

A leading lady lawyer of Chicago has been with her much of late, and, with the assistance of her legal husband, will assist Mrs. Lincoln's restoration to the world. She is decidedly better, sleeps and eats well, and shows no tendency to any mania, but whether the cure is permanent or not, the test of active life and time will prove.

Chicago Post and Mail, August 21, 1875, 1[*]

ROBERT LINCOLN, TELEGRAM TO
MRS. NINIAN W. EDWARDS
Farragut House, Rye Beach, N.H., Aug. 23, 1875

Do nothing whatever about proposed visit until you receive my letter of today. Robert T. Lincoln

NINIAN EDWARDS TO DR. PATTERSON,
written on RTL's Western Union telegram,

Springfield, Ill., Aug. 23, 1875

Dr. Patterson
Dear Sir:

We have not proposed any visit from Mrs. Lincoln except with the approbation of yourself and her son, not unless he should himself accompany her—whilst we would gladly receive her and do everything in our power to make her comfortable and happy, we think the responsibility and propriety of her leaving your institu-

---

[*] The author of this article was Mrs. M.L. Rayne, who previously had interviewed Mary Lincoln at Bellevue Place and published the report of her visit in the Chicago *Post and Mail* on July 13, 1875 (see chapter 6).

tion should be decided by you and her son and Mr. Swett—she herself proposed a visit to us.

Respectfully yours,
Ninian Edwards

Folder 17, Box 2, Mary Todd Lincoln Insanity File

"MRS. LINCOLN: STARTLING INTERVIEW UPON HER CASE WITH JUDGE BRADWELL"
Chicago Post and Mail, Aug. 23, 1875

He Considers Her a Wronged Woman and Her Mind Sound.

———

Probability That She Will Be at Liberty Within a Week.

———

While she lives the people of this grateful country will not cease to feel an earnest interest in the condition of her who was the wife of President Lincoln.

Mrs. Lincoln was found partially insane about three months ago by the Cook County Court, but it did not commit her to a public asylum or any other. The conservator appointed to control her movements, however, removed her to

A PRIVATE ASYLUM

for the insane at Batavia, kept by Dr. Patterson. There she was placed under a restraint that was virtual imprisonment.

THE POST AND MAIL is the only paper whose correspondent has ever interviewed her while there, and therein brought out many facts that enabled the public to see her as she was. And again on Saturday a correspondent of THE POST AND MAIL first announced that Mrs. Lincoln was about to make her sister, Mrs. Edwards, of Springfield, a visit.

In that correspondence of Saturday it was stated that "a legal lady of Chicago and her husband" (not to infer, however, that she had an illegal one), had taken steps for Mrs. Lincoln's release, it being implied that her contemplated visit to Springfield was the result of their friendly, if not professional, intercourse. Of course it was not necessary to guess twice to be sure that Mrs. Myra Bradwell and her husband, Judge Bradwell, were referred to.

This morning, therefore, a representative of THE POST AND MAIL called at the office of the *Legal News,* and soon found the courteous and humane Judge at leisure for an interview, though at first somewhat averse to it. Only the strong feeling of his good heart that Mrs. Lincoln was and that, as a President's widow, the public were interested in her personal welfare, and had a right to know the facts, induced him to talk upon the lamentable theme.

The following dialogue ensued:

Reporter—Judge Bradwell, is THE POST AND MAIL correct in inferring that yourself and Mrs. Bradwell are the legal gentleman and lady referred to by its correspondent as taking legal steps for the permanent release of Mrs. Lincoln from her confinement at Batavia?

Judge Bradwell—Well, I don't know, as I didn't see your correspondent. She certainly learned nothing from me. I have been to see Mrs. Lincoln several times of late, as also has Mrs. Bradwell; but no strictly "legal" steps have been taken, as it is hoped that her release from

HER UNJUST INCARCERATION

can be effected amicably. Do you want to write anything about this?

R.—Certainly; if you know anything about Mrs. Lincoln's condition and confinement at Batavia which the world doesn't know, and are disposed to tell it, THE POST AND MAIL, as always, will be inclined to enlighten the world by the publication of your information.

J.B.—Well, sir, I have no hesitation whatever in saying that Mrs. Lincoln ought not to be where she now is, and never ought to have been placed there. It was

A GROSS OUTRAGE

to imprison her there behind grates and bars, in a place understood to be for mad people. Why to be so shut up and guarded and locked up at night, with the feeling that it may last for life, is enough to make almost any aged and delicate woman crazy. She is no more insane today than you and I are.

R.—What makes you think so, Judge?

J.B.—I am as

THOROUGHLY CONVINCED OF IT

as of my own existence. I have had several business letters from her since she has been there, and Mrs. Bradwell has had letters of womanly friendship from her repeatedly; and she writes as straight and intelligible a business letter as she ever did, and as good, friendly letters as one need ask for. There is

NOT THE SLIGHTEST TRACE OF INSANITY

or of a weak mind about any of her writings.

R.—Well, a good letter is one of the best proofs possible of a sound mind. Will you permit one of more of her letters to be printed?

J.B.—I should hardly feel warranted in doing that without Mrs. Lincoln's consent; but you may take my word for it that they are good sane letters.

R.—When did you see and talk with her last?

J.B.—One week ago today.

R.—What did she say about herself?

J.B.—She sighed and plead for liberty like a woman shut up without cause. Said she to me: "Mr. Bradwell, what have I done that I should be kept here in this prison, behind these grates, my footsteps followed, and every action watched by day, and my bedroom door locked upon the outside at night, and the key taken away by my jailer? Surely 'I am not mad, but soon shall be.'

I WANT LIBERTY

to go among my friends."

R.—Is it not a pleasant place then?

J.B.—Oh, yes; the scenery is fine, and Mrs. Lincoln eats well and sleeps well, and has a healthy look. But she does not well brook the idea of being a prisoner. I sat in the room with her and looked out upon the Fox River with the forests and the flowers and the lawn, and said to her: "Mrs. Lincoln, this is very nice." She replied: "Yes, it is very nice to you who have your freedom to go and come as you please, but not so to me who can see it only through those window bars. Everywhere I go those hateful bars are before my mind, if not my eyes."

R.—She will be allowed to visit her sister will she?

J.B.—We hope so. Dr. Patterson

HAS SIGNED A CERTIFICATE

of her fitness to go; but she has not got it, and I have not, but he told me he had signed it. Mrs. Edwards wrote to her that she could come and live with her, and it is expected that when Robert Lincoln returns from the East, about the middle of this week, he will go to Batavia and accompany his mother to Springfield.* But I shall only feel safe when she is out.

DR. PATTERSON IS A VERY PECULIAR MAN.

I know that some letters she has sent have not been allowed to reach her friends, and some that have been sent her have not reached her. You can't tell what motives may tend to keep her there. Human nature is human nature. But if she is not soon out, there will be startling developments not to be mentioned now. Let her get out of danger first.

Chicago Post and Mail, August 23, 1875, 5

---

* Robert was with his family on vacation at Rye Beach, New Hampshire.

Chicago Times, Aug. 24, 1875

Mrs. Lincoln Will Soon Return from Her Brief Visit to the Insane Asylum.

For Her Physicians Pronounce Her as Sane as Those Who Sent Her There.

And She is Only Awaiting Robert's Return from the East to Set Her Free Again.

How She Talked With a "Times" Correspondent in a Recent Interview.

Her Recollection of Past Events and What She Had to Say of Them.

What Mrs. Myra Bradwell Has Been Doing in Her Behalf.

The public was somewhat shocked a few months since by the announcement that Mrs. Lincoln, the widow of President Lincoln, was insane; and further pained by the announcement of the fact that she had been confined in a private insane asylum at Batavia, in this state, owned and managed by Dr. Patterson. The proceedings before the court were reported with great fidelity, and published in detail in the newspapers of the city. The account of her subsequent departure from the city, was also given to the world with a painful minuteness. Occasionally some word has come up to the great busy world from the retired spot of earth, concerning the condition of the lady in whom all American people feel a kindly interest. These slight allusions to her were eagerly read, then the active affairs of life went on, and no one thought of the woman who had suffered so much in this world, and whose afternoon of life is filled with such a chilly atmosphere.

Recently a representative of THE TIMES, in quest of scientific facts by means of personal observation, visited the institution of Dr. Patterson at Batavia, and while there was

INTRODUCED TO MRS. LINCOLN

by a mutual friend who happened to be there at the same time,* not as a newspaper man but as a gentleman who knew her history and who took a friendly interest in all that pertained to her welfare.

The lady appeared in very good spirits, and her mind was clear and sprightly. After some preliminary conversation she invited the gentleman to her room to obtain a view of the pastoral landscape from that source, and to pursue the interesting conversation already begun. This opportunity, which had thus been presented by circumstances, was improved by the gentleman of the press, to discover the exact condition of her mind, so far as he was able to do so, by drawing her into conversation on all possible topics in which he deemed her to have been interested, either pleasantly or painfully during her life. If there were any weak points in her mind, he was determined to find out what they were. If she were brooding over any circumstance of her sad life, he was bent on finding out what it was. Her visit to London was alluded to, and thoroughly discussed. Little Tad was with her there, and she alluded to the child, now dead, but whose memory is very dear to her, with all the warmth and affection a fond mother might be expected to exhibit. There was, however,

NOT A SIGN OF WEAKNESS

or any abnormal manifestations of mind visible. She conversed fluently and rationally about her wanderings in England. She narrated her experiences in Germany, dwelling on the subject of her travels with much detail and interest to the end. During all this time she not only exhibited a sound and rational judgment, but gave evidences of the possession of uncommon powers of observation and memory.

Her attention was called to the time when the visitor had met her in Washington, in 1862. The occasion she remembered. Knowing that the death of little Tad and the assassination of Mr. Lincoln were two incidents in her life that were known to have made the most powerful impressions on her mind of any events which had ever occurred to her, these circumstances were adroitly introduced into the conversation. During all this her admirable mind maintained its poise with perfection. Concerning Mr. Lincoln she related anecdotes illustrating his extreme good nature. She conversed about the assassination. No mental weakness, under any possible test, could be discovered. She spoke of public men with whom she had become acquainted during her residence at the White House. She specially dwelt on the friendship which existed between Mr. Seward† and Mr. Lincoln and herself. It was the habit of the secretary to dine with Mr. Lincoln and herself informally, two or three times a week. She

---

* Myra Bradwell, who actually had gone to Chicago to fetch the reporter and bring him to Batavia specifically so he could write a story.

† Secretary of State William H. Seward—a man whom Mary did not trust, never liked, and with whom she never was friends.

whom she met in England, and spoke with great sensibility of their kindness, and told how badly she felt when the minister was removed. She very keenly described the characters she had met abroad, showing that she possesses great powers of analysis. She gave her views of foreigners, and foreign matters, concerning which she exhibited great apprehension and acuteness of mind. She also spoke of the books she was engaged in reading and the life she led. Her health at present, she observed, was superb. She had never been better. When she came to Chicago from Florida she had been suffering somewhat from fever, and her nervous system was somewhat shattered. She was prostrated, and any eccentricities she might have manifested then, if any, she attributed to this fact.

There were some light iron bars over the door, to which she called the attention of the gentleman. She said they seemed to menace her, and they annoyed her with the idea that she was in prison. She was somewhat apprehensive that the prison bars, and the presence of insane people in the house, whose wild and piercing cries she sometimes heard, might affect her mind so as to unseat her reason, in time. She commented upon journals and journalists with great intelligence. The conversation took the widest possible range, and from this the representative of THE TIMES became convinced that her mind was in

A PERFECTLY SOUND AND
HEALTHY CONDITION.

She made no complaint of her treatment. She thought she would like a little more liberty to drive out, and a little more liberty to receive her friends. She exhibited marvelous charity through the entire course of the interview for those by whose instrumentality she had been placed there. The gentleman departed thoroughly convinced that whatever condition of mind Mrs. Lincoln may have been in previously, she is unquestionably *compos mentis* now, and ought not to be deprived of her liberty.

A reporter of THE TIMES last evening called on

MRS. MYRA BRADWELL

at her residence on Michigan Avenue, and obtained from that lady some interesting particulars concerning Mrs. Lincoln. Mrs. Bradwell has been a warm personal friend of Mrs. Lincoln for some years, and has been in active correspondence with her during the past year. She has been associated with her intimately, and is thoroughly acquainted with her mental condition. During the past few weeks this lady has visited Mrs. Lincoln at Batavia several times, and has conversed with her for

---

* John Lothrop Motley, U.S. Minister to Great Britain, 1869–70, while Mary and Tad were touring Europe. President Lincoln appointed him Minister to Austria in 1861, where he served until 1869.

hours. She has occupied the same room and the same bed with her, and has received letters from her full of sensibility, affection, and pathos.

"What have you to say concerning Mrs. Lincoln's condition, Mrs. Bradwell?" asked the reporter after disposing of the preliminaries to the subject.

"I am extremely reluctant about saying anything about the matter at the present time," replied the lady, "on account of the unpleasant situation of things."

R.—I am informed that you have visited Mrs. Lincoln several times recently, and have had long conversations with her?

Mrs. B.—So I have. I have always had the tenderest regard and love for Mrs. Lincoln, and during her stay in Florida received many long and beautifully written letters from her. I was inexpressibly shocked when I learned of her alleged insanity, and of her confinement in an asylum at Batavia. I wondered what could have occurred to unbalance her mind so suddenly. It was a matter of the greatest surprise and astonishment to me.

R.—Do you think Mrs. Lincoln is insane?

Mrs. B.—I will be frank with you in answering that question. I think Mrs. Lincoln has no more cause for being confined behind bolts and bars than any other person whose sanity is not questioned. She is no more insane than I am.

R.—What was the object of your visit to Batavia?

Mrs. B.—I felt a deep interest in the welfare of Mrs. Lincoln. I went to see her and conversed with her for two hours. I obtained permission of Dr. Patterson to visit her again. I went again and again.

R.—What did you do upon your return to Chicago, Mrs. Bradwell?

Mrs. B.—Upon my return to Chicago from my first visit I obtained an interview with Mr. Robert Lincoln. I told him what I thought of the condition of his mother, and I referred to my long acquaintance with her. He acknowledged to me that he thought I was acting for what I deemed the best interests of his mother. If Mrs. Edwards, of Springfield, a sister of Mrs. Lincoln, would receive her, he would go himself to Batavia and conduct her there, provided Dr. Patterson would sign a certificate of recovery.

R.—Has Dr. Patterson signed such a certificate?

Mrs. B.—He has, but it has not been delivered to Mrs. Lincoln.

R.—Did you learn whether Mrs. Edwards would receive her sister?

Mrs. B.—I did. I made a visit to Springfield. I had a long conversation with her. She promised to receive her sister and take care of her. Mrs. Edwards is a lady of fine feelings and cultivation. She has a beautiful home, surrounded by lawns and flowers. It is just the place for a sorrow-burdened heart like Mrs. Lincoln's to find repose and peace. On my return here I had called to see Mr. Robert Lincoln, but he had gone east. Nothing can be done until his return. It is this circumstance which causes me to regret the publication of anything concerning this matter at the present time. It is premature and places me in a delicate position. It would have been better to have delayed it.

R.—Do you think Mrs. Lincoln's release can be obtained without an appeal to the law?

Mrs. B.—Unquestionably. I have no reason in the world to doubt Mr. Robert Lincoln's word. I believe he will do as he said he would. He informed me though, that he was very certain Mrs. Edwards would not consent to receiving her.

R.—What did Mrs. Lincoln say about a visit to her sister?

Mrs. B.—She implored me in the tenderest and most pathetic terms to go and see Mrs. Edwards and ask her to receive her.

R.—How did you find her situated?

Mrs. B.—I found her very comfortably cared for. When I first went there, there were bars over her windows and doors and this fact seemed to annoy her. I spoke to Dr. Patterson about it, and the next time I visited her she was in a room without bars. The bolt was not turned on the outside, which afforded her some relief.

The foregoing was the substance of the conversation with Mrs. Bradwell, who feels the keenest interest in the welfare of her friend. There seems to be no doubt that Mrs. Lincoln's mind is now sound and that she will be restored to the world in a short time. Mr. Robert Lincoln will return from the east next week, when he will act in the matter. The country will rejoice at the liberation.

Chicago Times, Tuesday, August 24, 1875, 4[*]

EDITORIAL

Chicago Times, Aug. 24, 1875

The public had read the harrowing tales of the imprisonment of sane men and women in asylums for the insane. Some of these were doubtless true, others fictions. That such things have been done does not admit of a doubt. The subject is brought forward again in a painful manner by an interview with Mrs. Myra Bradwell, editor of *The Legal News,* a lady of prominence and unquestioned veracity, who has several times visited Mrs. Lincoln at the retreat for the insane at Batavia, Illinois. Mrs. Bradwell is of the opinion, from a close study of the patient, that there is not the slightest trace of insanity about her. She thinks Mrs. Lincoln has been grossly abused, that she is today as sane as those who adjudged her otherwise, and should at once be restored to liberty and the control of her own affairs.

The case is a peculiarly sad one. It will be remembered that the jury which adjudged Mrs. Lincoln insane was selected with extraordinary care; that the ex-

---

[*] This article was written by Franc B. Wilkie based on his August 7 interview with Mary Lincoln at Bellevue Place.

amination of witnesses was reasonably thorough, and that the evidence presented was sufficient to convince even the most reluctant of her friends, of Mrs. Lincoln's mental aberration. But if she has since recovered her right mind, and is being held in duress unlawfully, and without good cause, the public will unite in a demand for her release and restoration for her proper place in society.

It would be strange if Illinois should furnish a parallel of the case of Lady Dudleigh, in Wilkie Collins' "Man and Wife."

Chicago Times, August 24, 1875, 4

EDITORIAL
Chicago Evening Journal, Aug. 24, 1875

We cannot but regard the efforts of certain persons and papers in this city to get up a "sensation" regarding Mrs. Lincoln as in very bad taste, to say the least of it. That unfortunate lady was last spring placed under medical treatment in a private insane asylum, at Batavia, near this city, the propriety of which step was apparent to all who were conversant with her sad condition. It would seem that, benefited by the seclusion and treatment she has experienced, under circumstances of the tenderest care and the least possible restraint, she has now virtually recovered her mental health, and asks to be permitted to leave the asylum and become a member of her sister's household at Springfield. We understand that Dr. Patterson, the proprietor of the asylum, is perfectly willing to gratify her wish in this respect if her friends desire it. And this is all there is of the matter. But why should the *quid nuncs** of the press ruthlessly and wantonly drag the lady's name and misfortune again before the public in a sensational style? It is an outrage upon common decency, of which no person having an appreciation of the simplest proprieties of life and conduct would be guilty.

Chicago Evening Journal, August 24, 1875, 2

"MRS. LINCOLN [IMPROVEMENT IN MENTAL CONDITION]"
Illinois State Journal, Aug. 25, 1875

The announcement contained in the Associated Press dispatches, based on the report of an interview of a reporter of the *Post and Mail* of Chicago with Judge J.B. Bradwell, of the material improvement in the mental condition of Mrs. Lincoln, is calculated to excite deep interest throughout the whole country, but nowhere more than in this city, where she is well-known, and where the remains of her honored and beloved husband and others of her family repose. While the theory of mental

—————
* Busybodies; gossips.

aberration affords the only reasonable, as well as charitable, explanation of some of Mrs. Lincoln's marked eccentricities since the tragic death of her distinguished husband, no right-minded man or woman in the nation can fail to be deeply affected by everything which concerns her welfare.

The loose talk which is finding its way into some of the Chicago papers, in the form of interviews, however, is calculated to do gross injustice to persons who have been compelled to perform a most painful duty, but who have endeavored to discharge it in the most delicate manner. For instance, Judge Bradwell is represented as saying "Mrs. Lincoln ought not to be where she now is, and never ought to have been placed there." Such a charge is a gross reflection upon the family and friends of Mrs. Lincoln who have suffered immeasurably beyond anything it is in the nature of their accuser to conceive. Her examination was conducted with the utmost delicacy, and the Judge of the Cook County Court, after listening to the evidence, felt compelled to declare that she was of unsound mind and should be placed under humane and prudent restraint. Events immediately following this investigation demonstrated beyond doubt the wisdom and the humanity of this decision, if those preceding it had not already done so. Equally inexcusable and unjustifiable, too, are the reflections cast upon Dr. Patterson, in reference to whom there is no evidence that his treatment of Mrs. Lincoln has been otherwise than most tender and considerate. That the Judge of the Cook County Court, with the evidence of her actual condition before him, and Dr. Patterson, with the opportunity of observing her condition daily, are far better qualified to judge of her needs, than the gentleman who thus presumes to criticize both, no one will be likely to deny.

Under all the circumstances, we do not hesitate to characterize these implied attacks upon Mrs. Lincoln's family and friends—and especially upon her only son, now absent from Chicago in the East—as extremely injudicious, as well as an unfeeling and gratuitous outrage. While there will be universal satisfaction to know that Mrs. Lincoln has been restored to her reason and her friends, these efforts of busy-bodies, whatever its motive, cannot hasten that result, but may impede it. The world may rest assured that Mrs. Lincoln does not stand in need of a self-constituted champion to protect her from friends who have the sagacity to perceive, and will rejoice to recognize the evidences of her restoration.

Illinois State Journal, August 25, 1875, 2

"MRS. ABRAHAM LINCOLN: HER RECOVERY DENIED"
Boston Globe, Aug. 25, 1875

The History of Her Insanity and Treatment.
[Special Dispatch to The Boston Globe]

CHICAGO, August 24—The attempt on the part of a newspaper in this city to work up a sensation in regard to Mrs. Lincoln is received with but little favor by the better class of citizens. The allegation that she is perfectly sane and that her imprisonment at Batavia is consequently an outrage, is not borne out by the facts, and is known to be utterly untrue by those who are familiar with the circumstances. At the time she was placed in the institution at Batavia, her insanity was very marked, though, as is usually the case, it was not apparent at all times. Since she has been under treatment, she has shown some improvement, and it is thought probable she will be allowed to visit her sister at Springfield. Like all insane persons, she is very certain that she is in the full possession of her reason, and letters written by her to meddlesome persons in this city have led to the report that she is improperly restrained of her liberty. Mr. Robert Lincoln, it is said, has been unremitting in his attention to his mother, and no one who knows the character of the man would for a moment accuse him of acting wrongfully towards her.

Boston Globe, August 25, 1875, 1

[MRS. LINCOLN'S RELATIVES ANNOYED AT EXPOSÉ]
Chicago Tribune, Aug. 28, 1875

A special dispatch from Springfield to the St. Louis *Republican* says:

"The relatives of Mrs. Lincoln here are greatly annoyed by the late obtrusion of her name in print and by the insinuations made that she is detained in the Batavia Hospital unnecessarily. For some time after her arrival at the hospital her prospect for recovery was very good, and it was hoped her health would be permanently restored. It is known that a belief in Spiritualism was one form of her mental disorder, and a visit made her by a Chicago lady who professes that belief has caused a recurrence of the most distressing symptoms. Her relations here regret the late unpleasant expose, but it is impossible to prevent such annoyance as long as the publication of sensational newspapers is a paying one."

The comment of the above dispatch is a timely one, and lacks only in severity. The scandal was set afloat by over-officious and intermeddling mischief-makers, who interfered in a matter which did not concern them, for purposes of sensation. The pretense made by them that she is sane and confined in the asylum against her will, is an atrocious libel upon her son and friends. If she were really sane, they would be the first to know it, and remove her at once, and no one would rejoice more than they to find that the unfortunate lady had been restored to health in body and mind. There is no scandal in this case, except so far as the intermeddling scandalizers themselves are concerned. Inasmuch as there are plenty of other objects upon which they can exercise their slop-over philanthropy and maudlin sentimentalizing, it is inconceivable why they have chosen Mrs. Lincoln for the exercise of their talents in this direction, except that it affords them an opportunity to wound the feelings of her friends, and to libel them atrociously besides.

Chicago Tribune, August 28, 1875, 8

"MRS. ABRAHAM LINCOLN: LETTER FROM DR. R. J. PATTERSON"
Chicago Tribune, Aug. 29, 1875

To the Editor of The Chicago Tribune:

Batavia, Ill., Aug. 28—It is no fault of mine that the sad case of Mrs. Lincoln has been again in all the papers of the land. But now that so many incorrect statements have been made, I deem it proper to correct some of them.

On the 19th of May last, Mrs. Lincoln, being in court, was declared "insane, and a fit subject for treatment in a state hospital for the insane." The warrant for commitment was at the request of her friends, directed to the undersigned, commanding him "forthwith to arrest and convey her to Bellevue Place, Batavia, Ill."

It has been publicly stated that I have "certified" to the recovery, or mental soundness, of Mrs. Lincoln. This is not true. She is certainly much improved, both mentally and physically; but I have not at any time regarded her as a person of sound mind. I heard all the testimony at the trial, May 19, and saw no reason then to doubt the correctness of the verdict of the jury. I believe her to be now insane.

The question of Mrs. Lincoln's removal from this place, notwithstanding her mental impairment, has received careful consideration from her conservator, Mr. Robert T. Lincoln, and myself. The proposition having been made that she should go and live with her sister, Mrs. Edwards, in Springfield, I at once said that if she would do this in good faith, and thus secure a quiet home for herself, I would favor it, "unless her condition should change for the worse." This was written to Mr. Robert T. Lincoln in a letter addressed to him on the 9th inst. And this is all there is of the "certificate" said to have been given by me of the "recovery" or "mental soundness" of Mrs. Lincoln. In accordance with the above conditional sanction of the proposition for removal, I have occasion to know that Robert T. Lincoln made efforts to perfect arrangements for the transfer of Mrs. Lincoln to Springfield.

It is well known that there are certain insane persons who need what in medico-legal science is termed interdiction, which does not necessarily imply restraint. If time should show that Mrs. Lincoln needs only the former, without the latter, all will rejoice to see any possible enlargement of her privileges. And now, although the conditions upon which, on the 9th inst., I favored her removal, have been modified by the presence of a greater degree of mental perturbation than at that time existed, I am still unwilling to throw any obstacle in the way of giving her an opportunity to have a home with her sister. But I am willing to record the opinion that such is the character of her malady, she will not be content to do this, and that the experiment, if made, will result only in giving the coveted opportunity to make extended rambles, to renew the indulgence of her purchasing mania, and other morbid mental manifestations.

In regard to the treatment of Mrs. Lincoln while under my care, it has been stated that she has been "kept in close confinement," "virtually imprisoned behind grates and bars," "locked by her jailer as a prisoner," "incarcerated," etc., etc. these and other like harsh terms are not used in the interest of truth. They are unjust, and do no credit to those who apply them to the case of Mrs. Lincoln. She need not remain indoors unless by her own choice more than two or three waking hours of any day. A carriage is always at her command. She may ride or walk when and where she pleases, on condition that she shall return at proper hours, and be accompanied by some suitable person or persons. She receives calls from ladies of her acquaintance in Batavia, and may return them. She has been called upon by Gen. Farnsworth, of St. Charles, and by some of her relatives in Springfield. She has had, until the 16th inst., private unrestricted personal intercourse with Judge Bradwell, who, in a threatening and insulting letter to me, calls himself "her legal advisor and friend." The wife of Judge Bradwell, until the date above named, has been permitted repeatedly to visit Mrs. Lincoln, write her numerous letters, bear messages and packages of letters to her, and lodge overnight with her in her room.

As to "guarded windows," I have only to say they are made as unobjectionable as it is possible to make them. A light ornamental screen was at first placed before Mrs. Lincoln's windows. These were subsequently removed. But when it is remembered that the same evening on which Mrs. Lincoln was declared insane she attempted suicide, all right-minded persons will agree that guarded windows were among the proper precautions against accident.

As to "barred doors," there are none at Bellevue Place. Mrs. Lincoln's doors leading to the outer world are never locked during the daytime. The outer door only is locked at bedtime at night by her private attendant, who sleeps in an adjoining room communicating with that of Mrs. Lincoln. This, to my mind, is the proper thing to do.

Mrs. Lincoln has been placed where she is under the forms of law, and, if any have grievance, the law is open to them. This sad case has commanded the constant endeavors of those who have the care of her unselfishly to do the best for Mrs. Lincoln.

R.J. Patterson

Chicago Tribune, August 29, 1875, 16

"MRS. ABRAHAM LINCOLN: WHAT HER PASTOR, PROF. SWING, SAYS ABOUT HER INSANITY"

Chicago Times, Aug. 29, 1875

The following from *The Alliance,* evidently inspired by Prof. [David] Swing, who was Mrs. Lincoln's pastor, deserves attention:

"The daily papers have, to say the least, awakened a large amount of inquiry regarding the lawfulness or humanity of Mrs. Lincoln's imprisonment. Many who read the evidences of her sanity as brought forward by parties so high in character as Judge Bradwell, are ready now to declare that the durance at Batavia was the result of fear and suspicion on the part of the son about property. There is room in this matter for an immense amount of injustice to be done Robert Lincoln, and we hope the public will decline accepting the opportunity. Mrs. Lincoln was sent to Batavia by a group of the best friends she has in the world, and a group of men who would not permit any wrong to be done the widow of the great president. Leonard Swett and I. N. Arnold are not the gentlemen to be participators in a plot that would wrongly deprive a valued friend of liberty.

"The case seems to our view about as follows: Mrs. Lincoln's mind is liable to spells of sinking and rising. For weeks it seems different from ordinary in being better than the average brain. She is much of her time witty, sharp, and playful, and has no more business behind bars than we all have who are allowed the freedom of the city. But it is also true that times do come when some strong arm should be near her by day and night to stand guard until the intellectual tide should rise again. There may be a few days or weeks in a year when her present home in Batavia would be the best possible place for her, but the rights to liberty and to be treated as a sane human being are so immense and so tender, that release should come the moment the mind straightens up again. Mrs. Lincoln's condition last spring was wholly new, and we think only temporary. The weakness of the mind revealing itself at times up to that date had such a shape that one could not well call it madness. If she kept her windows open that angels might come in, and that heaven might send her at times a whiff of its rare perfumes, this only indicates some harmless hallucination, and would suggest the idea of taking the iron bars also off her windows, so that the angels can come in if they so desire. No doubt upon the return of her son he will have the devoted mother removed to the house of some friend. He loves her more than the public does, and will do what is right as rapidly as the right shall make itself manifest."

Chicago Times, Sunday, August 29, 1875, 1

EDITORIAL
Chicago Times, Monday, Aug. 30, 1875

Prof. Swing, in his comments on the case of Mrs. Lincoln, has hit the truth. There are variations in her character; but the variations from the line of sanity are not either numerous or marked enough to demand her perpetual seclusion behind grated windows. It is probably the fact that, when sent to Batavia, she required the class of treatment which she received. It is also the fact that she has entirely recovered from this attack; and that her mental condition is such that her longer confinement against her will cannot be regarded other than an unlawful restraint. In the estimate of Prof. Swing, who knows her intimately, she requires only loving watchfulness and sympathy, and not enforced confinement.

It is somewhat strange, with reference to this matter, that *The Chicago Tribune,* without having informed itself as to Mrs. Lincoln's condition, has persistently treated her as if she were a confirmed lunatic; and has been guilty of scandalous vituperation of those who, from personal knowledge, have reached a different conclusion. *The Tribune* will do well not to permit its zeal to outrun decency and discretion. There are facts in reference to this prolonged confinement which, if made public, would not reflect credit upon parties who are closely related to its principals. The statement by *The Tribune* that Mrs. Lincoln, through the influence of spiritualism, is again insane, is either the result of a gross imposition on that journal, or else it is a malignant falsehood. There is a likelihood, and a very grave one, that a prolonged and unnecessary confinement would result in insanity, as has often been shown to be the consequence in other instances. Such a result may be attained in the present case; but, if so, there are capable witnesses who stand ready to establish that such a result was wholly unnecessary, and that, if produced, it came from the effect of a most mistaken intent, or a deliberate design.

Chicago Times, Monday, August 30, 1875, 4

On August 31, the Chicago Tribune *then continued the controversy by printing in full Dr. Patterson's August 18 letter to James Bradwell and Bradwell's combative August 19 reply.*

Chapter 8

September–December 1875

Robert Lincoln returned home from his summer vacation on September 1, and im-mediately began taking steps to investigate the possibility of removing his mother to the Edwards home in Springfield. Clearly, Robert had been considering this action while in New Hampshire, probably after receiving the letters from Patterson and Elizabeth Edwards while there. The first person he wrote was Dr. Patterson.

ROBERT LINCOLN TO R. J. PATTERSON

Sept. 2, 1875

Dear Sir:

Enclosed please find check for $72.66 for which please return a voucher.

I reached home on yesterday and have not yet had time to digest the extraordinary performances of the Bradwells.

I wish you would drop me a line so that I will get it early tomorrow morning as to my mother's present condition with your present views (for my information) of the probable safety in taking her to Springfield—find a letter from my aunt two weeks old, in which she says she will receive her if accompanied by a "competent white person."

I want to have a talk with Professor Swing tomorrow when he reaches here and suppose I will see you on duty.

LB 3:4:349

DR. PATTERSON TO ROBERT LINCOLN

Batavia, Ill., Sept. 2, 1875

R. T. Lincoln, Esq.
Dear Sir,

In reply to your note of Sept. 2nd, I am not able to report much change in the mental condition of Mrs. Lincoln since you last saw her. I do not hesitate to say that as a result of her intercourse with Judge and Mrs. Bradwell, she became worse; and since they have ceased their visits, she is again better and improving.

In regard to the "safety" of removal to Springfield, I can think of nothing better, than to call your attention to the enclosed extract.* Inasmuch as Mrs. Lincoln has had the promise that on certain conditions she can go and live with her sister, and as these conditions, so far as I know, have been complied with, I suppose the experiment ought to be made. I will see you on Saturday, and talk fully.

In haste for the mail,

R. J. Patterson

Folder 23, Box 2, Mary Todd Lincoln Insanity File

ROBERT LINCOLN TO DR. ANDREW MCFARLAND[†]

Jacksonville, Ill., Sept. 4, 1875

Note at top of letter:

Letter exactly the same as this written to A. J. McDill, supt. state asylum for the insane, Madison, Wisconsin

Dear Sir:

You are undoubtedly aware that on the 19th of May last, in consequence of a petition filed by me in the County Court of this (Cook) County, my mother, Mrs. Abraham Lincoln, was adjudged insane. Since that time she has been under the personal care of Dr. R. J. Patterson, at Batavia, Illinois.

For some time past she has been very urgent in the expression of a desire that I, (having been appointed to the custody of her estate and person) should permit her to visit her sister, Mrs. N. W. Edwards, at Springfield, Illinois. Mrs. Edwards has expressed a willingness to me to receive her, if properly attended.

As a guest of her sister, I do not think it possible that the same restraint could be exercised over possible irrational acts, should they occur as if she remained under the care of Dr. Patterson, but I am anxious that she should visit my aunt, if it is not probable that harm to her may come of it.

I am in possession of Dr. Patterson's opinion on the subject, (which I . . . [*illegible*] . . .) but I desire also the opinion of yourself and Dr. A. J. McDill, of Madison, Wisconsin, based on an interview with my mother, and on such further investigation as you shall choose to make. In this desire I have the concurrence of Judge Wallace of our County Court, whom I have consulted.

I have written a similar letter to Dr. McDill, and I desire very much that you should meet here at as early a day as possible and go to Batavia, which is ninety minutes

---

* Unknown.

† Superintendent of the private Oak Lawn Retreat Sanitarium, and former superintendent of the Jacksonville Insane Hospital.

distance by railway from here. If you will come, which I hope you can do, please do telegraph me at once the earliest day, and I will be able to arrange by telegraph your meeting Dr. McDill here.

Very respectfully yours,

Robert T. Lincoln

LB 1:1:145–46

"MRS. LINCOLN: IS THE WIDOW OF PRESIDENT LINCOLN A PRISONER?"

Chicago Courier, Sept. 4, 1875

No One Allowed to See Her Except By Order of Her Son.

An Account of a Remarkable Interview With Her Jailer and Physician.

The following communication has been reluctantly furnished us, after the most earnest solicitation, by a lady of this city,* who has, for many years, been an intimate friend of Mrs. Lincoln. The writer did not think of such a thing as publishing the result of her visit to Batavia, and from this fact, together with the high social position she occupies, great weight will certainly be accorded the statements made, and Mrs. Lincoln's friends be induced to have her case reopened—(Ed. *Courier*).

Anything which concerns the widow of our late lamented President is of interest to your readers. I have concluded, therefore, to give you an account of a visit I paid to Batavia yesterday. But first let me say, that I had no object in view in making this visit except to *satisfy myself* in regard to Mrs. Lincoln's insanity, of which so many have of late expressed doubts. The morning was a beautiful one. In passing over the country on my way to Batavia I was delighted with its loveliness. Nature did indeed have on her most regal robes. In due season I arrived at my place of destination, took a carriage to the hotel, and after a good dinner, inquired of mine host the way to the insane retreat. The building where Mrs. Lincoln is confined is a large stone building, with nothing to detract from its general appearance, except the bars at the windows, which, though diamond-shape, are none the less *bars.* The grounds around the house are beautiful, and are laid out quite artistically. I looked anxiously around, hoping I might possibly see my friend, Mrs. L., for I had learned she could

---

* Myra Bradwell.

walk in the grounds at her own pleasure, and I knew well how fond she was of such strolls. But not a person did I see anywhere around.

I ascended the steps of the house and rang the bell. Almost immediately the door was opened by a portly, fine-looking gentleman. I said: "Is this Dr. Patterson?" He said: "It is." I then introduced myself, and was courteously invited into his office. I said: "Doctor, I have called to see Mrs. Lincoln; she is a dear friend of mine and I thought I would like to see her a few moments, with your permission." I had no sooner spoken Mrs. Lincoln's name than a cloud passed over the doctor's face, and an expression, which I can best describe as *flinty,* took the place of what before was agreeable.

"Madam," said he, "have you a line from her son, Mr. Robert Lincoln?"

"No, sir," I replied, "I didn't suppose that was necessary."

"Where are you from, madam?" was his next question.

"From Chicago."

"Well, madam," said he, "you cannot see her unless you have such a paper."

"Couldn't I see her, doctor, in the presence of her attendant, my only object in coming here is to see her?"

"Well, madam," said he, "she may be out in a few days and you can see her to your heart's content." I said, "Do you consider her worse, Doctor? I understood from your letters to the public that she was allowed to see her friends."

"Well, madam, she is no *better*—for meddlesome people come here to see her, calling themselves her friends, when in reality they come out of self-interest only."

I said, "Doctor, please, don't attribute such a motive to *me.* I assure you my visit is only out of pure kindness to Mrs. Lincoln."

He replied, "I did not refer to you, madam."

"Well, doctor, as you are not willing for me to see her, will you allow me to leave a note for her?"

"No, madam, there is no necessity for that; it would only disturb her mind, and while she is under my care, I will not permit her to be disturbed, either by visitors or letters."

"If she is only permitted to receive letters except from such, she is virtually a prisoner, is she not?"

"Madam, she is no *more* so than other patients I have under my care."

While this conversation was going on, he kept looking at his watch, a gentle hint, probably, that I was trespassing on his time. "Doctor, it is some little time before the train leaves if agreeable, I will sit here till then, as it is not very pleasant sitting in the depot."

He hesitated a moment, and getting up, said, very graciously: "You can sit in here," and ushered me into what was, I suppose, the parlor of the establishment, leaving me there, and for the time I stayed I did not see him again, or any one else.

It struck me as being rather strange, inasmuch as I had heard his patients had the freedom of the house, but this, clearly, must be an erroneous impression of a good-natured public. I have no hesitation in saying that, if it should be my fortune to be placed in such an asylum, with the feeling within me that my friends placed me there with the desire to be rid of the trouble or care of me, or for some other end in view, or if I really believed they placed me there fully thinking me insane, and I saw no way out, and that speedily, it would take but a few days to make a raving maniac of me. Surrounded by those whose reason is dethroned, kept a prisoner to all intents and purposes, having no voice as to who shall see me or call on me, being left to one particular party, and that party's interest perhaps antagonistic to mine; knowing that I was constantly watched and every move known; soon, very soon, should all interest in life cease, and if death did not end the darkness that moved over me, the seal of insanity would surely be written upon my brain, and all that remained of life would go out in that hour.

I must add that Mrs. Lincoln recently said she would gladly surrender her bonds for her liberty, as money would not replace that nor give back to her the affection of those for whom she would be glad to live and for whom she would gladly lay down her life.

Chicago Courier, September 4, 1875

DR. PATTERSON TO ROBERT LINCOLN
Batavia, Ill., Sept. 7, 1875

Robert T. Lincoln, Esq.
My Dear Sir:

Now that so much is said about Mrs. Lincoln's removal to Springfield, I think it would be well if she could go at once.

As I have heard nothing from you since Saturday, in reference to the proposed medical consultation, I conclude there may be some delay in arranging for it. I do not myself see, that the proposed consultation is essential and I hope that the delay may not extend beyond a day or two.

In regard to a servant or waiting-maid, Mrs. Lincoln thinks that there need be no delay on this account, saying that a suitable person can be found in Springfield.

I enclose letters just received from Springfield.

Yours very truly,

R. J. Patterson

Folder 23, Box 2, Mary Todd Lincoln Insanity File

DR. ANDREW W. MCFARLAND TO ROBERT LINCOLN

Sept. 8, 1875

Sir,

Agreeably to your will I have this day visited Mrs. Abraham Lincoln, now under treatment at Bellevue Retreat, Batavia. My interview with her was protracted, confidential, and such as to possess me of all the facts and features of her case. My opinion being especially desired upon the expediency of her making a visit to her sister at Springfield; I should doubt the safety of the step unless she was, all the time, under the care of some discreet and responsible person; and see no good results likely to follow beyond gratifying an ardent desire to go, in which she seems to have been prompted by others. My fears are that a desire for further adventure will take possession of her mind, as soon as beyond the control of the present guardians of her safety, that may be attended with hazard if gratified.

It is fully my opinion that all the steps taken, growing out of her unhappy mental condition, have been absolutely necessary for her interests, her safety, and her hope of restoration. All the measures now in use in her case are no more than her helpless and irresponsible state of mind render unavoidable, and will bear the fullest inspection on the part of her innumerable sympathizers, the country over.

I am pained to add that there are features of her case that give me grave apprehensions as to the result unless the utmost quietude is observed for the few ensuing months, beyond which all reasonable hope of restoration must be abandoned, unless success within that period is achieved.

Andrew M. McFarland, M.D.

Folder 20, Box 2, Mary Todd Lincoln Insanity File

ROBERT LINCOLN TO A. J. MCDILL,

Chicago, Ill., Sept. 9, 1875

Dear Sir:

I am under great obligations for your prompt and kind response to my letter. Dr. McFarland did not await the arrangement to meet you but came at once on yesterday, saw my mother and addressed a communication to me of which I enclose you a copy. In view of the whole matter I have concluded to try the experiment, but with some apprehension as to the result. Inasmuch as Dr. Patterson thinks it ought to be done at once, if at all, I have arranged for her removal tomorrow and will therefore not put you to the trouble of coming here. Repeating my thanks for your letter,

Robert T. Lincoln

LB 1:1:149

ROBERT LINCOLN TO R. J. PATTERSON

Chicago, Ill., Sept. 9, 1875

Dear Sir:

Dr. McFarland's opinion (of which I will send you a copy) is very unfavorable to the hope of any good result from the proposed visit of my mother to Springfield. I intend however to make the experiment—at once.

If she will arrange her trunks so as to take not more than three of them to Springfield, giving the others into the safety deposit house and you can cause her to be properly accompanied by one of your female attendants up to the time of the train (9 p.m.) to S[pringfield] on Friday morning, and can see that she gets safely to Chicago, I will meet her at 3:40 p.m. Friday and take care of the rest. I will of course have the attendant promptly sent for and returned to Batavia the next day. I am engaged so that I cannot go out to B[atavia] today or tomorrow. You can say to my mother that I can allow only three trunks but those may be any she pleases [*illegible*] of those she has now or out of the vault. I cannot consent to burden my aunt with more.

I write hastily to catch the mail.

Very truly yours

Robert T. Lincoln

P.S. If this arrangement cannot be carried out I will have to come to your house on Saturday or arrange for an early day next week.

LB 1:1:147–48

Robert then received two letters from Dr. McFarland on September 10 and 11 about arranging a nurse for Mary Lincoln in the Edwardses' home. McFarland sent Miss Anna Kyle to Springfield, and told Robert that while the girl was not refined or cultured she has "willingness, good disposition, sagacity and presence of mind," and therefore would be a good companion for Mrs. Lincoln. McFarland also evinced surprise at the public indiscretions of James Bradwell, and suggested that Robert not "engage" him in the newspapers.[1]

"MRS. LINCOLN"

Chicago Tribune, Sept. 12, 1875

Springfield, Ill., Sept. 11—Mrs. Lincoln arrived here this morning in charge of her son Robert. She is to be the guest of her sister, Mrs. Edwards, and it is hoped that she will be improved by her stay here. She is not regarded as being any better in mind than when she first went to Batavia.

Chicago Tribune, September 12, 1875, 12

ELIZABETH EDWARDS TO ROBERT LINCOLN

Springfield, Ill., Sept. 15, 1875

My dear Robert,

Since sending you a note last evening, we have reconsidered, with regard to the girl, who is *somewhat* objectionable. Your mother thinks from her personal knowledge of *Amanda* she would well suit her—she does not wish to have Carrie. Ann[a] will remain until Saturday morning, or until the other arrives. The girl at Batavia told your mother, she received $16 per month from Dr. Patterson.

A trunk *has been sent by* express and she wishes you to send the longest Russian leather trunk, covered with duck, with the *mark* of a *tea cup,* in exchange. She wishes to know if two trunks have been sent from Batavia to you—please see to them—also note the number. The one now sent she says will make eleven (11) and a hat box, after withdrawing one, ten trunks and a hat box will remain.

Mary is delighted in meeting so many old friends, and I can truly say, that she never appeared to better advantage than she does now.

It will greatly cheer her to be with us I am sure.

Yours affectionately,

Aunt Lizzie

Folder 16, Box 2, Mary Todd Lincoln Insanity File

ELIZABETH EDWARDS TO ROBERT LINCOLN

Springfield, Ill., Sept. 15, 1875

Dear Robert,

I received your letter this morning, and am glad to say that the *attendant,* is now quite satisfactory to your mother, and she prefers to retain her.

A number of our friends have called and are delighted to see your mother looking so well, and in every respect acting in the most agreeable manner.

It will be a great benefit to her to be situated, where she will be urged to receive company, thus far she has readily acquiesced to every suggestion, of the kind, I have made.

She rode out this afternoon, with Lizzie, to make a call, up on Mrs. Dubois,[*] and at all times, seems to heartily enjoy herself.

I will certainly indulge the hope, that ere long, every one will be thoroughly convinced of her entire recovery.

I write in haste for the mail.

Yours affectionate

Aunt Lizzie

————

[*] Mrs. Jesse K. Dubois, the Lincolns' former Springfield neighbor.

(Enclosure)

Private

I have concluded to broach to you, a most painful subject. First-stating, that insanity, although a new feature, in our family history, first appeared within my knowledge, in the case of my own daughter, at the early age of thirteen. For six months, she was so decidedly flighty, as to be closely guarded. Her back from incidents is scarred its length. At the birth of each child, the same symptoms were shown, and severely felt, particularly by her husband, and myself.

At no time, has she ever been natural in her demeanor.

God pity those who are the victims, and who are the anxious sufferers in such terrible afflictions!

Folder 16, Box 2, Mary Todd Lincoln Insanity File

[MRS. LINCOLN: INDICATIONS OF A RESTORATION TO HEALTH]
Albany Evening Journal, Sept. 20, 1875

Mrs. Abraham Lincoln, since her arrival in Springfield, Ill., has given many indications of a restoration to health. She rides out frequently, is cheerful, and manifests much gratification at meeting her former friends.

Albany Evening Journal, September 20, 1875, 1.
This story was reprinted nationally, probably
by the Associated Press.

ELIZABETH EDWARDS TO ROBERT LINCOLN
Springfield, Ill., Sept. 22, 1875

My dear Robert,

I received your note, with check. Permit me to say that your mother's persisting upon the subject of paying board caused me to assent to her proposition, upon condition that she will look upon our home as her permanent one, at least for some time. I had expressly said to her, that $100 would cover every expense she would incur, except girl's wages, and insist upon it. The balance will be placed for her benefit.

I think that Amanda does not intend remaining here very long—should she return, to her former place, I can have your mother attended to, by my own servants. Lizzie sleeps in an adjoining room, and will take proper care, for she feels much interest in her Aunt.

We take daily rides, and your mother enjoys, without a doubt, the change in her habits. She has dined at Mrs. Smith's, taken tea at our sister Francis's, and received every visitor, with a manifestation of cheerfulness, and pleasure, as has surprised me.

When you write, please enclose letters in separate envelopes, that I may not feel obliged to show her your communications to me. She displayed some sensitiveness, in your wish to defer, to my judgment. Thus far, she has shown herself very clear-headed. Do not allow her to know, that I decline the large amount, she insisted upon. And I would advise, that you avoid as far as possible, any allusion to your belief in her insanity.

In haste,

Affectionately,

Your Aunt Lizzie

Folder 16, Box 2, Mary Todd Lincoln Insanity File

[MRS. LINCOLN: RESTORATION TO HEALTH?]
Lowell Daily Citizen and News, Sept. 25, 1875

It is stated that Mrs. Abraham Lincoln, since her arrival in Springfield, Ill., has given many indications of a restoration to health. She rides out frequently, is cheerful, and manifests much gratification at meeting her friends. There is no reasonable doubt that insanity in many cases is intensified by the rough treatment in asylums. Superintendents and hospital officials become impatient with their patients and often resort to severe methods of punishment, as though an asylum was a correctional institution.

Lowell Daily Citizen and News,
September 25, 1875, 2

No further mentions of Mary Lincoln appeared in newspapers for nearly one year after her transfer to Springfield; and no letters were written between Robert and his aunt and uncle for more than one month.

ELIZABETH EDWARDS TO ROBERT LINCOLN
Springfield, Ill., Nov. 5, 1875

Dear Robert,

I have not written to you recently, wishing to wait, until I could better understand your mother's mental condition. I have no hesitation, in pronouncing her sane, and far more reasonable, and gentle, than in former years. She bears up with great patience under the oppressive weight of restraint, which to her proud spirit, is very galling—awaiting the time, when the right of person and property, will be restored to her. Surely, the evidence of derangement exhibited last spring, must have arisen from physical disorder. She informs me that her health was poor before going to Florida, and during her stay there, and on her return, was often conscious, of the presence of fever—moreover, had used chloral very freely, for the purpose of inducing sleep. Those causes, had doubtless much to do, with producing the sad result.

As far as I can judge, she is capable of taking care of her interests. She assures me that from the income of every year, she has largely added to her principal.

To a person of any plain practical ideas it is surprising to look upon unnecessary purchases, but I have been startled, so often, by the extravagance of persons, of small means, as to judge leniently of those who can afford. Whatever her habits are in that respect, I would advise that you hereafter assume indifference, by doing so, you can quietly and unconsciously to her, gain such influence, as to keep her pecuniary affairs, in a proper state.

Above all, do everything, that will conciliate and make her as happy, as it would be possible to render her—for she has indulged her morbid ways so long, that it is impossible to prevent frequent reactions, to extreme sadness.

The reunion with her family, receiving the calls of former acquaintances, and returning visits, has already had a very beneficial [effect] upon her spirits.

As you desired me to be the judge of her necessities, I will state, that she is too much *herself,* to allow many suggestions. I quite agreed with her that her dust soiled veil bonnets and shawl, were too shabby for *her* to wear in visiting or church going. She stated, that she had no fresh substitutes in her trunks.

You understand her sensitive nature, and know why I hesitate to presume to oppose what I really think, she is entitled to enjoy. If I have ventured too far in giving my impressions, I hope you will pardon, and believe that I am intensely interested in your mother's future, hoping that it may be soothed with your tenderest love and forbearance, and occasionally refreshed, with pleasant intercourse, with your dear household.

I will not dwell longer, on this painful subject, and haste to a conclusion requesting you to enclose a reply to Mr. Edwards address. She knows nothing of my intention to write, to you, and may be present, on the delivery of the mail.

With sincere love,

Your Aunt Lizzie

Folder 16, Box 2, Mary Todd Lincoln Insanity File

MARY LINCOLN TO JAMES B. BRADWELL

Nov. 11, 1875

Private—

Judge Bradwell

My Dear Friend,

A long and weary time has passed since I last saw you—Knowing well the interest you have taken in my sad fate, I feel assured that you will be pleased to hear that

I am in perfect health, I am staying with my sister Mrs. Edwards, who has always been tenderly attached to me. I am now writing at the suggestion of Mr. N. W. Edwards, who is desirous that you should send me, the *will* you wrote for me many months since. You will remember, that I left it, in your charge. Please send it, by return mail. What can I say to your dear wife? The sorrow which has been mine for the last six months, has been in a measure alleviated, by the friendship of such noble hearts as yours. I feel assured you will reply to this *note* at once—without ever mentioning that you have heard form me. The paths of life have become very rough to me—since the most loving and devoted husband and children have been called from my side. In the great hereafter, when I am reunited with my beloved ones, we will then know, why the gracious Father, has caused such deep affliction.

Be kind enough to enclose the will to Mr. N. W. Edwards.

Yours very truly

Mary Lincoln

write me—quietly—

Both of you

Folder 2, Box 1, Mary Todd Lincoln Insanity File

ELIZABETH EDWARDS TO ROBERT LINCOLN
Springfield, Ill., Nov. 12, 1875

My Dear Robert,

I received your letter on yesterday, and after a careful reading with such reflection, must say, that I am convinced, that the only alternative in this case, for the sake of peace and quietness, will be to yield your mother the right to control her possessions. You will understand, that she is now pressing this matter, until the unpleasantness is such, that I am constrained to make the plea. She assures us, that she will pledge herself to place her bonds with Mr. Bunn, to be undisturbed during her life. In a conversation, some time since, she mentioned, that she had left a will with Judge B., had set apart $20,000 for little Mamie, leaving the remainder of her property to you. I cannot believe that she would ever divert it from you, and should she by resentment do so by will, you can well understand that your interests would not be injured.

With regard to Spiritualism she is wholly reticent. I would infer that she had no ideas upon the subject, and that it would not be an acceptable subject to one of her timid nature. She told me of a gift of plated ware, used in her early home marked "Lincoln," that she presented to some charitable home, which a friend of hers, *Mrs. Farwell* I believe was the name, felt interested in. It may be, that was, the silverware you referred to, and the destination, may have been misrepresented to you.

I perfectly understand you, with regard to her reckless expenditure of money, for the purpose, of adding to the contents of her trunks. It has always been a prominent trait in her character, to accumulate a large amount of clothing, and now that she has the means, it seems to be, the only available pleasure. Is it not best, that she should be indulged in it, as a matter of expediency? There is no evidence of derangement at this time, that would justify confinement in an asylum—and to impose restraint of any kind, would involve more contention, than could be endured.

As to what she could do, in her future movements, I do not know, and will not predict. Should she show again, a roving propensity—I would advise, that she should not be interfered with. If you determine, to become indifferent, to what you cannot prevent, you will insure yourself a greater degree of repose of mind, than you have known for years.

Excuse me for making such suggestions, as the experiences of long years, has taught me to be that most availing remedy in life's trails, where others are interested. Let them alone when you have done, what you could.

I am desirous to retain your mother's kindly feeling, *on her account,* realizing the loneliness of her situation, and believing that if any persons can influence her, we may find it possible. I do not know, that she desires any change. In dreading the approach of winter, she regretted that her plans for spending the cold months, in Florida, had been hindered. She is usually cheerful and enjoys every thing, which interests us, riding, visiting, etc. if she would take more pleasure in society, she would overcome the morbid state of mind, so long indulged. This is the place, where she is drawn out of herself, and I would be glad to see her better prepared to enjoy surrounding circumstances.

Even if I weary you, I am certain that you will appreciate my kind intentions. Remember me kindly to your wife, hoping that she will soon be well.

Very affectionately,

your Aunt Lizzie

Folder 16, Box 2, Mary Todd Lincoln Insanity File

NINIAN EDWARDS TO ROBERT LINCOLN

Springfield, Ill., Nov. 12, 1875

My Dear Robert,

Your mother wishes to know whether if she can establish before Gov. Palmer, Gov. Beveridge, Mr. Cullom, Mr. Hatch, and Mr. Dubois, or either of them, or before the County Court of Cook County, that she is now a fit person to have the care, custody, and control of her property, you will consent that said Court shall enter an order fully restoring her to all the rights and privileges enjoyed by her before you were appointed her conservator. If you are afraid that she will squander her means or use any portion of her principle, she is willing that Mr. Bunn shall hold the bonds in trust, paying her only the interest. He is willing to do so, and to reinvest in other bonds, as they fall due, without any change. And Mr. Smith will *give* her the use of a room in the 2nd story of the building occupied by him as a store, to keep her trunks in. I write this letter by her request and after consulting Mr. Stuart and Mr. Smith. Please answer as soon as possible as she will be certain to ask me if you have replied to my letter. She says she has no idea of leaving here this winter. She may wish in the future to make occasional trips but expects to make Springfield her home.

Yours affly

N. W. Edwards

Folder 17, Box 2, Mary Todd Lincoln Insanity File

ROBERT LINCOLN TO NINIAN EDWARDS

Nov. 15, 1875

My dear Uncle,

I would have answered your letter yesterday but I was kept in bed all day and am hardly able to write now.

Last spring after my mother came here from Florida I was so distressed in mind that I did not dare to trust to or act upon my own judgment. I [*illegible*] about two months in addition to taking the most competent medical advice I could get. I [*illegible*] consulted with friends here, but specifically I took no step without the full concurrence of Judge Davis, Mr. Stuart and Mr. Swett. The medical men told us that there was the greatest danger of personal injury unless she was protected and then could be but one opinion as to the danger to her property. There is no person upon whom lies the responsibility and duty of protecting her when she needs it, except myself. Whether it was then necessary to do this and how it should be done, I had to [*illegible*] first in my own judgment to decide and I acted entirely upon the judgment of the gentlemen I have mentioned. They decided that for the safety of both her person and her property, there was nothing left to do, except to place about her the safeguards provided by law. Whatever was done then was done not upon my own judgment alone nor by myself done but upon the most thorough consultation with and [*illegible*] consideration of the persons who I felt were nearest my father, to herself and to me and to whom under the distressing circumstances I could and ought to trust for counsel and assistance.

We have relaxed all the disagreeable personal restraint which was necessary six months ago. Whether it is now right upon my own responsibility to take away entirely these supposed so far as they relate to her property, I cannot decide without help. As I did not then deem to act upon my own judgment, so now I do not alone take the responsibility. I will consult with those upon whose advice and counsel in conversation and by letter I then relied and I still rely upon fully as soon as I have been able to do so.

I am as anxious as you can be to have every liberty and privilege restored to my mother at the earliest moment when it can be done with reasonable assurance that her protection and happiness will not be imperiled. I want to do everything I can which is really for her happiness and I have no wish to interfere with her expenditures further than to ensure her having money to expend as long as she lives. But if there is danger of her expending her capital and we should countlessly ignore it or imprudently contribute to it and she should impoverish herself we would be severely censured.

Of course you know that the suggested intervention of Mr. Bunn or anybody else as a mere custodian is impracticable and would be ineffectant as a protection. It would probably be impossible for my mother of this sort which she could not immediately undo. The question is simply whether she shall at once control and be able to dispose of all her means and whether you and my mother's sisters feel fully confident that there is no danger that in case I should act now upon your letter, she would not after a comparatively very little time find herself destitute of the resources which will probably for many years be necessary to her happiness and without which she will be very indebted.

Folder 2, Box 2, Mary Todd Lincoln Insanity File

ROBERT LINCOLN TO JOHN TODD STUART
Chicago, Ill., Nov. 15, 1875

My dear Sir:

Mr. Edwards, on Friday, sent me a letter, to which I was not able to reply as I was taken ill on Saturday evening and slept in bed until today. He states in his letter that it was written at my mother's request and after consultation with you and Mr. Smith. I wrote him today at length and I will be obliged if you will look at what I have said. I have two letters from my aunt Mrs. Edwards and they show plainly I think that the present state of things breaks up their domestic comfort, and that some change must be made.

Last Spring I relied and acted upon the advice and judgment of yourself, Judge Davis and Mr. Swett and I am fortunate in being able to go to three such men. I shall tomorrow send to Judge Davis the three letters I have received and a copy of mine to Mr. Edwards. You know the whole story and you can judge as well as anyone what would be the consequences to my mother of erroneous action on my part at this time. Her net annual income consists of . . . $8,500 [$4,000 in gold interest on $60,000 worth of bonds plus her $3,000 pension plus $1,500 total in monthly payments from Robert for her Chicago house].

I think from what I know of Judge Wallace that if the present *legal* status continues, he would authorize the expenditure by my mother in any way she chose of any sum per month which her friends thought right, without inquiring into detail.

I might add that personally I regard the continuance of the pension as at least precarious. My own opinion is that the composition of the House of Representatives is such that it would be stopped except by reason of the politics of the Senate.

I will be under several obligations to you if you will give me your counsel on the whole subject. On consultations with Mr. Swett and Judge Wallace and on hearing from Judge Davis, some suggestions may be made which do not occur to you or me and I may want to lay them before you before final action.

Affectionately yours

Robert T. Lincoln

Folder 2, Box 2, Mary Todd Lincoln Insanity File

ROBERT LINCOLN TO DAVID DAVIS

Chicago, Ill., Nov. 16, 1875

My dear Judge:

I know you will pardon me for again troubling you.

I enclose two letters from my aunt Mrs. Edwards and one from Mr. Edwards and a copy of my reply to Mr. Edwards. The trouble that my aunt is in is plain and of course she is to be relieved of it. In reference to her letters I want to note that by permission of Judge Wallace, I long ago told her that it was not necessary to scrutinize my mother's expenditures so long as they were not palpably outrageous, so that there was no need of her mentioning the bonnet and shawl purchase. I merely mention it to you to say that one of the last deliveries of goods to her before she went to Batavia was four new bonnets all of which are in her trunks at Mrs. Edwards and none of which she has ever worn. It is an indication to my mind that no radical change has taken place since last Spring but only opportunity is wanting to develop the same trouble. Her remark in her letter of Nov 12th as to my mother's will was caused by my saying in my reply to her first letter that I did not desire to limit her expenditures beyond the point where she would have neither capital or income to live upon, as I had no interest after her about understanding (as I did, and I must say still do) that she has by will otherwise disposed of her property.

My aunt is also misinformed about the silverware matter. The stuff is owned by a "Clairvoyant" woman who has a ranch on a side street a few blocks from my house. This I have been told of by three different persons. How grossly she misses on the general subject of my mother's devotion to Spiritualism, I think you know. She hardly thinks of anything else and almost her only companions were spiritualists. One other remark of my aunt and my "notes." She says that experience has taught, "that the most availing remedy in life's trials where others are interested. Let them alone when you have done, what you could." The trouble in my case is that I cannot abandon the matter if I would. The time will not come when I can end the trouble by saying I have done what I can, and if I let it alone, it would not let me alone.

You will of course keep this letter privately. I would not discuss my Aunt's letters with any one else. I cannot help feeling that she is taking a pretty short tone on me to relieve herself at all hazards of the trouble. How great the trouble is I well know; but last summer without speaking to me my aunt sent my mother a letter by the hand of Mrs. Bradwell inviting her to visit her. Of course I could only acquiesce.

Mr. Swett has been to see Judge Wallace since I wrote Mr. Edwards. The judge says (and we all concur) that under the statute he cannot "entertain an application for relief from the disability until the expiration of one year from the date of the appointment of the conservator" and that he had frequently so decided. That if he should entertain the application, before that time (next June) his opinion is that his order would not discharge the obligation on the Bond, of the Conservator or his sureties.

The Judge's authority as to maintenance seems sufficient to authorize almost anything, and practically he will order whatever Mr. Swett and I think best. Mr. Swett and I are discussing this proposition:

1. To remove all restraints upon travel and residence.
2. To pay to her to be expended by herself without scrutiny of any kind her whole income in monthly installments, at the present rate of gold and including a payment from me to her of $125 per month which will end April 1881. This monthly income will be about $700.
3. To have a competent person make an estimate on the annuity principle of what monthly sum can be paid her during her life so as to leave nothing at her death and if Judge Wallace will consent, to pay such sum to her monthly.
4. In addition to 1 and 2 or to 1 and 3, to deliver to her as being necessary for her comfort all of her personal effects which consist of clothing and jewelry.

The trouble with No. 3 is that her pension is to be regarded and personally I consider its payment for many years as uncertain.

If you have time to consider this whole matter and to counsel me you will add to the many obligations I am now under to you.

Please also to return to me the enclosed letter.

Most sincerely yours,

Robert T. Lincoln

P.S. Mr. Swett makes this further suggestion. Both he and I regard her as unsound in mind and not to be trusted with the power of impoverishing herself. Her course since the Inquisition has shown that in general she is able to control her impulses if she has an object in doing so. She has constantly kept in view her discharge and her aberrations during that time would make no case against her discharge probably. Supposing her to be insane, is it not better to utilize the six months which must intervene before she can be discharged, in giving her any opportunity (at least to the extent I have indicated) to develop her vagaries if she still has any, than to have her restrained and watchful with no opportunity, and then get her discharge and break out fully again and perhaps ruin herself before I could stop it?

Folder A-109, Box 7, David Davis Family Papers

NINIAN EDWARDS TO ROBERT LINCOLN
Nov. 17, 1875

Dear Robert

In my letter of the 12th inst to you, I was very careful not to proffer any advice, nor to make any suggestions in relation to your mother and to say that I wrote by *her request*. Except on the subject of her bonds and other personal property which she thinks she ought to have under her own control she is cheerful and happy, and in good health, and gives less trouble than any person I ever knew. She is very entertaining in conversation, enjoys the society of her friends and relatives and receives their calls. I have tried to assure her that her bonds were safe in your hands, and that you were willing to allow her as much of her income as she needs. Her proposition was that her bonds should be held in *trust* during her lifetime and so that she could not receive more than the annual interest—and she particularly complains that her trunks are withheld from her. I have no doubt but that you have acted from your best judgment and from a desire to do every thing in your power for the good.

Yours aff
N W Edwards

Folder 17, Box 2, Mary Todd Lincoln Insanity File

DAVID DAVIS TO ROBERT LINCOLN
Washington D.C., Nov. 20, 1875

My dear Robert,

You do right in always addressing me when in difficulty. No one sympathizes with you more, or is more willing to share responsibility with you, in whatever concerns your mother.

The present position of affairs is not encouraging but I was not unprepared for it.

I expected from the first the intermeddling of officious people, who do things in ignorance of the real situation. Mrs. Edwards brought the difficulty about when she sent a letter to your mother inviting her to visit her without consulting you in advance of the proposition. And I think your comments on her letter are eminently just and proper. She has no conception of your mother's real condition, and evidently does not believe that Spiritualism has anything to do with it, while you and I know differently. And her advice of indifference to you, though doubtless well meant is, to say the least, grounded on a total misapprehension of the relations between parent and child.

You cannot escape responsibility if you wanted to, and it would be esteemed by the world bad conduct if you should try. The trouble is on you and would not let you alone even (to suppose an impossible case) you were willing and should.

The embarrassments growing out of this visit to Springfield must be met, although you had no agency in creating them. Your mother has doubtless convinced Mrs. Edwards and her other relatives that she is unjustly restrained of her liberty. Persons in her condition, can generally restrain their impulses when they have an object in view. And I have no doubt your mother from the first has acted in a way to convince all who have been brought in contact with her that she ought not to be confined.

You cannot now send her back to Batavia and Mrs. Edwards must be relieved of the trouble.

It seems to me to be the right thing to remove restraints on travel and residence, and to pay her monthly, the amount of her income. The six months which must intervene before she can be discharged and you relieved, will develop her insane vagaries, if they still exist, which we all believe.

If she had remained undisturbed at Batavia there might have been a chance for her recovery, but I fear the intermeddling will prove disastrous to her, as it has already added to your trouble.

If she spends no more than her monthly income it is no matter. Should she contract debt beyond this with persons who do not know her to have been adjudged insane, it is not clear that they could not be severed because of her being discharged from the asylum and being left to go free and unrestrained. But this must be risked.

The annuity principle I don't think would apply. There is no necessity for it, and the judge would hardly be justified in paying her more than monthly income. If she is not insane, she would never spend as much as this. If the insanity remains, you can't tell what she will do. The six months can as you say be utilized for the purpose of ascertaining what is best to be done for the future. Of course her personal effects, including jewelry, she will want and it is best to give them to her. If she gives away any part of her clothing or jewelry, it is a small matter.

I think your mother would rest satisfied, if unrestrained and paid her income in monthly installments. At any rate, it is the only practicable thing to do, in the present emergency so far as I can see.

I took all day yesterday to reflect on the matter, and I cannot see any other course to pursue in justice to yourself and the future of your mother. She must not be impoverished and she may live as long as you do. There is no other way left since the Springfield visit. You could not get her back to Batavia and it is best to try freedom for restraint. I am glad that Mr. Swett is taken into counsel. Do nothing without his sanction. He is a wise counselor and a sympathetic man.

You know you have my sympathy.

Write me what you do.

Your friend,

David Davis

Folder 15, Box 2, Mary Todd Lincoln Insanity File

ROBERT LINCOLN TO DAVID DAVIS

Chicago, Ill., Nov. 22, 1875

My dear Judge:

Your exceedingly kind letter arrived this morning and I can only say that I am under renewed obligations to you.

I wrote to Major Stuart when I wrote you—not so freely of course—but soliciting his opinion from what he had seen. I got no reply from him but Mr. Edwards writes the enclosed letter, which is evidently intended as a reply to mine to Mr. Stuart. On looking again at Mr. Edwards' first letter which you have seen I cannot see that he was nearly as explicit in his disclaimer as he is now. I shall follow your advice in being guided by Mr. Swett and now think I will try to go to Springfield in a few days.

May I trouble you to return to me the enclosed letter and also the letterpress copy of my letter to Mr. Edwards. I may want to put my hand on it at some time.

I think I have not told you that we have a small girl baby two weeks old.[*] This makes three children for me and if I could count on them behaving themselves I would like them to be a dozen.

Very sincerely yours,

Robert T. Lincoln

Folder A-109, Box 7, David Davis Family Papers

ROBERT LINCOLN TO "MY DEAR KIMBLE"

Nov. 29, 1875

My dear Kimble,

I learn today that my mother has contracted a debt for goods at your house. I have no doubt she will pay it herself but I thought it right to say to you that she cannot in law make a valid debt and that the County Court here would not allow me to recognize such a thing. By permission of the Court I continually send her money to be used as she chooses and I have no concern how she expends it. I try

---

[*] Jessie Harlan Lincoln.

to keep her supplied with a sufficient amount of cash to gratify every reasonable whim, but there is nowhere any legal responsibility for any debts she may incur.

It is my duty to inform you of this but I beg that you will not let anyone know of my having written.

Very truly yours,

Robert T. Lincoln

LB 3:4:363

NINIAN EDWARDS TO ROBERT LINCOLN
Dec. 1, 1875

Dear Robert,

I received yours of the 29th ultimo, and will send you the voucher as soon as your mother hands me the check for $400.00. She sometimes retains those heretofore sent for several days. She is in fine health and spirits and is only agitated on one subject—the restoration of her right to control and manage her own property and bonds—and is determined to employ counsel to have the order of court depriving her of their control set aside. In order to keep her from doing this now I have told her that she can do nothing until one year from the 19th of May last. I have tried to assure her that every thing is safe in your hands, and that you are willing to allow her as much of her income as she wishes, but this does not satisfy her. You are the best judge of the right course to pursue, but we would all regret to have her resort to the law. I told her I knew you would be willing to do what Judge Davis and other friends of your father would advise.

What she does with the money you send we do not know, but as to that I refer you to the enclosed letter from your aunt.

Yours aff

N W Edwards

Folder 17, Box 2, Mary Todd Lincoln Insanity File

ELIZABETH EDWARDS TO ROBERT LINCOLN
Springfield, Ill., Dec. 1, 1875

My Dear Robert,

I read last evening your note to your uncle, giving a statement of your mother's expenditures, since she has been in our home. The recent demand surprises me. I had supposed, from her assurances, that she was *fixed* for the winter, that her shopping was over. She has protested against asking you, to send her winter wraps, and has consequently provided herself with new *waterproof* shawls etc. I do not really know anything about her purchases; we have never been with her in a store, and have never seen her open a trunk, therefore would be wholly ignorant of her needs. A few days ago, she said, that she had purchased a shawl and dress, to present to Mrs. Wallace for Christmas. The two articles, were purchased for less than $40.

I told her, she would find it difficult to have them accepted, and it proved so. You understand the proud nature of that Aunt. It is only in the seasons of her darkest sorrow, that Mr. Edwards, Mr. Smith, and their wives, have been able to contribute in a substantial way to her necessities. Let me here say, that the music box, sent by you, was presented to Fannie W., who was exceedingly pained believing that it had been withdrawn from you. We intend as far as possible to prevent any distribution of her money in our midst, and will not encourage any generous inclinations. At the time of the fair, for the home of the friendless recently held here, Mrs. Lamon caused a sofa cushion, flowers, etc., to be made a complimentary present to her. It gratified her, and in response, she enclosed $25 for the benefit of that charity.

The checks you have sent, have been enclosed to herself, she invariably requests Mr. E to hand her the amount, when cashed. We intended to receive her as our guest, not boarder, but she insisted that she could not feel contented, or make herself at home, without we received a board bill from her. She demands from you $150 a month for that purpose, although she knows, that I consented to $100, only. Amanda left at the end of her first month, and I felt that so liberal a sum for my trouble justified me in hiring the third female servant. Thus she has her washing, and every service rendered her. We hire when necessary additional assistance for our grounds, to be enabled to place our carriage at her disposal, at all times.

I am glad to state that she is unvarying in a polite, amiable, and affectionate manner towards every one.

I would gladly look forward to the pleasure of protecting her for life. It is only, when discussing the restraints imposed upon her that she exhibits the slightest impatience. I have ventured in a previous communication to express myself upon the subject of restraint, and the degree necessary. May I beg of you to regard my letters as confidential. I of course wish you to understand matters. In haste

Your affectionate
Aunt Lizzie

Folder 16, Box 2, Mary Todd Lincoln Insanity File

ROBERT LINCOLN TO JUDGE M. R. M. WALLACE

Dec. 10, 1875

To the Hon. M. R. M. Wallace,

The undersigned, conservator of Mrs. Mary Lincoln, respectfully shows that since the 11th day of September A.D. 1875 Mrs. Lincoln has been and is now an intimate of the family of her sister Mrs. N. W. Edwards at Springfield, Illinois.

That prior to the filing of the application in this cause Mrs. Lincoln had sent a number of trunks containing wearing apparel principally as he believes, to Milwaukee, Wisconsin. That he as conservator caused them to be brought back to this city and as he did not believe she then needed their contents for her personal use, he caused them, being nine in number, to be stored in the vaults of the Fidelity Safety Depository in this city for safekeeping. That upon her going to Springfield Mrs. Lincoln gave to the undersigned two more trunks of a like character which he caused to be stored in the same place. That the nine trunks first stored being then all in his possession, as mentioned in the Inventory filed by the undersigned in this Court.

The undersigned states that Mrs. Lincoln is very desirous that the above mentioned trunks with their contents should be sent to her at Springfield, she needing the same. The undersigned respectfully shows that he thinks it proper and safe that she should have them, and that she needs for her own a great part thereof, and that he does not believe that Mrs. Lincoln will not make any improper disposition of their contents and he prays the leave of the Court to send them to Mrs. Lincoln at Springfield and that the statement in writing of the Hon. Ninian W. Edwards with whom she is now residing that they have been placed in Mrs. Lincoln's care for her use shall be received by this Court in discharge of the responsibility of the undersigned for the same upon his final accounting.

Robert T. Lincoln
Conservator of Mrs. Mary Lincoln

Folder 33, Box 2, Mary Todd Lincoln Insanity File

ROBERT LINCOLN TO JUDGE M. R. M. WALLACE
Dec. 15, 1875

To the Hon. M. R. M. Wallace,

The undersigned, conservator of Mrs. Mary Lincoln, respectfully shows to the Court that Mrs. Lincoln is exceedingly anxious and desirous to have the custody and use of the articles of personal jewelry contained in a tin box which is mentioned by the undersigned in the Inventory filed by him. The box is now in the Fidelity Safety Depository for safekeeping and Mrs. Lincoln has its key.

The undersigned has consulted the Honorable David Davis of the United States Supreme Court and Mr. Leonard Swett, as friends, both of them being entirely familiar with the facts of Mrs. Lincoln's case and they have advised him that under all the circumstances, it would be well to comply with her request.

The undersigned states to the Court that he does not think that Mrs. Lincoln will not make any improper disposition of the articles contained in the box and he thinks that the possession and custody of the same will tend to benefit her.

He therefore respectfully prays that he may have leave to send the box and its contents to the Honorable N. W. Edwards at Springfield, Illinois, to be by him given to Mrs. Lincoln for her use, she being now an intimate of his family.

Robert T. Lincoln

Conservator of Mrs. Mary Lincoln

NINIAN EDWARDS TO ROBERT LINCOLN

Springfield, Ill., Dec. 18, 1875

Dear Robert,

I enclose receipt of box which was delivered yesterday by the express agent to your mother. In yours of the 16th inst you ask me to give you the best aid and advice I can for your mother's good and seem to think hard of both Stuart and myself for not having done so before. I have not done so because in several of your letters you said you would be governed by the advice of Judge Davis, Mr. Swett, Stuart and *others* of your father's friends.

Thus far you have done everything your mother has asked with the exception of restoring to her her bonds and you have with the approbation of Judge Wallace written to me that you would give her the entire income to do as she pleases with it. As this delicacy of the bonds is the only point of fire I will confine myself exclusively to it. It is true that the 39th section page 689 of the Revised Statutes provides that "no application shall be entertained for the removal of a conservator, within less than one year from the time of his appointment" and if the judge is unwilling with the consent of both parties to entertain such a notion within the year, of course nothing can be done until then.

If your mother could know this from him, she would probably not fret over it, nor find fault with you for not yielding to her wishes. As soon as she can legally do so, she says she will apply to have all her rights restored to her, and that she "is a fit person to have the care and control of her property," she says she will prove before the court how well she has managed it, how much she has given you, and how much she has added to the principal, and that she has already within a few days past, requested you to invest $2,000 of her income in bonds. She says she will show to the Court how much she would have lost if she had acceded to your request to allow investments to be made by you and John Forsythe. I wish if possible to prevent all this; and I would therefore advise as soon as it can be done for you to consent to what she proposes to do; that she shall by deed of trust place her bonds and monies in the hands of a trustee to pay over to her the income only and to hold the principle to be paid on her decease to those persons entitled by law to receive it. She has said she would do this and would consent that Mr. Bunn should be her trustee. Your aunt and myself both think that all her property should at her death go to you and your children.

Judge Bradwell has at her request sent her the will she made two years ago, and she has shown it to me. In it she left $20,000 to your daughter Mary, about $5,000 of the income to you until the year 1881, to be paid annually, and after 1881, the entire balance is left to you and your children. Whether she would do this now in a deed of trust I cannot say, as she is so much exasperated against you. If she has to go to the law she will summon a good many witnesses from here; and she is waiting for Governor Palmer to return for the purpose of seeing whether she can have her bonds restored to her now. I think she will consent that Mr. Bunn shall hold in trust the principal. When this is done, I think it is fair to say to you, that I believe she will go to Europe, to remain there.

You mentioned in one of your letters that such a deed of trust could not be made. In this I think you are mistaken. C. C. Brown is trustee under such a deed of trust, for my daughter Mrs. Baker. I would under no circumstances, advise that her bonds should be given up to her, or placed under her control, unless such a compromise is made. It is important however that whilst she is with us that she should not know that I have so advised. I have therefore written this in confidence. We fully sympathize with you and believe that you have done what under all the circumstances you thought it best.

Very affectionately yours

N. W. Edwards

When you write, send two letters one of which I may hand to her, as she always asks to see them.

Folder 17, Box 2, Mary Todd Lincoln Insanity File

ROBERT LINCOLN TO NINIAN EDWARDS
Chicago, Ill., Dec. 21, 1875

My Dear Uncle,

In reply to your favor of Saturday I have at your suggestion written you today a letter which my mother can see.

I am sorry you misunderstood my former letters about . . . [*line illegible*] . . . reply to me from you which I thought advised me to let my mother do as she would, and you afterward wrote me that in it you had explicitly refrained from advising me at all one way or the other. When I learned that you had not intended to express an opinion, I was desirous of knowing what your opinion was and I am much obliged for your reply.

In your last letter you say that you "would under no circumstances advise that her bonds should be given up to her unless such a compromise is made."

You and I agree entirely now in the end to be reached and the only question is how to attain it. I am thoroughly convinced in my own mind that my mother would permanently ruin herself in a comparatively short time if allowed to do so and I have not the slightest desire of restraining her from anything but that.

The present means of restraint is legally perfect and the question is can any other be [*illegible*]. It is a purely legal one and her present legal status has to be considered in determining it.

I said to you in one of my letters that I did not see the way to her doing any act of the way of getting her property in trust for her benefit which she could not as readily made. I have spoken about it to Mr. Swett and he is considering the possibility of such a thing. Judge Davis will be here in a day or two and I think he will take the matter with consideration. I wish that you and Mr. Brown would write to me the particulars of a plan which seems possible to you and will accomplish the object, with the authorities supporting it. I do not desire that any interest of mine or my children in the ultimate disposition of her property should be consulted and the only object I wish attained by any plan is her own protection.

I should regret very much the course proposed by my mother of going out in public all our relations for ten years. She would fail to show that I ever advised her to any investments, good or bad, except loans of money to myself on, I think, two occasions both of which were repaid. She has always been exceedingly generous to me in every way both in money and otherwise, and the delusion under which she hastened to Chicago last Spring was that I was in some [*illegible*] for money and she came expressly to give me everything she had. I am exceedingly gratified to her for it all and shall never hesitate to acknowledge it but being grateful merely will not discharge my duty to her even if necessary against her will.

I will write again as soon as I can see Judge Davis.

Very sincerely yours

Robert T. Lincoln

Folder 2, Box 2, Mary Todd Lincoln Insanity File

ROBERT LINCOLN TO NINIAN EDWARDS
Chicago, Ill., Dec. 21, 1875

My Dear Uncle,

Your letter of Saturday came yesterday and I would have replied then but I have been endeavoring to see Judge Wallace to ask him to [*illegible*] what he said verbally about an application for discharge from disability. I have been over there once yesterday and once today but failed to catch him. I cannot tell whether he will consider it proper in his official position to write an opinion on a matter not actually before him but there is no harm in asking him to do so. When I first spoke to him about the matter he said at once there was no question about it in his mind and that he has several times so decided in cases before him. I will try again tomorrow to see him.

I do not suppose it possible to convince my mother that I have absolutely no power in the matter. I am simply appointed as an officer of the court to convey to her the directions of the Court in such matters as lie in the discretion of the Judge. This matter of receiving and acting upon an application for discharge, the Judge says does not lie in his discretion but is governed entirely by the statute.

In all the matters in which the Judge has any power, exercised through me, I have obtained his consent so far as I could, in removing all the practical restraints which my mother has been under and I hoped that she would recognize that I could not [*illegible*] a thing in which I have neither power nor control.

Very sincerely yours

Robert T. Lincoln

Folder 2, Box 2, Mary Todd Lincoln Insanity File

J. M. PALMER TO ROBERT LINCOLN

Springfield, Ill., Dec. 21, 1875

Dear Sir,

At the request of Mrs. Lincoln I beg to call your attention to her situation and inquire whether in your judgment it is not possible to relieve her from her present situation which causes her so much annoyance.

It will be clear to you readily that I write to you on the subject with great hesitation feeling that you will do nothing not dictated by the best considered views of duty but at the same you will understand that I am only anxious to promote the comfort of your mother for which many of [us] feel a degree of solicitude only less than your own. She feels herself to be wholly competent to manage her own affairs and her conduct since she came to this city seems to justify a belief entertained by her friends that she is correct and my principal object in writing to you is to inquire whether your consent can be obtained to allow her to do so.

Of course this inquiry implies that you will at once or at the earliest day possible allow the proceedings in the County Court of Cook County to be set on the day her conservator be discharged.

I wish to be understood in calling your attention to the wishes of your mother to mean no more than to urge the matter upon you as one that causes her much uneasiness and no regard to which very much should be risked to relieve her.

She understands me to represent her professionally but I write under the influence of motives of a different character.

Respectfully,

John M. Palmer

P.S. Since writing Mr. Edwards showed me your letter to him. I find you are naturally embarrassed in regards to this subject. I hope you will regard this in the light of a suggestion and answer me in such way that I may log it before your mother.

J. M. P.

Folder 22, Box 2, Mary Todd Lincoln Insanity File

NINIAN EDWARDS TO ROBERT LINCOLN
Springfield, Ill., Dec. 22, 1875

Dear Robert

I have received yours of the 21st instant. Your mother for the last two or three weeks has been very much embittered against you and the more you have yielded the more immeasurable she seems to be. She is threatening to withdraw all of her possessions in your house, but your aunt is pleading with her not to do so, urging the inconvenience and expense of storing them elsewhere. I do not now believe that she will consent to the compromise she requested me several weeks ago to propose to you. As you propose to see Judge Davis, consult with him as to what is best to be done in the event of her insisting unconditionally of having her bonds restored to her. I believe on reflection and knowing her as I now do, and as in any event she will have the pension for life, I would give them up to her, for nothing else will satisfy her.

Gov. Palmer has shown me a letter he has written to you. Neither he nor I have any doubt but that the court would be justifiable by consent in allowing the order appointing a conservator to be vacated; and we also entertain no doubt but that she could make such a deed of trust as she proposed some time ago to make. If it should turn out that she was insane when she made it, it could be set aside on her decease. I am very anxious that there should be no controversy either before the courts or in the newspapers—I would also advise that she should know as soon as possible what she may expect. As I said in one of my letters, I do not believe she will remain with us a week after her bonds are restored to her. If any papers are to be executed by her I would advise that they should be either prepared or forwarded to Gov. Palmer.

Very affectionately yours,
N. W. Edwards

Folder 17, Box 2, Mary Todd Lincoln Insanity File

ROBERT LINCOLN TO J. M. PALMER

Chicago, Ill., Dec. 23, 1875

My Dear Sir:

Your letter dated Dec 21st reaches me on this morning. I have tried to the utmost limit to which Judge Wallace, our County Judge, would allow, to gratify every wish of my mother since she has been at Springfield. On the question of her discharge I have already written to my uncle Mr. Edwards the opinion as expressed to me entertained by the Judge of his power under the Statute. I called on him today and asked permission to say to you that he will write to you his views on any points you may suggest. He said he would do so. I did this because what I have said heretofore seems to be taken as *my* opinion of his power instead of his own. I wish you would write to him (Hon. M. R. M. Wallace) and learn from himself his views.

I will be very glad to resign my office, and relieve my sureties from their responsibility and myself from embarrassment and perplexity in endeavoring to do my duty, which are nearly overwhelming.

Mr. Henry F. Eames and Mr. [Edward] Isham are on my bond for $150,000 and they are in no way [*illegible*].

Under the views which Judge Wallace has expressed to me I see no way for my relief except by resigning. This I will do at any moment. I suppose it would not be accepted until my successor qualified and I will be gratified to you for aid in finding a successor.

If you are confident in your view that the question of vacating the proceedings in the County Court depends upon the consent of the Conservator, will you not as I resign take my place as conservator and then act on your own [*illegible*] as representing my mother's interests?

Very truly yours
Robert T. Lincoln

Folder 2, Box 2, Mary Todd Lincoln Insanity File

NINIAN EDWARDS TO ROBERT LINCOLN

Springfield, Ill., Dec. 28, 1875

Dear Robert,

I enclose receipt for $300. Your mother did not hand me the check until today. I am sorry to say that she is still very impatient and unhappy about her condition being under a conservator. It is impossible to reason with her on the subject. I write in haste.

Yours aff,
N. W. Edwards

Folder 17, Box 2, Mary Todd Lincoln Insanity File

State of Illinois, } ss.   In County Court of Cook County.

COUNTY OF COOK

To the Hon. M. R. M. WALLACE, Judge of said Court:

The petition of _Robert T. Lincoln_

would respectfully represent that _his mother, Mary Lincoln, widow of Abraham Lincoln, deceased,_ a resident of Cook County is insane, and that it would be for _her_ benefit and for the safety of the

community that _she_ should be confined in the Cook County Hospital or the Illinois State Hospital

for the insane. The facts in _her_ case can be proven by _Ralph N. Isham_

a regular practicing physician, and by _Willis Danforth, Samuel M. Turner, Maggie Gavin, J. R. Albertson, E. S. Isham, James P. Stone, E. L. Groff, I. C. Matlack, James P. Stone, C. J. Maloney, S. _____, Nathan S. Davis, Hosmer A. Johnson, R. J. Patterson, J. S. Jewell, Chester J. Smith, and other witnesses except the clerk J. Patterson who reside in Cook County,_ all whom are residents of this County, and that the said _Mary Lincoln_

has property and effects consisting of _negotiable securities and other personal property_

the value of which does not exceed the sum of _Seventy-five thousand_ Dollars,

and that the said _Mary Lincoln_ is absolutely non compos mentis

and incapable of managing _his_ estate, wherefore your petitioner prays that a Warrant be issued for

said _Mary Lincolns_ and that a Venire may be issued for

a jury of _twelve_ good and lawful men, to determine the truth of the allegations in the

foregoing petition contained; and also, that a subpœna be issued for the witnesses named, returnable at

such time as may be fixed by your Honorable Court, and that said _Mary Lincoln_

be declared an insane person after due hearing and proof, and that a

Conservator be appointed to manage and control _her_ estate. _Robt T. Lincoln_

Robert T. Lincoln being duly sworn, deposeth and says that the foregoing petition

by _him_ subscribed is true, to the best of _his_ information

and belief.

Robt T. Lincoln

Sworn to and subscribed before me, HERMANN

LIEB, Clerk of the County Court, this _19th_

day of _May_ A. D. 187_5_

_____ CLERK.

Ayer & Kales, and Leonard Swett, Of Counsel for Petitioner.

Petition of Robert Lincoln to have Mary Lincoln declared insane, May 19, 1875. Courtesy Allen County Public Library.

State of Illinois,
COUNTY OF COOK.
ss.

In the County Court of Cook County:

THE PEOPLE OF THE STATE OF ILLINOIS,

To the Sheriff of said County :—GREETING:

Whereas, it has been represented to the Honorable M. R. M. WALLACE, Judge of this Court, by *Robert T Lincoln* in a petition duly verified, that *Mary Lincoln widow of Abraham Lincoln deceased* is believed to be insane, and whereas said Judge has appointed the hearing of said petition for the *Nineteenth* day of *May* A. D. 18*75*, at *2 OClock* P. M.

You are therefore hereby commanded to arrest said *Mary Lincoln Widow of Abraham Lincoln deceased* to have her on the *19th* day of *May* A. D. 18*75*, at *2 Oclock* P. M., before our County Court, and then and there to await and abide the result of the trial.

And have you then and there this Writ, and make due service as the law directs.

Witness, HERMANN LIEB, Clerk of our said Court, and the Seal of said Court at Chicago, in said County, this *19th* day of *May* A. D. 18*75*

Hermann Lieb Clerk.

Order to arrest Mary Lincoln, May 19, 1875. Courtesy Allen County Public Library.

State of Illinois, ss.
COUNTY OF COOK.

Be it Remembered, That on the *19th* day of *May* A. D. 187*5*, the same being one of the days of the *May* Term, 187*5*, of the COUNTY COURT OF COOK COUNTY, present thereat:

M. R. M. WALLACE, *Judge*,
FRANCIS-AGNEW, *Sheriff*,
HERMANN LIEB, *Clerk*,

the following among other proceedings were by and before said Court had, and entered of record, to wit:

IN THE MATTER OF THE ALLEGED INSANITY OF

Mary Lincoln

And now comes the said *Mary Lincoln* who is alleged to be insane, in custody of the Sheriff of Cook County; also comes *B. F. Ayers Esq on behalf of Robert T. Lincoln* at whose instance *s*he was arrested; and thereupon also come the jurors of a jury of good and lawful men, to wit: *S. C. Blake* a doctor of Medicine, and *Wm Stewart* *C. B. Farwell C. M. Henderson S. M. Moore B. M. G. Adams Jas A. Mason H. C. Durand L. B. Parkhurst T. R. Cameron Thos Cogswell L. J. Gage*

who, after being duly empaneled and sworn according to law, and having heard the evidence adduced, and the arguments of counsel, retire in charge of an officer of the court to consider their verdict; and thereupon return into court, and in the presence of said *Mary Lincoln*

deliver their verdict in the words and figures as follows, to wit:

STATE OF ILLINOIS, ss.
COUNTY OF COOK.

We, the undersigned, jurors in case of *Mary Lincoln* alleged to be insane, having heard the evidence in the case, are satisfied that the said *Mary Lincoln* is *insane* and is a fit person to be sent to a State Hospital for the insane; that *s*he is a resident of the County of Cook, in the State of Illinois; that h*er* age is *fifty six* years; that h*er* disease is of *unknown* duration; that the cause is ~~supposed to be~~ unknown; that the disease is not with h*er* hereditary; that *s*he is not subject to epilepsy; that *s*he does not manifest homicidal or suicidal tendencies, and that *s*he is *not* a pauper. Which verdict is signed by each of the jurors above named.

Whereupon, upon the verdict aforesaid, it is considered and adjudged by the Court that the said *Mary Lincoln* is an insane person; and it is Ordered that said *Mary Lincoln* be committed to *a State* Hospital for the Insane. ~~And it appearing to the Court that it is necessary that said~~ ~~be temporarily restrained of h liberty, it is therefore ordered that, pending h admission to said Hospital, he be confined in~~ And it is further Ordered that *a summons be issued* ~~execute this order~~ *to the said Mary Lincoln, commanding her to appear before this Court & show cause if any she has or can show, why a conservator should not be appointed to manage and control her Estate.*

Verdict of jury declaring Mary Lincoln insane, May 19, 1875. Courtesy Allen County Public Library.

LETTERS OF CONSERVATORSHIP. Cameron, Amberg & Co., Printers, 84 Lake St., Chicago.

State of Illinois, } ss.
COUNTY OF COOK,

In County Court of Cook County.

The People of the State of Illinois, to

Robert T. Lincoln of said County, GREETING:

WHEREAS, you were by the County Court of this County, on the _Fourteenth_ day of _June_ A. D. 1875, duly appointed Conservator for

Mary Lincoln

NOW THEREFORE, trusting in your fidelity, the said Court do by these presents constitute and appoint you to be Conservator for said Insane person, and authorize and empower you to take and have the care of _her_ person and the custody and management of _her_ property, frugally, and without waste or destruction, to improve and account for the same in all things according to law.

Witness, HERMANN LIEB, Clerk of the said County Court, and the Seal of said Court, at Chicago, in said County, this _fourteenth_ day of _June_ A. D. 1875

Hermann Lieb Clerk.

Appointment of Robert T. Lincoln as conservator for estate of Mary Lincoln, June 14, 1875. Courtesy Allen County Public Library.

Chicago June 15. 1876.

State of Illinois, } County Court of
Cook County } Cook County

We the undersigned jurors in the case wherein Mary Lincoln who was heretofore found to be insane and who is now alleged to be restored to reason having heard the evidence in said cause, find that the said Mary Lincoln is restored to reason and is capable to manage and control her estate

R. M. Paddock M. D.
D. J. Heathenhead
H. F. Knowles
Cyrus Gleason
W. L. Heron
D. Kimball
R. F. Wild
Wm. J. Tyon
C. H. Chapin
H. Dahl
W. S. Dunham
Wm. Roberts

Verdict of jury declaring Mary Lincoln restored to reason, June 15, 1876. Courtesy Allen County Public Library.

Chapter 9

January 1–May 21, 1876

The holiday season and start of a new year did nothing to change Mary's condition. In fact, as 1876 began, Mary seemed to grow worse. She not only threatened her son's life, but also started to carry a pistol in her pocket. Robert had to decide whether to allow his mother to continue living in Springfield or return her to Bellevue Place sanitarium.

NINIAN EDWARDS TO ROBERT LINCOLN
Springfield, Ill., Jan. 14, 1876

Dear Robert,

I am sorry to say that your mother has for the last month been very much embittered against you, and has on several occasions said that she has hired two men to take your life. On this morning we learned that she carries a pistol in her pocket—we also hear from others that she has had a great many dresses made, and is still purchasing largely for her *own* use. She has everything she buys sent direct to her rooms. She says she will never again allow you to come into her presence. We do not know what is best to be done. Your aunt says nothing will ever satisfy her until she has possession of her bonds, and her advice is that all her rights should be restored to her as soon as possible. She does not believe that she will expend her income, and she can never come to want as she has her pension for life. Nothing else will satisfy her. Gov. Palmer advises me to inform you of her threats and of her carrying the pistol. He is of opinion that by consent her bonds may be restored to her. If you think it best to come down, you had better not come direct to our house but advise me where to meet you. Except on the subject of the restoration of her bonds and her purchases, she is as rational as I ever knew her. Please do not let her know that I have written to you on the subject. The information in regard to the pistol you can learn from others.

N. W. Edwards

She spends nearly ½ of every day with dressmakers and in the stores.

Folder 17, Box 2, Mary Todd Lincoln Insanity File

NINIAN EDWARDS TO ROBERT LINCOLN
Springfield, Ill., Jan. 15, 1876

Dear Robert

I wrote to you on yesterday that your mother carried a pistol. Your aunt thinks she could get it from her, but she fears in so doing that my daughter Mrs. Glover would know of it and would be alarmed. We do not think she would use it to the injury of anyone. Do you know whether she [*illegible*] presented to your father in her trunks? She has given to Mrs. Dubois, Mrs. Hatch and myself a cane, with a request that Charlie (my son) should have mine at my decease but I intend to keep it to be disposed of as you wish.

Besides a dress and shawl to her sister Frances, she has made no present except a few toys to the children, in all including the dress and shawl not to exceed fifty dollars.

Your aunt still thinks that she should have all her rights returned to her and especially is she would put her bonds in trust and that she ought not to be sent to an asylum. If this is done she would probably be again reconciled to you. The danger is that she might visit or [*illegible*] her bonds, and they might be stolen.

Yours affectionately

N. W. Edwards

Folder 17, Box 2, Mary Todd Lincoln Insanity File

ELIZABETH EDWARDS TO ROBERT LINCOLN
Springfield, Ill., Jan. 16, 1876

My dear Robert,

Your uncle is perhaps unnecessarily excited upon the subject of the *pistol*. There may be danger to herself and others. I think that it will be best, that you write to her, saying that you have obtained such information from outside parties—at the same time, write to Mr. Edwards, it will give him an opportunity of investigating and demanding the weapon, without exciting the suspicions, of our being the informants.

She has been very petulant for the past two months, but I will endure very much, for the sake of seeing her occasionally cheerful. There is no doubt that her chief enjoyment consists in purchasing and storing. She is very secretive—errand boys go to her room—and the merchants, disguise from me, the extent of the mania.

Your uncle has represented, as is true, that my affectionate interest, would prompt me to secure if possible her freedom from restraint, of course, I see the propriety of it being conditioned.

I can truly sympathize with you, in this very difficult case.

In haste,

Your affectionate

Aunt

Folder 16, Box 2, Mary Todd Lincoln Insanity File

ROBERT LINCOLN TO NINIAN EDWARDS

Chicago, Ill., Jan. 17, 1876

My dear Uncle,

Your letters of Friday and Saturday are received, and also one from my aunt, and they give me great concern, not for myself but I fear that something unforeseen may happen. The doctors whom we consulted last spring were very urgent in expressing their opinion that no one could foretell the possible freaks which might take possession of my mother and that the ideas she then had rendered it necessary that she should be placed where no catastrophe could happen.[*]

In her last letter to me received last week she asked me to buy $1,500 in U.S. Registered bonds for her and I have ordered them. In no letter has she ever asked or suggested my sending her bonds to her and since I sent her the trunks and jewelry box I do not think there has been a word in her letters indicating animosity towards me. I heard from Springfield last week that she is constantly making large and unnecessary purchases and *giving her notes* to various merchants. My information was by letter from a friend whose name I am not now at liberty to give. It was written not in answer to any letter from me, and urged me to come to remonstrate with the merchants. For several reasons I regard so doing as of no use. The principal one being that I regard her actions in this regard as merely one of the evidences of the real trouble. The sending her the bonds even if I would do it, would really ease this great trouble as little as stopping her purchases from any dealers.

In regard to sending her the bonds, I had a full consultation with Judge Davis and Mr. Swett and they unhesitating in their opinion that I would commit a grave and dangerous breach of trust to the suretors on my official bond, in allowing them to go out of my hands except to a successor in office or to my mother herself upon

---

[*] In the first draft of this letter, Robert here wrote, "I do not know where she obtained the pistol and do not recollect that I have ever seen one in her possession." He omitted the statement from the final letter.—Ed.

her discharge. They were also of the opinion that the trust proposition suggested by you could not be carried out, Judge Davis saying that such an arrangement would be a mere nullity. I will not commit such a breach of trust. I suggested to Gov. Palmer that he should become my successor in office so that he could deliver over the securities if he thought it his duty to his ward to do so and safe to himself and his suretors but he did not reply.

I have not the slightest idea that doing so would help any of us who are responsible for right action in this trouble and I have not the slightest doubt that the result would prove to be an act in the highest degree censurable.

I [*illegible*] what you tell me about the pistol business and her purchases and from what I have been told by others in addition to the letter I have mentioned, I am afraid the situation will as it did last spring move from bad to worse. If it would get better it would relieve me from an anxiety which is overwhelming. She was removed from the care of Dr. Patterson against my judgment as to the safety of such a step and she remains out of professional care contrary to my judgment. No catastrophe has yet occurred, but remembering what was told me by the physicians last spring, I live in continual apprehension of it. It is not now my expectation that without the development of something extraordinarily serious, to exercise the power which I have as her conservator to return her to the care of Dr. Patterson, without the concurrence of my aunt and yourself in the necessity of so doing. The [*illegible*] of any such necessity will appear to you before it does to me.

Affectionately yours,

Robert T. Lincoln

LB 3:4:384–87

ROBERT LINCOLN TO ELIZABETH EDWARDS
Chicago, Ill., Jan. 17, 1876

My dear Aunt,

Your letter of yesterday and two from my uncle are received. I have written him quite at length and need not repeat from what I have said. I am very much afraid that things are going from bad to worse as they did last spring, and that if they get worse it will be necessary to place my mother again under Dr. Patterson's care. It is not now my expectation that in any probable event I would exercise the power I have of doing so without your concurrence in the propriety of so doing.

I believe I have told you that in the height of my mother's mental troubles last spring, she usually appeared to me personally to be perfectly calm & sane when I saw her in the evening, except that she constantly denied (usually) having been out of her room. She seemed able, admirably able, to control herself before me but her conduct before others was [*illegible*] incompatible with any idea of her being sane.

I mention this again to suggest that possibly her actions in shops and elsewhere may have no likeness to her actions in your presence.

I think it also possible that you have a wrong idea of what is implied by her being under the care of Dr. Patterson. Aside from the idea of the place, there was I think nothing unpleasant about it. She had two rooms to herself (not large but comfortable) and was in no way under any necessity of meeting other patients. At my request Dr. P removed the wire nettings on her windows and there was as I think nothing suggestive of imprisonment. Of course the fact was there but if your influence cannot restrain her what are we to do? Josephine* can tell you more about the place in a few minutes than I could with a good while.

Affectionately yours
Robert T. Lincoln

LB 3:4:382–83

ROBERT LINCOLN TO EDWARD ISHAM
Jan. 17, 1876

My dear Edward,

Here are two letters—one from my aunt and one from my uncle—which please read and preserve. I think it about time to suggest the remedy for all this trouble and I send you my replies. If you think them prudent please seal the envelopes and send over to office of Stuart, Edwards & Brown. If you think them imprudent or ill advised bring them back.

R. T. L.

Folder 1, Box 2, Mary Todd Lincoln Insanity File

ROBERT LINCOLN TO MARY LINCOLN
Chicago, Ill., Feb. 7, 1876

My dear Mother,

In reply to your letter of the 3rd, asking me to send you the paintings. The Sleeping Christ, The Madonna, Cupid, Rebecca, Ruth, Winter, and The Woman of Summer. The picture dealer Mr. Coppersall has taken them to pack and will try to have them go by tonight's express, but they may not start until tomorrow. I hope you will give credit to my taste in the framing of the first three named.

The clock and candelabra I have had packed in my house. In unpacking you will find in your trunk:

---

* Josephine Remann, daughter-in-law of Ninian and Elizabeth Edwards.

2 candelabra boxes

2 candelabra tops

2 storks

1 pendulum

1 key

In one small wooden box you will find bronze [*illegible*]. In the other small wooden box you will find the clock proper.

You asked also for the large size Shakespeare, Dickens works, Coopers works, Balwers works, [*illegible*], Mrs. Browning, Whittier, Pope.

In the large wooden box you will find a complete set of Dickens 48 vols., complete set of Balwer 21 vols., complete set of Cooper 20 vols., Mrs. Browning 5 vols., Whittier 4 vols., Hearth's Shakespeare 6 vols.

I can find no such book as [*illegible*] and never heard the name before. [*Illegible sentence*] I never had Mr. Pope's works in my possession and I send Mrs. Herman's instead.

I send also three other books:

World [*illegible*] Women, 1 vol., Queens of England, 1 vol., Histories of Shakespeare, 1 vol., as there was just room enough in the box.

All the above mentioned things will go by U.S. express tonight and I trust will reach you in good shape.

Affectionately yours

R. T. L.

LB 1:1:162–64

ELIZABETH EDWARDS TO ROBERT LINCOLN
Springfield, Ill., Feb. 9, 1876

My dear Robert,

I overheard your mother last evening giving directions to our servant man, respecting boxes, that were to arrive by express, saying, that she wished them left in the office, until she secured a room for storing them. I at once concluded that she was carrying out her threat, to remove from your house her paintings, etc. I have in vain expostulated with her and regret her course for many reasons.

Can you not as conservator refuse to give her possession of such goods, as would be injured by removal, and storage? The box of books, you sent her, are in her way, and altogether needless, as we have 5,000 volumes of the most varied literature, in our home. I am exceedingly pained to so thoroughly understand her motive.

She has been much calmer, since, she was informed, in a positive way, that she could entertain no hope of release until *May*. As to the manner, in which she spends her money, others can better inform you. Mr. Edwards learned from Coleman & Kimber, that she had given them no notes for purchases.

I am sure that you will regard, my communications as confidential, being unwilling to incur your mother's displeasure, and anxious to secure as much peace as possible.

Love to your wife,
Yours affectionately
Aunt Lizzie

Folder 16, Box 2, Mary Todd Lincoln Insanity File

ROBERT LINCOLN TO ELIZABETH EDWARDS
Feb. 12, 1876

My dear Aunt,

Your letter of the 9th was only received by me late on yesterday. I am sorry the things I sent down incommode you. I believe I have told you that my house is filled with all sorts of things—presents from my mother to my wife and myself during the past eight years. In a letter of February 3rd she asked me to send her a few books, she named, a clock & half a dozen pictures—all [*illegible*] for her room. Although I considered these things as much my own as though I had bought them, I gave them to her desiring to gratify her as far as I can. There came at once from her another letter more than a dozen pages long filled with demands for "my this" and "my that," almost without end. Everything that we can recognize was a present at one time or another, many things neither my wife nor I remember ever seeing, many other (dress goods and the like) are worn out and forgotten. Apart from these considerations the whole demand is so unreasonable in the light of any service that the things could be to her or that she could properly make of them in her situation that it is plainly irrational and the emanation of an insane mind. Even if the things were not my own, I agree with you that they should not be sent.

In the hope of making her more contented and thus aiding her mental condition, I have with great trouble obtained from the Probate Judge the permission from time to time to relax in various ways the legal restraints imposed upon her and I am so satisfied that so doing has worked harm instead of good that I do not propose to go any further. Her demands have gone on from one thing to another as you know, until they indicate such a state of mind that it is a serious question for us as whether we will not have to take the back track.

Affectionately your nephew
Robert T. Lincoln

LB 1:1:165–66

Feb. 16, 1876

My dear Aunt,

I did not reply to the letter of my mother which I mentioned in mine to you and I have not since heard from her. I glanced at her letter again today and I find on one of the crossed papers that she asks for a number of things, a whip, some shells, some engravings and chromos [chromolithographs], etc., as being at 375 Washington St., her old residence. I ought therefore to qualify what I said about *all* the things she sent for being presents, as the things at 375 were stored there by her, at various times in a small locked room which I have not been in for a year and a half. These things now there are her own and were never given me. They are of little value and properly safe and I propose not to go near them, and certainly do not intend to send them down to burden you with them.

Affectionately yours,

Robert T. Lincoln

LB 1:1:167

NINIAN EDWARDS TO ROBERT LINCOLN
April 18, 1876

Dear Robert,

Your mother is again *very much excited* on the subject of having her bonds restored to her. She has employed Governor Palmer in the case, but if you do not intend to resist the application it would be better for her on several accounts to employ no one, *and it would be a great relief to her to know immediately your decision.* As she can never cease to want having a pension for life amply sufficient for her support both your aunt and myself would advise that she should have her bonds and the privilege of going where she pleases and I would in your case do as I advise you. I also feel confident that she would not spend all her income. She says her bonds are all registered and not due until 1881. She is rational on all other subjects and has been for several months, until within a few days, in good spirits and health, and not an unpleasant word has passed between her and any member of our family. If her bonds are given up to her I believe she would again be cheerful and happy. After a visit with Fannie Wallace to Kentucky she proposes in the fall to go again to Europe and I think she ought to [be] gratified in all her wishes.

Yours affly,

N. W. Edwards

P.S. She understands that it will require an order of court after the expiration of a year from the time of your appointment to have you as conservator removed and her property restored to her.

Folder 17, Box 2, Mary Todd Lincoln Insanity File

ROBERT LINCOLN TO JOHN M. PALMER
April 20, 1876

My dear Sir:

Your favor of yesterday is received. There seems to be a little misapprehension as to the time when the application can be made. The Inquisition was held May 19 but I was not appointed Conservator until June 14. Nearly two months must therefore intervene before the Court will entertain the application.

In answer to your question as to what I shall do then, I can only say that unless my duty to my mother, backed by the strongest evidence, forbids it, I shall gladly aid her in procuring her discharge from the disabilities which are so unpleasant to her.

Information from several of my relations that she is very much embittered against me has prevented my visiting her, from a sense that it would be injudicious. I should be very glad to consult you freely and candidly and if you come to Chicago please do not fail to let me know it.

Very truly yours,
Robert T. Lincoln

LB 3:4:412–13

ROBERT LINCOLN TO NINIAN EDWARDS
April 24, 1876

My dear Uncle:

Your letter was received on Saturday. You do not seem to be aware that I send my mother every cent of her income as fast as it comes in.

The matter of parting with the custody of some $75,000 worth of securities, for every cent of which I must account in a few weeks, is so serious that whatever may be my opinion as to its propriety, I could under no circumstances do it without the consent of the gentlemen who signed my bond for $150,000. My own affairs are such that any great loss could fall upon them. I tried to see one of them, Mr. Eames, President of the Commercial National Bank, on Saturday but could not. I saw him today and gave him your letter. He desires to think over the matter and will see me tomorrow.

If Mr. Bunn is willing to take any part in my mother's affairs, why will he not come up here and be appointed Conservator? I will resign and will aid him in every way.

Affectionately yours,

Robert T. Lincoln

LB 3:4:415–16

HENRY F. EAMES TO ROBERT LINCOLN
April 25, 1876

Dear Sir:

I return to you the letter of Mr. Edwards, which I have considered with care. The securities in your custody as conservator belonging to your mother are easily convertible by her under the present unfortunate circumstances and should not be subjected to any possible outrage.

I can see no possible good in sending them to Springfield and I think that trouble and embarrassment might very easily come of it to all of us. As surety on your official bond I think it decidedly more prudent that they should be retained here within the immediate control of the Court to which you must account.

Truly yours,

Henry F. Eames

LB 3:4:417

ROBERT LINCOLN TO NINIAN EDWARDS
April 25, 1876

My dear Uncle:

Mr. Eames sends me today the enclosed note. I am absolutely bound to follow his wishes in the matter, as I think you will agree with me that after having procured him as a friend to be my surety, to do anything which in his view would put him in danger or make him dissatisfied would be violating his confidence, and in bad faith on my part. If Mr. Bunn is willing to bother with this matter to the extent you mention why will he not take my place in form as well as in fact? The change could be made in five minutes and would relieve me very much.

Affectionately yours,

Robert T. Lincoln

LB 3:4:418–19

ROBERT LINCOLN TO ELIZABETH EDWARDS

May 17, 1876

My dear Aunt,

Your letter was delivered at my house so that I did not receive it until last evening.

You entirely misunderstand my powers. A year ago my mother was so out of her mind, showing it in many ways that it was absolutely necessary for her personal safety that she should be placed for a time under proper care. Under the laws of this state no person could take this course without the order of the County Court. When this was had, the law compelled the court to appoint a Conservator of her property and it appointed me on June 14, 1875.

The same law provides that the Court *shall not hear* any application for the removal of the Conservator for one year. I had to give a bond of $150,000 with two gentlemen here as suretors, to deliver up all her property at the end of the year. It would not only ruin me but besides be a heavy loss to my friends on my bond if next month, I should for any reason whatever not be able to place their bonds (being in value more than $70,000) in the hands of the court.

From what you say about her expressed intention to throw away everything she has to spite me, and to depend upon the government for support, I should hardly think her as sound in mind as you do, as the sane way of punishing me for trying to take care of her, would be to make a will and give me nothing. If she is so unreasonably exasperated against me, her anger might now easily lead her if she had the power, to waste or give away her property and then next month call on me and my suretors to account for and pay over every cent. I think anyone would admit that I would be very foolish to run such a risk, with no possible good to come from it. I send her every penny of her income as fast as it comes in. She has never asked me for the bonds and nobody has ever suggested my sending them to her except Mr. Edwards. I have repeatedly urged that some one should become conservator in my place who might be more daring in running risks than I am, but I get no reply and there is nothing for me to do but await my discharge.

No scandal or trouble will be avoided by my doing or not doing anything. Plenty of it will probably come and I can only hope that my aunts, who now have charge of her, will have less trouble on that score than I have had for many years.

Affectionately yours,

Robert T. Lincoln

LB 1:1:168–69

Chapter 10

Trial of 1876

As June 1876 approached, Mary Lincoln—with the assistance of her brother-in-law Ninian Edwards—continued to push avidly for a second trial, the removal of her conservator, and the return of her bonds and power to control her own property. The records show that Robert Lincoln had no plans to oppose a second trial, especially after receiving advice to the same effect from his mentor David Davis.

DAVID DAVIS TO ROBERT LINCOLN
Bloomington, Ill., May 22, 1876

My Dear Robert,

By appointment Mr. Edwards came to see me today, and I am satisfied, that you had better consent to the discharge of your mother at the end of the year. This is my advice on the theory that her money is squandered by her. She cannot come to want, as the pension of $3,000 will in any event be enough for her support.

Mr. Edwards and his wife both believe her to be sane, and that she ought to be discharged. They will testify to her sanity. Can we oppose it? Ought we to oppose it? Can we afford to have a general fuss, which is sure to come? I think she has enlisted Marshal O. Roberts in her behalf who has employed a lawyer in New York to assist Gov. Palmer if the discharge is resisted.

Mr. E says she still purchases things, chiefly dresses that she does not need, but he says she always did this. Mr. E does not believe that your mother will squander the principal. She says she intends to spend her income hereafter but not to touch on the principal.

I have after mature reflection come to the conclusion that it is better for your happiness to give a free consent to the removal of all restraint on her person or property and trust to the chances of time.

And I would suggest that you see the Judge of Probate to ascertain what evidence he needs to grant the discharge. Edwards testimony would be enough. Of course, the ten days notice by law you could waive. I have heard nothing from Gov. Palmer. Let me hear from you or you can write Mr. Edwards. In haste,

Your friend,
David Davis

ROBERT LINCOLN TO NINIAN EDWARDS
May 24, 1876

My dear Uncle:

I have today arranged with the Judge of the County Court that on Thursday June 15 at 2 p.m. my mother's application for my removal as Conservator will be presented to him,—I am waiving all notice and that the matter will be heard at once. The Judge will wish you to testify. There will be no offering evidence. Immediately upon my removal, I will present my account so that my sureties may be discharged and the whole matter ended. I will previously send down to say . . . [*illegible*] . . . of the account so that . . . [*illegible*] . . . examined before being presented to the Court.

There will be no need of anybody being present except you and myself. You will of course propose a short application under section 37 of Chapter 86 Rev. Stat. and have it signed by my mother. If it were known that the matter were to be disposed of on that day, probably a large crowd of loafers would be on hand expecting some sensation. To avoid this the Judge and Clerk of the Court will say nothing of the appointment. Please be particular about the date for the Court takes [*illegible*].

Affectionately yours,
Robert T. Lincoln

LB 1:1:170

"MRS. PRESIDENT LINCOLN: HER RESTORATION TO REASON AND PROPERTY"
Chicago Tribune, June 16, 1876

Yesterday afternoon, in the County Court, Mrs. Abraham Lincoln filed a petition asking that the management and care of her estate, which was taken from her about a year ago by the same tribunal, be restored. Mr. Swett appeared for her, and her conservator, Robert T. Lincoln, interposed no objection, waiving the statutory demand of proper notice. Mrs. Lincoln's brother-in-law, Ninian W. Edwards, of Springfield, also appeared in the interest of the petitioner. The whole hearing occupied a very few moments, more time being consumed in impaneling the jury than trying the cause.

The petition was as follows:

STATE OF ILLINOIS, COOK COUNTY—In the County Court—To the June term, A.D. 1876—To the Hon. M. R. M. Wallace, Judge of the County Court of the County of Cook, State of Illinois—Your petitioner, Mary Lincoln, respectfully represents unto your Honor that on the 14th day of June, at the June term of 1875 of the County Court, in and for said county, that Robert Lincoln, whom your petitioner prays may be made defendant to this petition, was appointed under the provisions of Chapter 86 of Revised Statutes of said State, now in force, her conservator. Your petitioner showeth to your Honor that she is a proper person to have the care and management of her own estate. Your petitioner therefore prays that her said conservator may be removed, and that your Honor may enter an order full restoring her to all the rights and privileges enjoyed by her before her said conservator was appointed, and that her said conservator may be required to restore to her all the money, estate, title, and pension papers, United States bonds, leases, and other effects with which he is chargeable as her conservator. MARY LINCOLN.

[Mr.] Ninian W. Edwards was the first witness called, and testified as follows:

Mrs. Lincoln has been with me for nine or ten months, and her friends all think she is a proper person to take charge of her own affairs. That she is now in said condition; that she can manage her own affairs. She has not spent all that she was allowed to spend during the last year, and we all think she is in a condition to take care of her own affairs.

The case was then given to the jury, which, after being absent long enough to attach their respective signatures to a verdict, reported as follows:

"STATE OF ILLINOIS, COOK COUNTY—County Court of Cook County—We, the undersigned jurors in the case wherein Mary Lincoln, who was heretofore found to be insane, and who is now alleged to be restored to reason, having heard the evidence in said cause, find that the said Mary Lincoln is restored to reason and is capable to manage and control her estate."

After the above section was had, the conservator, Robert T. Lincoln, filed his report, accompanied by an inventory of the property of Mrs. Lincoln placed in his hands on the 14th of June 1875. It showed that in cash there was $1,029.25; United States stocks and bonds, $58,000; personal obligation of conservator, $8,875; lace curtains, $549.83; wearing apparel and personal jewelry, $5,000; other items, $7,936.17, making a total of $81,390.35. The report covering the period between May 19, 1875, and June 15, 1876, showed that the conservator's receipts had been $11,140.35, and the disbursement $6,875.97 for Mrs. Lincoln's personal expenses, and $4,264.38 for investments in United States bonds. The report was approved, and upon the conservator turning receipts from Mrs. Lincoln into Court, he will be discharged.

Chicago Tribune, Friday, June 16, 1876, 8

Mrs. Abraham Lincoln Restored to
Her Reason and Freedom.

And by Action of Court is Again Placed in
Possession of Her Property.

Which Amounts to the Snug Sum of Eighty-One Thousand
Three Hundred and Ninety Dollars and Thirty-Five Cents.

A year ago Mrs. Abraham Lincoln was adjudged insane by the county court of this county and sent to Batavia to a private asylum for care and treatment. After remaining there for a time, three physicians, one from Madison, Wis., another from Jacksonville, and the third from this city, called upon her by previous arrangement, with a view of ascertaining the advisability of allowing her to visit her sister at Springfield, in compliance with her urgent and repeated requests, and the result of their examination was a report that the journey and visit could be safely and beneficially made. Mrs. Lincoln at once joyfully gathered her baggage together, bid adieu to the institution, and sought Springfield, where she remained the guest of her sister, Mrs. N.W. Edwards. The kind care and

DEVOTED ATTENTION

shown to her there, seems to have had a very excellent effect upon her mind and spirits, and the improvement was very marked. Her friends were highly gratified over the indication of a restored mind; and resolved to secure from the county court an order to restore her the control of her property, which was in the hands of her son as conservator. Although at times she was somewhat eccentric, yet there was nothing to indicate a positive product of lunacy, and they determined to take no time to again entrust her with the management of her own estate. So confident have her friends been of her sanity that they carried their proposition into practical effect on yesterday afternoon, and fully evinced their faith in her ability to wisely and judiciously handle the property. The form of the procedure was in the nature of a petition by herself, and the application of her warm friends to secure the discharge of the conservator. The property is quite large, when it is considered that generally the relics of the presidents of the United States are left only a small pittance, and amply sufficient to enable her to live in an elegant and comfortable manner.

THE ESTATE

consists mostly of United States bonds, which yield a very handsome income, and a quarterly pension from the government of $750. According to the report of her conservator during the year of her [commitment], the estate amounts to $81,390.35, and additions are being annually made in the shape of government bonds, which are purchased with the surplus of her income. This year over $4,000 worth of bonds were added, and but for the great outlay incident to the unfortunate position in which she has been placed, a large investment could have been made.

The gentlemen who appeared in court yesterday afternoon were Hon. Leonard Swett, counsel for the conservator, Mr. Ninian W. Edwards, her brother-in-law, and her son, Mr. Robert T. Lincoln. Mrs. Lincoln remained at home in Springfield, and left the consummation of her desires to the above gentlemen.

After Judge Wallace had disposed of several small cases, he rested his eyes upon the gentlemen, who had a lien upon the clerk's desk, and awaited their pleasure.

Mr. Leonard Swett said that if the court pleased, Mr. Edwards, of Springfield, desired to present a petition from Mrs. Mary Lincoln.

MR. EDWARDS

adjusted his eyeglasses and proceeded to read the following:

STATE OF ILLINOIS, COOK COUNTY—In the County Court—To the June term, A.D. 1876—To the Hon. M. R. M. Wallace, Judge of the County Court of the County of Cook, State of Illinois—Your petitioner, Mary Lincoln, respectfully represents unto your Honor that on the 14th day of June, at the June term of 1875 of the County Court, in and for said county, that Robert Lincoln, whom your petitioner prays may be made defendant to this petition, was appointed under the provisions of Chapter 86 of Revised Statutes of said State, now in force, her conservator. Your petitioner showeth to your Honor that she is a proper person to have the care and management of her own estate. Your petitioner therefore prays that her said conservator may be removed, and that your Honor may enter an order full restoring her to all the rights and privileges enjoyed by her before her said conservator was appointed, and that her said conservator may be required to restore to her all the money, estate, title, and pension papers, United States bonds, leases, and other effects with which he is chargeable as her conservator. MARY LINCOLN.

Mr. Swett then stated that the friends of the petitioner had been anxious to restore her to the management of her estate some time ago, but as that could not be done under the statute until the expiration of one year, they had deferred making the application until this time. Her friends had conferred together upon the matter, and now asked for a jury to pass upon the case.

A JURY

was accordingly selected and Mr. Edwards was sworn. He made a statement, which was short-handed by a reporter and subsequently put into the form of an affidavit.

The statement is as follows, and rather singularly contains a number of repetitions:

STATE OF ILLINOIS, COOK COUNTY—In the County Court—June term, A.D. 1876—Mrs. Lincoln has been with me for nine or ten months, and her friends all think she is a proper person to take charge of her own affairs. She has been with me about nine months, and her friends all of them recognize that she is a fit person to take care of and manage her own affairs. That she is now in said condition that she can manage her own affairs. She has not spent all that she was allowed to spend during the last year, and we all think she is in a condition to take care of her own affairs. N. W. EDWARDS.

THE COURT

said that unless the conservator waived process, the discharge could not be made until the expiration of ten days.

Mr. Lincoln replied that he waived the service of the usual notice, and desired immediate action. To that end he had prepared his final report of the account of the estate, and therein asked to be relieved from further responsibility.

The jury then retired and returned shortly with the following

VERDICT:

STATE OF ILLINOIS, COOK COUNTY—County Court of Cook County—We, the undersigned jurors in the case wherein Mary Lincoln, who was heretofore found to be insane, and who is now alleged to be restored to reason, having heard the evidence in said cause, find that the said Mary Lincoln is restored to reason and is capable to manager and control her estate.

The verdict was signed by R. H. Paddock, M.D., D. J. Weatherhead, S. T. Knowles, W. R. Heron, D. Kimball, R. F. Wilds, W. G. Lyon, C. H. Chapin, H. Dohl, W. S. Dunham, and W. W. Roberts.

Mr. Lincoln then filed his

ACCOUNT OF THE ESTATE

from the 19th day of May, 1875, to the 16th day of June, 1876. The receipts were $11,140.35, and the disbursements $6,875.97 for personal expenses of Mrs. Lincoln, and $4,264.38 for investments in United States bonds. The inventory of the property of Mrs. Lincoln, when it was placed in his hands on the 14th of June, showed that in cash there was $1,029.25; United States stocks and bonds, $58,000; personal obligation of conservator, $8,875; lace curtains, $549.83; wearing apparel and personal jewelry, $5,000; other items, $7,936.17. Total, $81,390.35.

THE ACCOUNT

was approved and an order was entered discharging him as conservator of the estate.

The parties then left the courtroom, and immediately a dispatch was sent to Mrs. Lincoln by Mr. Edwards as follows: "All right. We will send them."

A few days ago a copy of the report of the conservator was sent to Mrs. Lincoln, and the following reply was received:

I have received the amount forwarded by Robert T. Lincoln for the last year and subscribe my name to it as being perfectly correct. MRS. ABRAHAM LINCOLN.

Chicago Times, Friday, June 16, 1876, 3

After reading the newspaper reports of the trial, Ninian Edwards was so embarrassed by the doddering and repetitious nature of his testimony that he wrote three letters in one day to Robert Lincoln to explain himself.[1] These letters—like the testimony—are repetitious, but they also include insights into Mary Lincoln's attitudes in the wake of the trial. The last letter in particular is interesting in that Edwards makes clear that not only was the jury not supposed to decide the state of Mary's sanity or insanity, only the status of her property rights, but that Mary herself was angry that she was declared "restored to reason," since she never conceded she had lost her reason.

NINIAN EDWARDS TO ROBERT LINCOLN
Springfield, Ill., June 17, 1876

Dear Robert

Your mother is in much better spirits today and was much pleased with the notice of her case in the Illinois State Journal of this morning and has requested Lewis Baker to send copies to the Chicago Times and papers in New York, Philadelphia, San Francisco and other cities.

I mentioned in my letter to you that I never would have signed the statement of my testimony published in the Times if I had not supposed it was only intended for your private use. Whatever I may have said I certainly would not have written a paper containing so many repetitions one of which was caused by the judge asking me to speak louder. I too for some cause was very much embarrassed. It may be better, however not to notice it, and especially if the reporter should insist upon its correctness; but if he is willing to have the explanation made as requested without comment I would be very much pleased to have it done. Your mother is in good humor again, and we are in hopes that she will in a very short time be reconciled to you.

Yours affy

N. W. Edwards

Folder 17, Box 2, Mary Todd Lincoln Insanity File

NINIAN EDWARDS TO ROBERT LINCOLN

Springfield, Ill., June 17, 1876

Dear Robert

If Mr. Storey makes the explanation requested you to ask him to make, in regard to the evidence I gave in your mother's case, I hope it will be published in the Times and Evening Telegraph. I used the word "proper person" because the jury was summoned "to try the question whether she was a fit person to have the care, custody and control of her property." They were not called upon to try the question of her sanity, and [I] regret very much that the verdict stated that she was "restored to reason." This was what excited her so much on yesterday morning. A person may be insane and yet capable of taking care of his property.

Yours aff uncle

N. W. Edwards

Folder 17, Box 2, Mary Todd Lincoln Insanity File

Chapter 11

June–September 1876 *

Even though Mary Lincoln now had control of her own property, her antipathy toward her son had not lessened. She, in fact, immediately sought to exact revenge against Robert for his actions by printing accusations against him in the newspapers, by accusing him of thievery and double dealing, by threatening lawsuits against him, and, ultimately, by cutting off all communication with him.

MARY LINCOLN TO MYRA BRADWELL
Springfield, Ill., June 18, 1876

My dear Mrs. Bradwell:

Your most welcome letter, was received last evening and I am quickly demonstrating the pleasure it afforded me by replying at once.

God is just, *retribution,* must follow those who act wickedly in *this* life, sooner or later compensation surely awaits those, who suffer unjustly, if not here, in a brighter and happier world. The most villainous plot, has come to a close, but on Friday morning, when the young man, who perpetrated it came down to S[pringfield] when I looked into his face (at a slight distance you may be sure), I saw the reluctance, with which he yielded up what he so ignominiously fought for—my poor pittance, as the world goes—so far as wealth is concerned—"a widow's mite," my bonds. Prayers will scarcely avail in his case I think. My heart fails me, when I think of the contrast between himself and my noble glorious husband, and my precious sons, who have only "gone before" and are anxiously I am sure, awaiting the reunion, where no more separation comes—and so I told him (R. T. L.) he could not approach us in the other world—on account of his heartless conduct, to the wife of a man who worshipped me—as well as my blessed sons did. *This one* as my beloved husband always said was so very different from the rest of us. Prided himself on his philosophical nature—not satisfied with the fortune I bequeathed him *in one* morning,*

---

* This probably refers to the division of Tad's estate upon his death in July 1871. By state law, Mary was entitled to two-thirds of his $35,750 estate and Robert to one-

desiring the rest, brought false charges against me. The only trouble about me, in all my sorrows and bereavements has been that my mind has always been too *clear* and remembrances have always been too keen, in the midst of my griefs. As to *Swett* he has proved himself to be, the most unmitigated scoundrel and *hell* will be his portion and *doubtless,* he will have company. Never could such a creature approach my husband, who loved me so devotedly—in the other life—I have my dear friend, a very great favor to ask of yourself[,] your good husband and the gentleman who called with you at B[atavia] the City Editor, of the Times.[*] If I were to tell you *three, all* the utterances of this man R. T. L. you would *not refrain* from writing the *latter* person up, *without* a day's delay. Your pen is sharp, so is Judge Bradwell's, so is the Editor's, just named, of course you would not wish your names to appear, but you will not fail me, I am sure, *now* is the time, have justice rendered me, my dearly loved friend, see the City Editor of the Times, before the close of the day, when you receive *this* letter. I have been a deeply wronged woman, by one, for whom I would have poured out, my life's blood.

R. T. L.'s *imprecations* against you all, have been very great, only on account of your being my true friends. *Do not* allow a day to pass, before this writing *is done* and forwarded in every direction. Let not *his wickedness* triumph. It appears there is no law for the widow—in this land, and I solemnly pledge you my word as an honorable woman, that *not one* word shall ever escape my lips—not a person in *this* house or elsewhere about any article or the probable author, that may be published. My sister Mrs. E. sat by me on Friday for about an hour and a half and in a quiet composed and I trust lady like manner I gave expression to my feelings as to sins he had committed against a broken hearted woman who had been called upon to give up, all her dearly beloved ones, for *the time* being only—and I asked him to look upon my bleached hair—which he *had entirely* created caused with the past sorrowful year.

Write, fail me not, I pray you, *any delay* will be grievous, I assure you. So much I have to tell you. Kiss your sweet lovely daughter for me. Would to heaven, I could see you. Best regards to your husband—*fail me* not.

Always your most affectionate friend,

Mary Lincoln

I enclose this article from yesterday's journal. Phillips,[†] I believe wrote it—write stronger. I am sure you will. M. L.

---

third, but she chose to split the amount equally with her oldest son. Robert called this "very generous," as it "makes a difference of about $7,000." Robert T. Lincoln to David Davis, September 21, 1871, Folder A-109, Box 7, David Davis Family Papers.

[*] Franc B. Wilkie.

[†] David L. Phillips, editor, publisher and co-owner of the *Illinois State Journal* from 1862 to 1878.

[*on front of letter*]: Burn this scrawl. You will, especially on the last page, be unable to decipher it, I fear.

Folder 1, Cont. 8, Part 2,
Robert Todd Lincoln Family Papers

MARY LINCOLN TO ROBERT LINCOLN
Springfield, Ill., June 19, 1876

Robert T. Lincoln

Do not fail to send me without *the least* delay, *all* my paintings, Moses in the bulrushes included—also the fruit picture, which hung in your dining room—my silver set with large silver waiter presented me by New York friends, my silver tête-à-tête set also other articles your wife appropriated and which are *well known* to you, must be sent, without a day's delay. Two lawyers and myself, have just been together and their list, coincides with my own and will be published in a few days. Trust not to the belief, that Mrs. Edward's tongue, has not been *rancorous* against you all winter and she has maintained to the very last, that you dared not venture into her house and our presence. Send me my laces, my diamonds, my jewelry—My unmade silks, white lace dress—double lace shawl and flounce, lace scarf—2 bl[ac]k shawls—one bl[ac]k lace deep flounce, white lace sets ½ yd in width and eleven yards in length. I am now in constant receipt of letters, from my friends denouncing you in the bitterest terms, six letters from prominent, *respectable,* Chicago people such as you do not associate with. No John Forsythe's and such scamps, including Scammon.[*] As to Mr. Harlan[†]—you are not worthy to wipe the dust, from his feet. Two prominent clergymen, have written me, since I saw you—and mention in their letters, that they think it advisable to offer up prayers for you in Church, on account of your wickedness against me and High Heaven. In reference to Chicago you have the enemies, and I chance to have the friends there. Send me all I have written for, you have tried your game of robbery long enough. On yesterday, I received two telegrams from prominent Eastern lawyers. You have injured yourself, not me, by your wicked conduct.

Mrs. A. Lincoln

My engravings too send me. M. L. Send me Whittier, Pope, Agnes Strickland's Queens of England, other books, you have of mine—

Louise Taper Lincoln Collection. Printed in Turner
and Turner, *Mary Todd Lincoln,* 615–16.

---

[*] Unclear if this refers to Robert's mentor Jonathan Y. Scammon, one of Chicago's most respected attorneys, or his alcoholic son, Charles Scammon, Robert's first law partner.

[†] Former U.S. Senator James Harlan, Robert's father-in-law.

LEONARD SWETT TO NINIAN EDWARDS

Chicago, Ill., June 20, 1876

Hon. N. W. Edwards

The recent attitude of Mrs. Lincoln towards Robert, and her drastic intentions, expressed in letters and verbal conversations, have induced him to consult me as his, and his father's friend, in regard to attacks which she proposes to make upon him. I therefore take the liberty of addressing to you this note.

Before her recent mental troubles Mrs. Lincoln was exceedingly kind to her children. She had an income larger than she needed for herself, and therefore since the death of her husband she has been [*illegible*] in making presents to them. About the time Robert was married in 1868, she was in England, and feeling kindly towards him and his wife, she sent them a great variety of personal gifts. These were accomplished by letters, full of affectionate regard and presenting the things, and fortunately most of the letters I've seen preserved.

While Mrs. Lincoln was in Chicago in 1866, she bought and furnished a house, but soon tiring of this mode of life, she broke up her home, and stored most of her smaller household ornaments and furniture, and a large number of trunks containing a great variety of personal articles.

As Robert contemplated housekeeping after his marriage, Mrs. Lincoln wrote to him and his wife repeatedly saying that she had no imaginable use for her household goods, and asking them to go where they were stored, and take such articles as they might need, and buy nothing which they could find of use there. Her letters also named certain specified things such as unmade material for dresses, and these they were asked to take and use.

As this afforded to Robert an opportunity to save expenditures in commencing his housekeeping, it was a material matter, and they as young people would do, took these things as they were directed, and such of these as are not worn out are now scattered through Robert's house.

About 1873 Robert collected for his mother $5,000, and at her request kept it awhile, she saying that she would determine by and by what to do with it. Finally she said she had no use for it and gave it to him, and he used it, largely in purchasing his law library, and for other purchases.

After leaving her house, bought in 1866, she, in 1874, at her own urgent request, took from Robert a contract to pay certain installments for seven years, and deeded to him the house, it being practically a handsome gift to him. These payments have been made for the two years which have expired, and thus the matter stands. The title to this property is now in litigation, a certain grantor in the chain of title insisting that her deed was forged, and if this shall be established the subsequent deed to Mrs. Lincoln of course will be void.

At the death of Taddie, his estate descended by law two-thirds to Mrs. Lincoln and one-third to Robert. Mrs. Lincoln generously insisting upon dividing this evenly, it was done.

About 1867 Mrs. Lincoln bought a house upon speculation. This was found difficult to rent and was finally traded for, among other things, a vacant lot. In 1873, she gave this lot to Robert, and he still owns it.

In the Fall of 1874 she went to Florida and during the winter Robert was in receipt of most pleasant letters from her, but in March she telegraphed to Mr. Isham, his law partner, that Robert was dying and that she would come on the first train. This was followed by telegrams to Robert begging him to live for her sake. Notwithstanding dispatches were immediately sent by Robert and Mr. Isham both, and received by her, stating that in his usual health, she was not shaken in her delusion, but came immediately to Chicago.

Upon her route home she thought she was poisoned by rebels, and so insisted to physicians who saw her after her arrival here. After her arrival at the Pacific Hotel she imagined she was pursued by men who were plotting her destruction, and that she could hear a mythical man talk to her when she would stand upon a certain spot on the carpet, and after such communications she would hunt the man throughout the house. She also heard voices speaking to her through the walls of the house and in the night. She was afraid to be in her room alone, and imagined that enemies bent on her destruction, were lurking about the halls of the hotel. At other times she imagined that the city was about to burn, or was burning, and on one occasion drove in great haste to Robert's office, urging him to put his valuables in a satchel which she brought to him, and escape from the city. Under this delusion she had nearly a dozen trunks sent in great haste to Milwaukee, and took from the Fidelity Safety Deposit some $56,000 in bonds, and concealed them upon her person. She was accustomed to be driven out by strange carriage drivers and studiously concealed where she went, and knowing the large amount of valuables carried upon h[e]r person, and ascertaining that suspicious and unknown persons were coming about her, it was feared she might be murdered for her money.

Under these circumstances Robert sought the advice of friends, and the conclusion was to summon a council of physicians, and submit to them two questions: 1. Whether she was insane; 2. Whether her personal safety required that she should be restrained. Seven of the most eminent physicians of the city unanimously gave it as their opinion that she was insane and should be restrained.

At Batavia where she was sent three rooms were allowed to her. She was a member of the physician's private family; was separated from all other patients; had her own meals when she desired, served in her own rooms; rode whenever she pleased; had every comfort that money could buy and entire liberty except the liberty to go away.

In a few months, by the kindness of family, was removed to your house and has been there since.

During the year her income has been paid over to her except certain amounts which have been invested in bonds. Her bonds have been kept just as they were, simply having been kept in a vault and recently as you know they have been handed over, nothing being charged for the expenses of the conservatorship, or for attorneys who conducted legal inquiries involved.

Notwithstanding these acts she harbors towards Robert an insane hatred because he caused her to be pronounced insane.

For about two months she has been demanding from him the return of personal gifts, described by this letter, at first specifying certain things which she desired. All that were asked for in her last letter were sent, but as he yielded she demanded more, and finally was said to him, by letter and verbally, that she must immediately have "all her things;" things which she gave to Robert "you remember" otherwise she says "my lawyers" will immediately commence suit; and that unless the things are returned scandalous publications will be immediately made.

A moment's reflection will show that very many of the things cannot be returned. A part of them are baby clothes and dress materials worn out, and household ornaments broken or gone. The watch presented to Mrs. Robert Lincoln before her marriage, which is especially demanded, was a beautiful gift, the presentation being engraved on the inside of the case; but in a railroad car years ago a thief stole it.

As to the things of value you and I both know that we have committed acts of doubtful propriety in causing to be returned to her what has been returned already. Recently through our agency, you in making it, and I in the request of Robert not opposing it, more than $10,000 has been handed over to her which there is great danger will never be of any benefit either to her or her friends, and that too upon the distinction which you drew in your testimony and in your letter received today, that while she is not in her right mind, she is able to manage her business. What ought to have been done, as common prudence most plainly dictated, was to place the bonds in some safe deposit and let her spend the income and all the principal she needed.

What she does, as we both know, is to buy dresses and be almost constantly employed in making and fitting them, and then placing them in trunks never to be again unfolded or taken out. In this way most of her income for the past six months has been spent. Now this is very harmless, and as long as she has the money she should be gratified in it, for it does her good in employing her mind, and does good also to those who are paid by her. I have always advocated therefore that she should have monthly all her income which I understand to be about $700 per month, and if she could spend it, enough of the principal also each month so that at such a time as her life should terminate according to ordinary calculation it would be all gone.

Robert is her only son, and he has had enough to give him a start, and now let him for his own good make his own way. He is in a most excellent law firm, has now an assured permanent business which must give him, I should think, $5,000 a year, and such a position is improved none by giving it work than by giving it money. Now assuming that we have done right in our doubtful experiment of giving to her, to keep her quiet, all her fortune in bonds, have we not gone far enough in that line?

If any misfortune happens to her, Robert must support her, and is it not proper that being given her $70,000 to experiment upon, when we all know that she is not in her right mind, he should keep something for her in case of misfortune. Besides, Robert cannot now without injury pay back the money she has given to him, and to turn over to Mrs. Lincoln a law library which he needs and which she can have no use for would prove her to be insane in accepting it, and ourselves very weak and foolish in being permissive.

Robert is a young man of whom any mother might well be proud. He is making excellent [progress] in his profession, commands the respect and confidence of the whole community, and is growing, I think I may providently say, as fast as his father was growing at his age in life.

Now with such a son bearing patiently for ten years, after all his past sad family history, the troubled burden of his mother's approaching insanity, putting off any steps restraining her until seven of the most prominent physicians say to him professionally there is danger of her jumping out of her window to escape from fire and from imaginary rebels, visiting his mother every week at Batavia, permitting her to be restored the first day the statute permits it, mainly at your request, and when you yourself say that she is not in her right mind; giving her also, mainly at your request, every dollar of her principal and all the interest accrued, when it was his judgment that it should be better to pay it in monthly installments—I say with such a son and such a mother, shall we, friends of the family, permit her to go about with a pistol, avowing her purpose to shoot him, or shall we permit her to break him down and ruin him by harassing and annoying him.

If Mr. Lincoln could speak to us what would he say? If Mrs. Lincoln, who in her right mind was the kindest of mothers, clothed with proper reason could see herself trying to ruin her son, would she not cry out, "hold me! hold me!"

The question with us is not one of judgment; but one of courage. We yield to her step by step when we know it is wrong and makes the situation worse, simply because we are afraid of her, and afraid while we are really trying to save her from herself, we ourselves will be misrepresented and misunderstood by the public, because the public don't understand the facts.

Now for one I am determined to do this no longer, and therefore I write you this note.

If Mrs. Lincoln wishes specific articles of property such as a picture or orna- ment or thing of like character which she has given Robert or his wife, and will ask them returned recognizing the gift and not demanding them as right; he will return them if it can reasonably be done, but he cannot return them upon the theory that they were improperly procured, and have been improperly retained, or under denunciation and threats. There has been an effort by meddlesome people to cast upon Robert, because he wanted his mother's money saved for his mother, so that it might be spent by his mother, the imputation of selfish motives. I am happy to say however that this feeling has been universally disavowed by all persons who know him and who know the facts, and especially by you and your family, who on all occasions have explained to him your sympathy and confidence. He cannot therefore for his own reputation allow his poor insane mother to charge him with getting her things improperly, and then half acknowledge the charge by yielding and returning them to her.

You may say what can I do about it?

I will tell you what I will do about it. We both know that the removal of civil dis- abilities from Mrs. Lincoln is an experiment. It has been done to err upon the side of leniency towards her, if we should err at all. It has been done with the hope that she would be quiet. If she will this is all right. If she will not, but turns upon her only remaining child to destroy him, knowing that she is insane, I shall, as a citizen, irrespective of Robert, or any one, in discharge of what I know to be my duty to her and her dead husband, at the proper time, have her confined as an insane person whatever may be the clamor or consequences. Please communicate to her, kindly but firmly, my intentions.

Since writing the above I have conferred with Judge Davis, who happens to be in town, and he approves of this letter, and my determination.

Since this writing also Robert has received another characteristic letter in which she calls for things, some of which were sent to her a month ago and in which she characterizes him as a "monster of mankind."

Yours truly,

Leonard Swett

Folder 27, Box 2, Mary Todd Lincoln Insanity File

MARY LINCOLN TO JAMES BRADWELL
Springfield, Ill., June 22, 1876

My dear friend:

Swett has written a letter to Mr. Edwards, which has been received this morning, filled with the most voluminous falsehoods. Amongst other things Swett writes that the title to the house 375 West Washington St.* is in litigation, the title being imperfect. You remember well the article I showed you, which Robert T. Lincoln drew up in regard to this house which I gave him, subject to the rent to be paid for seven years, from the time I deeded it to him. It is evident that after these long years it is rather late for a flaw to be in the lease.

May I employ your services to examine this lease. It is evidently gotten up to prevent the monthly payment of the rent. *Ascertain correctly* and write me all the facts in the case. The lease was examined and considered perfect at the time of the purchase. It was purchased from a man by the name of *Cook,* who resides near Batavia, Ill. I presume the people who reside in the same block feel very easy as to their titles—Cook—building all the houses. There is beyond question, the most unmitigated villainy in the case. *Do not* delay an hour, my dear Judge Bradwell, in regard to this involving such a loss. It appears that I must see yourself and Mrs. Bradwell. Pardon blots and everything—fail me not—*at once* write.

Your friend

Mary Lincoln

Folder 1, Cont. 8, Part 2,
Robert Todd Lincoln Family Papers

NINIAN EDWARDS TO LEONARD SWETT
Springfield, Ill., June 22, 1876

My Dear Sir:

I have received yours of the 20th and hasten to reply to it. Mrs. Lincoln authorizes me to say that all she asks Robert to return to her are some paintings she left in his house for safekeeping, and her case of silverware. You are correct in saying that all persons, and especially myself, my wife and her other sisters, who know the facts, do not believe that Robert has acted from selfish motives. We have expressed to him and others our confidence and sympathy and when she implored Mrs. Edwards and myself to allow her to make us a visit we had so much confidence in him that we declined to receive her unless the consent and approbation of him and Dr. Patterson, nor unless he would bring her to our home. I have never from considerations of policy expressed any opinion in regard to her sanity for I knew that the words "insanity and restoration to reason" were very offensive to her, and that it was not necessary, under the statute, that any verdict should be rendered by the jury, except that in the language of the 3rd section of chapter 86 of the Revised

---

* Mary bought the house in May 1866 for $18,000 after Congress paid her the remaining $22,000 of President Lincoln's salary. She was forced to leave the house and rent it out in the spring of 1867, due to high costs. Pratt, *Personal Finances,* 184.

Statutes of the State, it should be that she was *a fit person to have the control of her property* and before I consented to present her application to the court I exacted a promise from her that she would deposit her bonds with Mr. Bunn. This I believe she will this day do. Both Mrs. Edwards and myself have commiserated with Robert assuring him of our regard and sympathy, and I felt it my duty to inform him of her threats which I, however, believed that she would never carry into execution. I have reason now to believe that the story in relation to the pistol was not true. When I read to the court her petition which is in my handwriting, and also when I made my statement to the jury I was suffering very great pain in one of my eyes.

You are correct, as to the manner in which she has expended her income. Since she has been at my house she has occupied herself with constant and secret shopping and in having drapes made and fitted. Her sister Mrs. Wallace has been in poor circumstances since the death of her husband. When Mrs. Lincoln became conscious of this fact and learned that her sister Mrs. E and Mrs. Smith had been contributing for the past 8 or 10 years to her support she determined to brighten up Mrs. W home with new carpets, having contributed in that way about six hundred dollars. Mrs. W being the only member of her relatives who needed or would accept anything from her.

She promised me in the presence of her sister and niece Mrs. Glover, that she will neither bring a suit against Robert nor make any attacks on him and I think in course of time she will be reconciled to him. She, however, insists that he shall pay her the rent from the house on Washington Street. Mrs. Edwards desires me to say that we approve of your letter.

Very Truly Yours,

N. W. Edwards.

Folder 17, Box 2, Mary Todd Lincoln Insanity File

NINIAN EDWARDS TO LEONARD SWETT
Springfield, Ill., June 24, 1876

Dear Sir,

Mrs. Lincoln has deposited her bonds with Mr. Bunn and has given him power of attorney to receive the interest and to collect her rent from Robert. She was very much excited and angry with me when I informed her what you would do if she carried out her threats against him. She is now calm and says if he will send her the pictures and the silver engraved in her name and which was presented to her, he may keep everything else. She wished me to notify him that Mr. Bunn would expect him to remit the rent, but I declined doing so, preferring to write to you to let him know that she seems determined that he shall pay it whether he loses the property or not. I feel confident that she will manage her estate so as to add annually 3 or

4 thousand dollars to the principal. I have never thought otherwise since she has been at my house, not even if it was a doubtful experiment I was in favor of trying it and especially as she has a pension of $3,000 per annum. We wish you to reassure Robert that we have never for one moment believed that he has been actuated by any motive other than for her interest and happiness; and from the testimony of the physicians, and others of his father's friends we do not see how he could have done otherwise. He has had from the first our sympathy, love and confidence.

Very truly yours,

N. W. Edwards

Folder 17, Box 2, Mary Todd Lincoln Insanity File

NINIAN EDWARDS TO ROBERT LINCOLN
Springfield, Ill., June 26, 1876

Dear Robert,

To humor your mother I write anything she requests me to write to you, that is not offensive. She proposes to return to you Dickens works which she says have your name in them provided you will send her the picture of Moses in the bulrushes, which she says is a favorite picture and was presented to her when in Europe. I wrote to Mr. Swett that she had deposited her bonds with Mr. Bunn and your aunt and myself have no doubt but that she will leave them with him until 1881—for she today remarked that she will not return from abroad until then. She is afraid that you are not going to pay her the rent for which she has given Mr. Bunn power of attorney to collect.

Is all her interest in bonds payable in Chicago?

I would add more but suggested to Mr. Swett to show you my letters to him.

Yours affy

N. W. Edwards

Folder 17, Box 2, Mary Todd Lincoln Insanity File

LEONARD SWETT TO NINIAN EDWARDS
June 28, 1876

Dear Sir:

Your two letters have been received.

Tomorrow morning Robert and I will meet and this I will send to you at length.

I expect Mrs. Lincoln would be annoyed at my letter and my determination. This makes no difference. The determination comes from a sense of duty and all she has to do to avoid the effects of it is to behave herself within the bounds of propriety. If she does the determination will not injure her and if she does not I am determined to carry it promptly into effect.

As to the articles specifically named in your letter I will determine nothing until my conference with Robert, but my inclination will be simply to abide by the conditions of my first letters.

Yours Truly,
Leonard Swett

LB 3:4:430–31

LEONARD SWETT TO NINIAN EDWARDS
Chicago, Ill., July 1, 1876

Dear Sir:

Your two letters of the 22nd and 24th ultimo, in regard to Mrs. Lincoln's pictures and silverware in the possession of Robert, have been received and considered by us. I should have answered sooner but for the press of professional business, which has given me scarcely a moment of time.

Robert has no pictures and no silverware, that he is aware of, belonging to his mother in store at his house or elsewhere. I will relate the facts and you will then see the difficulty which your requests presents. In yours of the 22nd you say: "She asks Robert to return to her some paintings she left in his house for safekeeping, and her case of silverware;" and in yours of the 24th you say: "If he will send her the pictures and the silver, engraved with her name and which was presented to her, he may keep every thing else."

A few evenings since Robert came to my house bringing a package of letters, received mainly by Mrs. Robert Lincoln, and I took time in a general way to go through them. The silver, which possibly you refer to, is covered by these letters.

Before Mrs. Lincoln went to Europe she placed in the vault of Solomon Smith's bank, a box of silverware. While in Europe she wrote repeatedly in regard to it; presenting it to Mrs. Robert Lincoln, and urging that it should be taken by them and used. She describes this in these letters as being merely at Mr. Smith's bank near the Tremont House. There was a difficulty at first; from the indefinite description, in finding it, for at Mr. Smith's bank they at first thought they had no such package. It was finally discovered in their vault they having forgotten to whom it belonged. This was in fact the consummation of a wedding present to Mrs. Robert Lincoln, and the letters of Mrs. Lincoln cover it explicitly, and press it upon them in affectionate terms and urge them to accept the present.

As to the pictures the following are in substance the facts, as shown by Mrs. Lincoln's letters. I previously stated to you that Mrs. Lincoln in breaking up housekeeping in 1866, stored her household ornaments. While in Europe she wrote to Mrs. Robert Lincoln repeatedly, asking her and Robert to go where these were stored, and get them, and not to buy anything they could find there. She said that the things were going to decay and soon would be of little value, and that she had no use for them, as she did not expect to keep house again. She therefore urged in the most affectionate terms that Robert and his wife should go there and take whatever they may desire, and specified many things to which she particularly called their attention. Among these were a portion of the pictures Robert has in his house now.

At the time of Mrs. Robert Lincoln's marriage, Mrs. Lincoln sent to her at Washington as wedding presents, among other things several engravings and pictures; these are also at Robert's house.

When Mrs. Lincoln came here from Europe she brought with her a great variety of personal ornaments and pictures. Some of these she brought to Robert's house and presented them to Robert and his wife. These were not framed, and upon this basis he had them framed and they have been in his house now for five years.

Most of the pictures which Mrs. Lincoln brought from Europe, were asked for in the first letter which she wrote to Robert, and were boxed up and sent to her last winter. Several however are left and still in his house.

From the above you will see that Robert cannot comply with the general and indefinite request to send "my pictures" and to send "my silverware."

There is another reason why this request, in its present form, cannot be complied with. Robert is in receipt of letters from Mrs. Lincoln, such as none but an insane mother would write to her son, accusing him and his wife of having obtained pictures, clothing and household ornaments improperly. This surprised and pained him and he began to consider whether he had evidence which to other persons would refute these charges. Affection between child and parent makes them partly careless of natural rights, and at first he doubted whether, in the lavish and affectionate manner in which his mother for years had been presenting to him and his wife the tokens of her regard, he could produce such evidence as would show the real facts involved. Nothing could show so plainly the utter wreck of Mrs. Lincoln's mind as the reading of letters in which one time and another she sends these things, and comparing them with the recent letters demanding their return. For instance take any specific article which Mrs. Lincoln directed to be brought from where her things were stored in Chicago. The original letter, directing the act and presenting the article, is in the most affectionate terms. She seems gratified that she had children worthy of her affection, means to gratify her desire to be constantly bestowing gifts upon them. She therefore sends a gift, describing it, and then asks if it is acceptable; and finally in substance accuses her children of stealing it.

While of course, owing to her condition of mind, this unkindness is to be forgiven and forgotten, the fear of being misunderstood by strangers has induced Robert—and I think wisely—in reference to the things referred to in your letters, not to return them, demanded as a matter of right, accompanied with the assertion that they were obtained improperly. Therefore if Mrs. Lincoln shall desire these things under the terms named in my first letter, she must ask for them, recognizing the fact that they were given to her children, and that they are rightly in their possession.

By reference to my first letter which was deliberately written, you will see that I am but repeating what I then said. I do not desire to change the terms of that letter, and if Mrs. Lincoln wants anything under it she must comply with its conditions.

LB 1:1:172–79

MARY LINCOLN TO MYRA BRADWELL
Springfield, Ill., July 7, 1876

My dear Mrs. Bradwell:

I have received no letter from you, am I forgotten? If you ascertain any facts in relation to 375 West Washington St. please inform me.

A weak "invention of the enemy" united with villainous falsehood. That Swett, should become so debased as to try and drag down to his own debased standard the son of the noblest, most honest man, who ever lived. None of my treasures in the way of rich and rare presentations, that were made me, have been returned to me. As I truly told R. T. L. villains, could not venture to approach my dearly beloved husband in the other world. *His* reply I gave you.

My husband always told me, that he only liked those whom I did and when I remember the contrast between R. T. L. and my other blessed sons, the latter so lovely, gentle and noble and my darling husband, who worshipped me so greatly, that often he said, that I was his weakness.

We conversed very unreservedly together when you were in S. Anything you said to me will be held sacred—some little communications I made you *please* breathe to no living soul. We discussed Prof. S.* who between ourselves I think amounts to very little. The subject of Mrs. E. etc please erase from your memory, as an honorable woman I entreat you to cast *all thoughts* of either of these persons from your mind or *mention.*

What are your plans, believe me, I am deeply interested in them, for the next *six weeks or two* months. Write me dear friend, when you receive this scrawl I am so anxious to hear from you.

---

* David Swing.

My pen is refusing its office, so I must bid you adieu, until I hear from you. Please present my love to all your family whilst I remain

Your very affectionate friend

Mary Lincoln

Folder 1, Cont. 8, Part 2,
Robert Todd Lincoln Family Papers

MARY LINCOLN TO MYRA BRADWELL

Springfield, Ill., July 14, 1876

My dear Mrs. Bradwell:

Your expected letter has been received. As to the abstract, I suppose R. T. L. has it. Mr. Cook from whom 375 West Wash. St. was purchased, resides somewhere in the country, near Chicago, doubtless transacts business in the latter place.

Mr. Phillips made me a very pleasant call a few evenings since. Is very vehement against two of the greatest scoundrels of the age R. T. L. and Swett. The last of whom he pronounces a very profligate man and says that my husband had become thoroughly disgusted with S. (Swett and so expressed himself to P.) Certainly as the wife I heard enough against S.

We speak of you so frequently. Would that we could daily meet, converse together. Will not Judge Bradwell return west by way of Springfield? I, so much wish to see him before the sail, "down the bay." If you still have Mrs. Ellen Johnson (colored)* address—please forward it to me—also, please drop her a note to call to see you—as she would like to hear—that a *faithful, devoted* son failed in his attempt to render a deeply bereaved mother *insane. Do* see her for my sake, my dear friend.

Will write you again soon. My sister is well and cheerful—Too much kindness of heart is the only trouble of the *other party*—I assure you—easily imposed upon an innocent by those who make a representation of want of means. Others justly require what is thus bestowed. Much love to you and yours. Write and do not act *quite so mean* by your silence.

Affectionately yours, M. L.

Folder 5, Cont. 8, Part 2,
Robert Todd Lincoln Family Papers

---

* A laundress hired by Mary Lincoln when she lived in Chicago.

MARY LINCOLN TO MYRA BRADWELL

Springfield, Ill., Aug. 2, 18[76]*

My dear Mrs. Bradwell,

Tomorrow morning, Fannie Wallace and myself leave for San Francisco, to be absent, four weeks. I trust you will not start East, before our return, as I am anxious for your company, "down the bay," about the middle of Sept. My movements are of course, *entre nous*. I shall not feel satisfied, if I do not see you, before my departure. You have been so dear a friend to me, as well as your husband, that my heart has gone out *entirely* to you. We must meet again, before long, and I *do hope,* you will defer your Eastern trip, until the time I mention.

Doubtless your very sweet daughter is enjoying herself in Brooklyn. Letters received, assure me of the death of one of my dearest friends Mrs. Judge Roosevelt. I shall write her sister, Lady Dudley of England, a letter, when I reach the Continent. Do not disappoint me or my expectations.

With much love, believe me, your affectionate friend,

Mary Lincoln

My dear sister sends her warmest love to you M. L.

privately owned

---

* The letter was misdated by Mary as 1867, but the reference to a trip with Fannie Wallace (previously mentioned by Ninian Edwards in an April 18, 1876, letter to Robert Lincoln) and the death of Cornelia (Van Ness) Roosevelt, wife of New York Supreme Court Justice James John Roosevelt, who died in February 1876, proves this to have been written in 1876. Unfortunately, in a previous article about this letter I accepted Mary's erroneous date. Emerson, "New Mary Lincoln Letter Found," 315–28.

Chapter 12

October 1876–June 1882

There is no evidence that Mary Lincoln traveled to California with her sister in August 1876 as she proposed, but in September she did leave Springfield—secretly, in fear that Robert would have her arrested and returned to Bellevue Place—for what was a self-imposed exile in Europe. "I cannot endure to meet my former friends Lizzie," she supposedly told her sister Elizabeth Edwards. "They will never cease to regard me as a lunatic. I feel it in their soothing manner. If I should say the moon is made of green cheese they would heartily and smilingly agree with me. I love you, but I cannot stay. I would be much less unhappy in the midst of strangers."[1] Mary traveled the continent as she had on her previous European sojourn in the 1870s, but stayed mainly in Pau, France. She would not return to America for four years.

MARY LINCOLN TO EDWARD LEWIS BAKER

Havre, France, Oct. 17, 1876

My dear Lewis:

I find myself, sufficiently recovered from my sea voyage, to write you, concerning my safe arrival, on a foreign shore. Tomorrow I sail on a new Steamer, the Columbia, for Bordeaux. Such kindness, deference, and attention, as I met with on my arrival here, it is impossible for me to describe to you. Our elegant and kind hearted friend Louis de Berbieu, had written several letters to the agents here and they immediately took me in charge, without opening an article of baggage. They were equally as gentlemanly and distingué in appearance as Mr. De Berbieu, the latter, I am told, is of royal descent, is a widower, certainly, a very cheerful looking one, with a beautiful young daughter, an only child. Every where, reverses of fortune are met with. Perhaps it has not been *his* fate financially. Each day, since I have been here, about eleven in the morning, a carriage with a coachman and footman and livery, has called for me to drive, accompanied always, by the owner. It is pleasant to be *thus* received, although of course, I am aware, it is entirely my own fault, as in *NY* and *Phil,* in keeping myself aloof from dear friends, who love me well. I propose to act in a more *civilized* manner in the future, which conclusion will greatly please your *very dear* Grandma. I fear the small sum of $27 scarcely, returned you, my dear Lewis, to S. *Words,* are impossible to express, *how* near you are to my heart. Such attention, such kindness, as you have shown me in the past year I can say no more, I am indeed a broken hearted, bereaved woman, but God in his "Own Time," will restore me to my beloved one.

Please write at once and direct to Pau, France. Present my best love to your precious home circle—Write me every thing. I have just received from Galignani's at Paris, Guizot's History of France in 5 large volumes, handsomely bound, the latest history, of this beautiful land.

Do not fail to write me and tell my dearly loved sister to do the same. Love to all friends,

Most affectionately, your aunt,

Mary Lincoln

Lincoln Collection. Printed in Turner and Turner,
Mary Todd Lincoln, 617–18.

ELIZABETH EDWARDS TO ROBERT LINCOLN
Springfield, Ill., Oct. 29, 1876

My dear Robert,

I owe you an apology for not having written to you before, or immediately after your mother's departure. She so strictly enjoined upon me, not to inform you of the time of her leaving, and her questionings were so close, that to keep peace, I failed to write, full well knowing that you understood her plans, and intended to allow her to carry them out. This I assured her, but her resentful nature found it necessary to place the ocean between you and herself. I predict that it will not be long before she wearies of the isolation.

It surprised me at the moment of parting, to witness her gush of anguish saying, "I go an exile, and alone! Will you not join me in Europe next year?" I told her then, as often before, of the very great mistake she was making, in going abroad, when she had the liberty of making her headquarters wherever she pleased, and not necessarily confining herself to Springfield, which place she insists, is too full of sad memories, to be agreeable to her.

Lewis Baker had contemplated going to the Centennial, and was her escort for about ten days. They first visited Mammoth Cave, and Lexington, where she enjoyed herself for a day or two in visiting scenes of her childhood, not omitting *there* the cemetery. The Centennial afforded her entertainment for a short time. I think that she was nearly a week in New York, spending much of the time in driving, and I presume as is her unfortunate custom, to much time, and money, shopping. I never refer to that painful point, in her monomania, without a sigh and a tear.

Her recovery from it, seems so utterly hopeless, any exclamation of surprise at a purchase that seemed useless, on my part invariably called forth angry words from her, thus I was prevented, exerting any influence. As many as six trunks were added to those you sent down. I have been surprised to learn of the statements of merchants and dressmakers. It is lamentable, but what can be done in so difficult a case?

Be assured of one thing, that the contents of those trunks, will be guarded with the most miserly care, and no human being will be able to look into them. Not long before she left, she drew from them a white silk dress having never been worn, to present to Lulu T. who has been recently married to Mr. Keyes, a very desirable young man.[*] The silk had become a creamy white, but made a beautiful garment, and was greatly appreciated by the *beautiful* bride.

I often wonder, dear Robert, if the course, I have been constrained to pursue has at all dissatisfied you. The truth is I only, from the beginning of this unpleasant matter, wished to do my duty, depending upon the judgments of others for guidance. It may yet turn out, that all parties have been too indulgent, if so, the consolation will be, in having erred on the side of humanity. I am still of the opinion that she will not expend her income, and also believe that a sense of loneliness, will cause her return, sooner than she contemplated. The improvement in her social feeling, was quite manifest, during the stay here, and among strangers, she will yearn for home ties. It was her intention to make her quarters for the winter at Pau, France. She sailed on the Labrador, destined for Havre and the Captain assured Lewis that every possible courtesy and assistance, should be extended. By the way she says that she has American and English friends at Pau and elsewhere, who will be kind, among them, the several members of the Orleans family, whom she knew in W. and met afterwards in England.

I fear that I have made myself tedious to you, but could not resist giving you as many particulars, as I have done, with my impressions. When I hear from her as I expect to, I will write again.

With much love,
Your Aunt Lizzie

Folder 16, Box 2, Mary Todd Lincoln Insanity File

---

[*] Edward D. Keyes was a Springfield, Illinois, banker. His wife, Louisa Todd Keyes, was Mary Lincoln's niece, the daughter of Mary's oldest brother, Levi O. Todd.

MARY LINCOLN TO ELIZABETH EDWARDS

Pau, France, Mar. 19, 1877

My dear Sister:

I wrote you a letter a few days since, on receipt of the [Illinois State] *Journal,* containing the afflicting intelligence of the death, of dear, sweet, affectionate little Florence,* whom I loved so well. The information saddened me greatly and rendered me quite ill. I have drank so deeply of the cup of sorrow, in my desolate bereavements, that I am always prepared to sympathize, with all those who suffer, but when it comes *so close* to us, and when I remember that precious, happy child, with its loving parents—what can I say? In grief, words are a poor consolation—silence and agonizing tears, are all, that is left the sufferer. Immediately, on the receipt of your most welcome, tender letter, with the enclosures of dear dear Florence's beautiful photograph, some weeks since, I wrote you a long letter and sent a loving kiss, to the sweet child—Do write me, when you can, every thing. What a fearful winter, my dear Sister—you have had—I have never received a line from Lewis Baker—and I often feel, that letters are sent, when I do not receive them. Yet, at this Hotel, they are very attentive. There is a carelessness, I fear, at the P.O. here. The French are a superficial people, yet, I live, very much alone, and do not identify myself with them—have a few friends and prefer to remain secluded. My "*Gethsemane,*" is ever with me and God, can alone, lighten the burden, until I am reunited to my dearly beloved husband, and children. Write as soon as possible.

Most lovingly, your sister,

Mary Lincoln

Lincoln Financial Foundation Collection. Printed in
Turner and Turner, *Mary Todd Lincoln,* 626–27.

How completely Mary Lincoln had severed her oldest son from her life during these years is shown in a statement Robert made in November 1877. In response to a request for his mother's signature, Robert responded, "My mother is now somewhere in Europe but she has for unfortunate reasons ceased to communicate with me and I do not know her present address."² And yet Mary Lincoln continued to send presents from Europe to her little granddaughter, Mary "Mamie" Lincoln.

---

* Florence Edwards, daughter of Elizabeth's son Charles, died on February 21, 1877, at the age of four.

ROBERT LINCOLN TO ELIZABETH EDWARDS

April 18, 1879

My dear Aunt,

I have your kind letter of Wednesday and I found on reaching home last evening that the things sent up by express had arrived safely. Mamie was not at home I am sorry to say to receive them but they will be sent to her at once. We thought it best some ten days ago to send her to her grandfather's in Iowa, to get her out of the smoky air here and let her play out of doors. She will write to her grandmother thanking her.

As to writing to my mother myself I appreciate the kindness of your suggestion but I am afraid a letter from me would not be well received. If I could persuade myself otherwise, I would write to her at once and not think I was making any concession, for I have not allowed her anger at me to have any other effect upon me than regret that she should so feel and express herself towards me. As to interfering to control her in any way, I assume you and I hope you will so write to her, that under no possible circumstances would I do so. If I could have foreseen my own experience in the matter, no consideration would have induced me to go through with it, and the ordinary troubles and distresses of life are enough without such as that. I therefore hope that no fear of me will prevent my mother from returning to America and that if she expresses any apprehension of my assuming to interfere with her actions, you may be able to convince her that such apprehensions are idle; that not only I have no reason to think that such interference is now or will hereafter be proper but that whatever I might think hereafter, I would under no circumstance do anything.

I am very glad that she has sent the things to Mamie for it makes it seem probable that the time will come when her great animosity toward me will cease and I am very anxious that it should. Its existence has been very distressing to me.

Affectionately your nephew,

Robert T. Lincoln

Lincoln Financial Foundation Collection

Mary Lincoln returned to the United States in October 1880 and resumed her residence in the Edwardses' home in Springfield. By this time, at age sixty-one, Mary suffered from numerous medical problems, including chronic inflammation of the spine, chronic kidney disease, migraine headaches, bodily swelling, eye cataracts, and loss of sight. She needed assistance to walk, and could not descend the stairs. Her doctor, world-renowned orthopedic physician and childhood friend Dr. Louis A. Sayre, also said she suffered from "great mental depression." Mary's medical condition was constantly reported on in the national newspapers.[3]

Robert Lincoln and his mother did finally reconcile in May 1881 after five years of estrangement. Robert was at that time President James A. Garfield's secretary of war, and in mid-May left Washington for an official visit to Fort Leavenworth, Kansas. He stopped in Springfield from May 26 to May 27 on his way west, and spent an entire day with his mother at the Edwardses' home.

ROBERT LINCOLN TO SALLY ORNE

Washington, D.C., June 2, 1881

My dear Mrs. Orne,

Just arriving from the west I find your kind letter of Sunday. That day I spent with my mother in Springfield where she is with her sister, Mrs. Edwards. The reports you have seen about her are exaggerated very much. She is undoubtedly far from well and has not been out of her room for more than six months and she thinks she is very ill. My own judgment is that some part of her troubles is imaginary.

I take pleasure in sending your letter to her and I know she will be glad to hear from you.

I thank you heartily for your kind words to myself.

Very sincerely yours,

Robert T. Lincoln

Robert Todd Lincoln Papers

Chapter 13

Posthumous

Mary Lincoln died on July 16, 1882, after suffering what was probably a stroke. Her body was laid out for viewing in the parlor of the Edwardses' home, the same room in which she was married, and her funeral was held in the First Presbyterian Church of Springfield on July 19, 1882. It was characterized as nearly the largest funeral in the city's history, second only to that of her husband.[1] Mary's casket was placed in the Lincoln tomb in Oak Ridge Cemetery.

DAVID DAVIS TO MISS ADDIE BURR

Washington, D.C., July 19, 1882

My dear Addie,

In the hurry and distraction of business of the Senate I cannot except on Sunday write you a long letter. This I am writing from my desk in the Senate. . . .

Poor Mrs. Lincoln! She is at last at rest. She has been a deranged woman, ever since her husband's death. In fact, she was so, during his life. The selling of her clothes [in 1867] was an act of insanity. On my remonstrance to her, she plead that she had to do so as she was in danger of becoming a pauper. She really had the insane delusion that poverty stared her in the face and this too in the face of owning $75,000 in Govt Bonds.

A lady friend of mine in Springfield once told me that Mr. Lincoln would never have been president if he had not had such a wife. He was a domestic man and not naturally ambitious. With happy family relations, he would have eschewed politics. His wife's disposition drove him from home and into politics. Peace be to her ashes. Had I not been President of the Senate I would have gone to Springfield to attend the funeral. And I regretted greatly my inability to go.

I will tell you more on this subject when we meet.

Adeline Ellery (Burr) Davis Green Papers

After his mother's funeral, Robert Lincoln had her nearly six dozen trunks of clothing and house decorations shipped to his Chicago home. His wife, Mary Harlan Lincoln, went through everything and decided what to keep for herself and her children, what to give to friends and family, and what to donate to various institutions and organizations.[2]

ELIZABETH EDWARDS TO ROBERT LINCOLN
Springfield, Ill., Nov. 9, 1882

My dear Robert,

The boxes, sent by express arrived safely. When I *saucily* suggested that if you found more furs, than you could protect from moths, to send some to the [*illegible*]. I scarcely anticipated that you would furnish them so liberally. Please accept our united thanks and with the icy breath of winter we will bless your *precious* name. I sent Lizzie who is at Racine, the warmest wrap, gave Josephine one and kept the silk garment for myself. You have been most lavish in your distribution of various articles, and the parties, who have shared the bounty, are truly grateful. I wrote to your wife, while feeling nervous, and weary, and fear that I was not sufficiently enthusiastic in my praise, for her kind and laborious effort, in giving pleasure and comfort to so many, and to some, who are in depressed circumstances. It is a sad fact, that the young members of our several families, have been lamentably unsuccessful, and greatly embarrassed those who should not have been made uncomfortable.

You wrote me of some illustrated books, you desired to send Josephine and Mary Baker, the latter promised me to write to you, accepting for both parties. I trust that no mistake will be made in sending them, else I may be called upon to act as peace-maker.

What an amount of trouble, you are having in the disposition of things, that must excite your thorough disgust, in looking upon them. I wish they were in a sensible, and substantial form. But your consolation must be, that you yielded to your mother's irrational ways, rather than deprive her of the freedom she so arbitrarily insisted upon. I know that you have the approbation of the general public, upon that subject.

I fear that I trespass upon your time in writing too long notes.

With renewed thanks, for all your kindness,

Believe me, ever your

Affectionate aunt

E. T. Edwards

Folder 16, Box 2, Mary Todd Lincoln Insanity File

A few years after Mary Lincoln's death, Leonard Swett, the man who acted as Robert Lincoln's main legal advisor and mentor during the 1875–76 insanity period, began preparing an article about the case to be published in The Century *magazine. He wrote to Robert to ask for assistance in recalling the facts of those events.*[3]

ROBERT LINCOLN TO LEONARD SWETT
May 25, 1884

My dear sir:

Your letter of May 17th reached me at Sandusky just as I was leaving there for Washington, and I have been so pressed since my arrival on Friday night, that I have not been able to answer it. . . .

Now, in answer to your specific inquiries,—I can, away from my personal papers at Chicago, only say about this: As to the verdict, I have no copy of it. It is, of course, on record in the Probate Court, under date of May 19th, 1875. It was not a verdict of seven doctors, but a verdict of six jurors, of whom one or two were doctors. You may remember that C. B. Farwell, S. M. Moore, and J. McGregor Adams (of Crerar, Adams & Co.), were three of the jurors.

As to the bonds, which you ask about,—my memory is this: She had $56,000 of registered bonds on her person. After the hearing, upon returning to the hotel, she refused to give them to me, but said she would give them to Mr. Arnold. As that was of no consequence, with my assent Mr. Arnold took them, and the next day gave them over to me as her Conservator. With her income, and after paying outstanding accounts which remained after I returned a considerable quantity of useless goods purchased by her,—such as jewelry, curtains, etc.—I was able to purchase for her, I think, two more registered bonds, for $1,000 each. At about this time, she was very anxious that her whole income should be sent to her; and with the assent of Judge Wallace, I thereafter sent her, as it came in, her total income.

On the 19th of May, 1876, I rendered a full statement of account to the Probate Court, which ought to be on file among the papers, indexed under the insane cases. One of your clerks could step over to the Court House and get a copy of the verdict, the names of the jurors, and a copy of this account, all in half an hour. Mr. Isham is not in Chicago, as I understand, and I am not sure of the names of any of the clerks in our old office, or I would write out and have this done for you. You are correct in your understanding that there never was a time from the death of my father until my mother's death, in which her settled income was not at least $500 a month; and it was so small as that only after the rate of interest on bonds was reduced from six percent to four percent. Her own personal expenses, aside from indiscreet and useless purchases, were insignificant.

After I was discharged from the conservatorship, I delivered her bonds, augmented, as I have said, by the purchase of two $1,000 bonds, to herself in person. Mr. Edwards afterwards wrote me that he and Mrs. Edwards had persuaded her to place them in the hands of Mr. [Jacob] Bunn. Mr. Bunn very kindly acted for her in collecting her pension money, and in receiving from me a monthly payment due from me on account of the purchase of a house from her, until after her return from Europe, late in the fall of 1880, when he rendered his accounts to her and delivered her securities to her.

I cannot give you a statement of the things which were found in her room in the Pacific Hotel, beyond what you yourself say. There were large numbers of lace curtains; several trunks of fancy merchandise, mainly from Gossage's, of a character entirely useless to her, as they were gaudy things, while she herself used nothing but black. There was a very considerable quantity of jewelry, which she had procured mainly from Matson's, on approval, as it is called, and which she had refused thereafter either to pay for or to return. These articles of jewelry consisted of lockets, chains, and things of that sort, of quite considerable value. All of them were, I think, returned to Matson's, and the charge on their books against her was thereby cancelled.

There was also in her room a considerable number of carpet-covered footstools, such as are made in furniture stores to use up remnants of carpets. She had a large number of these, and when she was getting ready to go to Batavia, she took a number of carpet bags with her; and I had the curiosity, when her back was turned, to look into some of them; and I found that each of the bags which I opened contained nothing but one of these footstools. I said nothing, but let them go, with the rest of her baggage, to Dr. Patterson's at Batavia.

You are very kind indeed to take the trouble you do about this matter; and I want to have you know that I appreciate it in the highest degree.

Very sincerely yours,

Robert T. Lincoln

LB 11:16:277–86

ROBERT LINCOLN TO LEONARD SWETT
June 2, 1884

My dear sir:

In reply to your letter,—there was no written opinion of the physicians who met at your office. I think, but do not know, that one of them suggested to you a meeting of themselves and Mr. Ayer at your office, and then I was sent for. The delusion my mother was then under was not fear of rebels, but fear of fire. I remember the doctors said that in such a delusion she might suddenly jump out of a window; although they said that of course no one could predict what an insane person might do. They were all pronounced and earnest that the time had come when her personal safety had to be assured. This opinion was not, as I remember, given in writing, but orally to us at the meeting.

Very truly yours,
Robert T. Lincoln

LB 11:17:329

In May 1887, Leonard Swett gave an interview to a newspaper reporter about Mary Lincoln's trial. The origins for the article are unknown: the reporter may have simply wanted to revisit an interesting story; Swett may have been promoting his upcoming article; or the emerging boom for Robert Lincoln to be the 1888 Republican presidential candidate may have had something to do with it.

"ROBERT TODD LINCOLN"
Los Angeles Times, May 21, 1887 [excerpt]

[Special correspondence, Chicago, May 13]

For the tender, manly and judicious manner in which he deported himself through the ordeal of his mother's failing reason, Robert Lincoln deserves more credit than for anything else he ever did. His was a most unenviable situation. Convinced on the one hand that his mother was irresponsible and that some action was absolutely necessary, and at the same time struggling against filial affection, family pride and a fear of adding fuel to the flames of insanity which the shock of the assassination had started, he knew very well what his duty was, and yet found it a very hard duty to perform. Mrs. Lincoln was then boarding in a Chicago hotel, having $70,000 or $80,000 in United States bonds and currency secreted in her clothing. Placing the matter in the hands of his father's friends—Judge David Davis and Leonard Swett—the son endeavored to do the best thing possible under the circumstances—have his mother judicially declared insane and placed under restraint. Mr. Swett and Judge Davis found Robert most patient and tender, and at the same time judicious and courageous. "In that trying time," says Mr. Swett, "we almost leaned upon the boy instead of his leaning upon us, and we always found his judgment good and his plans perfect." What an afternoon he must have passed when he waited in a room near that in which Mr. Swett struggled for three long hours to induce Mrs. Lincoln to go quietly to court without an escort of police! Across the street stood two officers, to whom Mr. Swett called Mrs. Lincoln's attention, saying: "If you will not go with me quietly I must call those men." Of course the unfortunate woman flew into a passion, and declared that those who should be her friends were trying to rob her of her money and liberty, but Mr. Swett persisted, firmly but gently, until at last the widow yielded. In the private room of the judge there was another scene, and it was only after another hour's struggle that she was induced to give up the bonds and money in her possession. Even then it was necessary to call her attention to the fact that in the corridor outside stood two women, commissioned by the court to search her person.

Mrs. Lincoln died in the home of her sister at Springfield, and her body is now at rest beside that of her husband. But even at this late day there are writers willing to blacken her memory, by unkindly recalling incidents which occurred after her mind had been unsettled by the shock of the assassination. Still another faction, including a number of prominent persons in this city, have blamed the son for the course he pursued with his mother, and in answer to all these injustices, Mr. Swett is now preparing a paper to be printed in *The Century* magazine, defending the unfortunate wife and widow and the son who was ever tender and true.

Los Angeles Times, May 21, 1887, 10

In the 1880s, a young Indiana lawyer named Jesse Weik began interviewing numerous people throughout the Midwest who had known Abraham Lincoln. These interviews he planned to use to supplement the research and recollections of William Herndon—Lincoln's former law partner—with whom Weik was collaborating to write a book on Lincoln that would be part biography, part reminiscence.[4] One interview Weik conducted by mail was with the physician who attended Mary Lincoln on her deathbed, Thomas W. Dresser.

THOMAS W. DRESSER TO JESSE WEIK
Springfield, Ill., Jan. 3, 1889

Dear Sir,

. . . . It is probable that I will be unable to give you such a sketch of Mrs. Lincoln as you desire.

She died in this city July 16th 1882. In the late years of her life certain mental peculiarities were developed which finally culminated in a slight apoplexy, producing paralysis, of which she died. Among the peculiarities alluded to, one of the most singular was the habit she had during the last year or so of her life of immersing herself in a perfectly dark room, and for light using a small candle light, even when the sun was shining bright out of doors. No urging would induce her to go into the fresh air. Another peculiarity was the accumulation of large quantities of silk and dress goods by the trunk and cart load, which she never used, and which accumulated until it was really feared that the floor of the store room would give way. She was bright and sparkling in conversation and her memory remained singularly good up to the very close of her life. Her face was animated and pleasing; and to me she was always an interesting woman; and while the whole world was finding fault with her temper and disposition, it was clear to me that the trouble was a cerebral disease.

Yours truly

Thos. W. Dresser

Herndon-Weik Collection of Lincolniana. Printed in Wilson and Davis, *Herndon's Informants*, 671.

Robert Lincoln was the guardian of the Lincoln family legacy for his entire adult life, and for sixty years he contributed in untold and unparalleled ways to posterity's understanding of his father. His mother's legacy, however, was another matter. Robert found her mental illness embarrassing not only to himself, but also to her and her husband's legacies. And so at some point in the years after his mother's death, Robert decided not only to suppress any writings about the insanity trial and period, but also to collect and burn any of his mother's correspondence that he could that reflected her insanity.

ROBERT LINCOLN TO ABRAM WAKEMAN[*]

Nov. 28, 1908

My Dear Mr. Wakeman,

I have taken several days to think over your letter, and am now writing to say that I would very greatly prefer that my mother's letters should be left out of the proposed articles.[†] Of course, I do not know their contents, but upon the subject which you mention, I do not think that there is any very great public interest, nor any great controversy. It is very unpleasant for me to think or to hear of any anticipation of publication of her letters, because, as you know, the shocking circumstances of my father's death completely deranged her, and she spent most of

---

[*] Abram Wakeman's father, a New York City politico, had been a friend and confidant of Mary Lincoln during the period between Abraham Lincoln's reelection in 1864 and his assassination in 1865. She wrote Wakeman numerous letters during this period about federal appointments, and later claimed he owed his position as postmaster of New York City to her influence.

[†] The subject of these articles, or if they ever were published, is unknown.

the years afterwards in writing countless letters, which could only have been written in such derangement, and which were a source of great unhappiness to me. I therefore should be very sorry to see the subject opened up again, and I hope that you will avoid doing so.

LB 41:71:430

ROBERT LINCOLN TO LE GRAND VAN VALKENBURGH
May 26, 1913

Dear Sir:

I find here your letter of a week ago on my return from a short absence and I greatly appreciate your thoughtfulness. Of course I regret the existence of these relics of the long years of the distressing mental disorder of my mother but it is idle to think of gathering them up. Hundreds of them have been kindly sent me for destruction and I am quite sure that there exists still other hundreds. All that I have known of are of the same tenor; many have been printed in newspapers and catalogues; and I long ago came to the conclusion that one could not imagine a more hopeless work than an effort to collect them or even a large fraction of them.

With many thanks I am,

Very truly yours,

Robert T. Lincoln

Lincoln Collection

Rev. William Eleazer Barton, a Congregationalist minister in Illinois and amateur historian, was a prolific writer of Lincoln studies in the 1920s. In both his two-volume Life of Abraham Lincoln *(1925) and his subsequent* Women Lincoln Loved *(1927), Barton investigated and wrote about Mary Lincoln's insanity case. He not only uncovered the original trial documents, but sought and received a recollection of Mary Lincoln's 1875 insanity trial from one of the original jurors.*

LYMAN J. GAGE TO WILLIAM E. BARTON
Point Loma, Calif., Jan. 20, 1921

Dear Sir:

I have to acknowledge receipt of yours of January 9th, with its inquiry concerning the examination of Mary Lincoln for insanity before the court in Chicago, in 1875.

I remember the fact of that trial or examination quite distinctly, although I could not possibly name any one of the other eleven men who constituted the trial jury, nor could I name the judge who presided.

The prosecuting witnesses were Robert T. Lincoln, Mrs. Lincoln's son, and I think a nurse or companion of Mrs. Lincoln's. Little or no effort was made to defend the accused. Beside the two witnesses named above, there was one or two medical men, alleged experts, who testified that in their opinion Mrs. Lincoln was suffering from aberration of mind, and ought to be confined in some hospital.

There seemed to be no other course than for the jury to find the lady guilty as charged, and she was, as you may know, sent for treatment to Batavia, Ill., where she was put under the charge of a Dr. Patterson, who had [an] institution for the treatment of such cases.

The trial was privately conducted, and I doubt if there was any press publicity given to the case. It did not appear the accused was violently insane, but suffered from phobias or occasional insane delusions. She imagined at times that the city was afire and became greatly excited. She also had a kind of phobia for purchasing on credit goods for which she had no use. The evidence went to show that she bought large quantities of things, had them sent to her rooms, where they were thrown into her closet and the wrappers containing them never taken off.

I knew the lady before the circumstance above named occurred, but not very intimately. She seemed to be a woman of rather superior mind, and of high nervous temperament, and susceptible of intense feeling.

It is rather a startling fact that the leading physician who testified against her [Dr. Willis Danforth], afterwards told me privately that there was no doubt whatever of the fact of her mental aberration. He told me in substance that it was a case of dementia, or degeneration of brain tissue, that she would steadily degenerate and that within a year or a year and a half, or two years, she would die.

However, as I was afterwards informed, she was discharged by Dr. Patterson as fairly well balanced in her mentality, went to a friend's somewhere in the East, and continued to be fairly sane and well balanced for four or five years afterwards.

This is about all I can say in this connection.

Truly yours,

Lyman J. Gage

William Barton Scrapbook, vol. 47, Barton
Collection of Lincolniana

In late 1926, the famed vaudeville actor Eddie Foy published an autobiographical article in Collier's *magazine, in which he related his mother's experiences as Mary Lincoln's personal nurse and traveling companion from 1872 to 1875.*

"CLOWNING THROUGH LIFE"
Collier's, Dec. 25, 1926

. . . Soon after we returned to Chicago [in 1872] Mother was employed as a sort of nurse, guard and companion to Mrs. Abraham Lincoln. Mrs. Lincoln had always been a woman of rather unusual disposition, and it will be remembered that she had had some spells of "temperament" even while she was in the White House. After her husband's assassination she fell into deep melancholy, and after her son Tad died in Chicago in 1871 (the third son she had lost) she suffered from periods of mild insanity.

She had many strange delusions at these times. She thought gas was an invention of the devil, and would have nothing but candles in her room. At other times she insisted on the shades being drawn and the room kept perfectly dark. Mother was with her at Springfield* most of the time, but made one or two southern trips with her in winter.

The position was a trying one, and Mother gave it up twice, but each time the kinsmen induced her to come back after she had had a short rest. She remained with Mrs. Lincoln until the close of the latter's life, when that unfortunate lady became so much unbalanced that the family thought it best to place her in a private sanitarium.[†] Mrs. Lincoln died in 1882.

Foy and Harlow, "Clowning Through Life," 30.

From late 1932 to early 1933, a columnist for the Aurora, Illinois, Beacon-News *newspaper wrote a series of articles about Mary Lincoln's time living at Bellevue Place in nearby Batavia. He investigated the case, toured the sanitarium, looked at records, interviewed employees (including the superintendent of nurses), and received letters from local residents sharing their reminiscences of the time.*

"MRS. LINCOLN IN AURORA"
Aurora Beacon-News, Dec. 18, 1932

I remember of seeing Mrs. Lincoln [in Aurora] several times before I knew her identity. She was a very distinguished looking woman, faultlessly attired; of modest manner and refinement; of medium stature and quite active. Her complexion was very light with a noticeable pallor. While erect and dignified of bearing, her coun-

---

* Chicago, not Springfield.

[†] Foy is correct that his mother left her position as Mary Lincoln's nurse after the former first lady was committed to Bellevue Place sanitarium, but this occurred in 1875, not 1882.

tenance was pleasant, smiling and friendly, as I recall. By inquiry I learned who our distinguished visitor was and thereafter took more particular notice of the former mistress of the White House.

One day Mrs. Lincoln, with her attendant, came in our store and I waited upon her, without intimating that I knew her identity. She purchased some gents' hosiery, for a gift to one of the hospital attaches I gathered from her conversation incidental to the purchase, and in her familiar and cheerful discussion with her companion I was impressed with her refined, considerate and democratic manner.

Herman Felsenheld to Lutz White, Aurora, Illinois, February 14, 1926. Printed in "Now and Then," *Aurora Beacon-News*, December 18, 1932, 4.

"MORE ABOUT MARY LINCOLN—MISS STIMPSON'S STORY"
Aurora Beacon-News, Dec. 25, 1932

"Of course I never knew Mrs. Lincoln," said Miss [Lena] Stimpson [superintendent of nurses], "but I did know Mrs. Ruggles, who was matron here at the time Mrs. Lincoln was a patient. She was matron when I came in 1893. I was interested in the tragic story and Mrs. Ruggles used to relate her experiences with the distinguished patient. What I repeat to you is as I heard it from the former matron.

"Most of the tales that filtered to the outside were fabulous or grossly exaggerated. The letter you printed recently, written by Dr. Patterson,* at the time, explains that phase quite satisfactorily, and the stories best be forgotten. Dr. Patterson and Mrs. Lincoln got along very well. He ruled with kindness, and with understanding, without sacrifice of dignity or institutional discipline. His patient was treated as one of the family and took her meals at the family table.

"Mrs. Lincoln suffered with hallucinations. Otherwise she was normal except for an uncontrollable temper. She quarreled with everyone she came in contact with; nothing suited her and no one could please her. She was ever an aristocrat, proud and arrogant, and for this there is some excuse. Once the first lady of the land, and sentenced to Bellevue by the court, she was humiliated. She held no interest in Batavia or those surrounding her. Her thoughts and interests were far away.

"During Mrs. Lincoln's stay she always had her private horse and carriage at her disposal. The sanitarium maintained a stable and equipages for accommodation of patients, but Mrs. Lincoln used a livery outfit. Robert Lincoln arranged for a horse and carriage for her own special use, at the Greene stable and every day she took her drive in pleasant weather. Sometimes she would storm at the livery man for delays or fancied neglect. In her drives she was always accompanied by her attendant.

---

* Letter to the editor, *Chicago Tribune*, August 29, 1875 (see also chapter 7).

"In the hospital record of her case set down daily by the attendant these drives are always mentioned. We see such notes as 'drove today for an hour and a half' or 'drove today for two hours,' and in some instances we see records such as this— 'drove today for two hours and had a hard time to induce the patient to go home.'

"Mrs. Lincoln's one consuming passion seemed to be dress. Her whole time seemed to be taken up with her wardrobe. She was always richly and tastefully attired and employed a regular dressmaker at Batavia, and I believe a woman at Aurora did some work for her. It was well that she enjoyed this hobby, as it kept her mind occupied."

Miss Lena E. Stimpson, interview by Lutz White,
"Now and Then," *Aurora Beacon-News,*
December 25, 1932, 4

The final reminiscence given by one who knew Mary Lincoln occurred in the 1950s, when Mary Edwards Brown, age 86, gave her recollections of the last days of her great aunt Mary, with whom she was then living in the Edwardses' home in Springfield, Illinois, during 1881–82.

"AN OLD LADY'S LINCOLN MEMORIES"
Life, Feb. 9, 1959

I was a girl of sixteen when Aunt Mary was ill in Grandmother Edwards' house, the winter before she died. A few years before that her son Robert had to have her committed to a sanitarium because she did queer things like getting into an elevator in a hotel when she was undressed; she thought it was the lavatory. Mother went to call on her at the Sanitarium and Aunt Mary said, "Tell Elizabeth"—that was Grandmother, Mrs. Ninian Edwards—"to come and get me and I won't be any trouble." But she was, a lot of trouble.

She kept writing letters all the time to rich men in the country saying how poor she was and living in despicable circumstances and the nation should be ashamed. She often told my mother, "Robert says I'm crazy, but he is crazy too. He was bit by a mad dog when he was a boy." It was very hard on cousin Robert. He suffered a lot and his mother wouldn't speak to him and she said he was a robber, that he had stolen her silver and her jewelry. But Mother always told us that we mustn't say anything unkind about Aunt Mary in her last years because she wasn't herself.

She had a lot of money that she kept in a money belt, even under her nightdress, but sometimes she hid it in other places. One day she said Grandmother had stolen her money. Mother was there (she always got along with Aunt Mary because she never argued with her like Grandmother did). Well, Aunt Mary had a commode with a piece of Oriental carpet on top—she kept it beside her bed. Mother and

Grandmother got her up on that and Grandmother dived her hand in under the mattress and there was a big roll of bills.

In the room next to her, Aunt Mary had sixty-four trunks. Grandmother's maid left because she was afraid to sleep under that room, with all that weight. The trunks were filled with bolts of curtain materials and dress goods. Aunt Mary had a lot of clothes in her trunks made out of elegant foreign material she bought abroad, and she had basted it together to look like dresses—to escape the customs duty. She wouldn't stop buying. Once she bought three hundred pairs of kid gloves at one time and two dozen watches. She had about a hundred shawls. Every day she got up and went through those trunks for hours. Grandmother said it was funny, if Aunt Mary was so sick, that she was able to be up all day bending over her trunks.

She had terrible headaches, and she was puffed up. She took a lot of bottles of "restorative," it was called, and it had paregoric in it, same as opium, but you could get those things without a prescription then. She didn't know much about diseases, but what she thought she had was a condition where her blood was turning to water, and when too much water hit her heart she would die. Her fingers swelled up so she had to take off her wedding ring—it was a wide ring and worn very thin. After Aunt Mary died, Mother hunted it up and got it back on her finger. Mother laid Aunt Mary out too. The newspapers wrote about the ring when she was lying in her coffin in Grandmother's parlor with the wedding lamps lighted, how the ring was Etruscan gold and it was shining on her finger and there was a smile on her face.

Mary Edwards Brown, interview by Kunhardt,
in "An Old Lady's Lincoln Memories"

Appendix
Abraham Lincoln's Comments on His Wife's Sanity

There are three known recollections of Abraham Lincoln supposedly commenting on his wife's mental health. The earliest is creditable; the other two are dubious in their authenticity.

The first of these was written by Mary Lincoln's White House *modiste,* Elizabeth Keckley, in her 1868 memoir. It is a believable reminiscence because at the time Lincoln was not the secular godhead he is considered today, and Keckley was not trying to write herself into his heroic story by peddling lies and fantasies (as many later writers did). Her purpose was to show the country the true and admirable character of Mary Lincoln, explain the former first lady's unhappy post-Washington life, her dire financial situation, and the reasons she tried to sell her old White House clothing in New York in 1867. Keckley hoped the book would help her friend pay off her large debts, either by convincing rich readers to donate money to Mary or by sharing the book's profits. Neither happened.

Keckley's description of Lincoln commenting on his wife's mental state occurred while describing the aftermath of son Willie Lincoln's death in 1862:

> Mrs. Lincoln's grief was inconsolable. The pale face of her dead boy threw her into convulsions. Around him love's tendrils had been twined, and now that he was dressed for the tomb, it was like tearing the tendrils out of the heart by their roots. Willie, she often said, if spared by Providence, would be the hope and stay of her old age. But Providence had not spared him. The light faded from his eyes, and the death-dew had gathered on his brow.
>
> In one of her paroxysms of grief the President kindly bent over his wife, took her by the arm, and gently led her to the window. With a stately, solemn gesture, he pointed to the lunatic asylum.
>
> "Mother, do you see that large white building on the hill yonder? Try and control your grief, or it will drive you mad, and we may have to send you there."
>
> Mrs. Lincoln was so completely overwhelmed with sorrow that she did not attend the funeral.[1]

The next comment, written by William Herndon, Lincoln's former law partner, occurred in 1882, after Herndon read the news that Mary Lincoln was severely ill and financially destitute. Even though Herndon's statements were made in a private letter and not meant for publication (and indeed never published), his deep and well-documented disdain for Mary Lincoln makes anything he ever said about her automatically suspect.

> Mrs. Lincoln is a curious woman—an unfortunate one, and to a certain extent a despised one. Mrs. Lincoln is in part an unbalanced woman—her mind is—and more—unhinged, and has been for years.
> *Private*—Mr. Lincoln held his wife partly insane for years and this shows his toleration of her nature—his great forbearance of her outlandish acts, otherwise not understood by the great world.[2]

The last known comment on Abraham Lincoln's opinion of his wife's sanity was by William P. Wood, superintendent of the Old Capitol Prison during the Civil War, and later chief of the U.S. Secret Service. Wood wrote in an 1887 newspaper article that President Lincoln once confided to him that Mrs. Lincoln's embarrassing and at times unethical conduct as first lady went deeper than mere bad judgment. Abraham Lincoln, however, was an intensely private man, and Wood was merely an acquaintance, not a friend, so it is highly doubtful that the tight-lipped Lincoln would have shared so personal a thought—about his wife, no less—with Wood.

> The troubles of President Lincoln were not confined to political issues or exclusively to military operations. There were several things about the White House which annoyed him far more than the reader can conjecture.
> A survivor of Buchanan's administration retained position under Lincoln. The position was apparently an insignificant one. The favored one was Thomas Stackpole, a subtle partisan, Yankee Democrat. He had an eye to business and he was anxious to make an extra dollar whenever occasion offered. If a permit was possible in those ticklish times Tom Stackpole could obtain it, and a customer with ready money had only to call upon John Hammack to secure the coveted paper.
> John Hammack was the keeper of a restaurant then on the northeast corner of Pennsylvania Avenue and 14th Street. John wore good clothes and belonged to that class of idlers known as sporting men. His shortcomings in book education were counterbalanced by his experience as a local sport. He was a Virginia-bred Democrat and a rabid secessionist. Stackpole had the ear of Mrs. Lincoln. He and Hammack were bosom friends. The latter should have had quarters in the Old Capitol [Prison], but was allowed his liberty because he was the silent partner of Stackpole, who secured permits for Hammack's customers through the "lady of the White House."
> The bargain and sale of trading permits, official favors and Government secrets, chargeable to Stackpole's influence with Mrs. Lincoln, was so extensive that I

deemed it my duty to inform Secretary Stanton of the fact. I discovered through whom certain applications would be presented. The subject became so notorious that President Lincoln's attention was speedily called to the matter by Secretary Stanton, who suggested that the President should send for me for all the details of the nefarious practice.

After a long private interview with the President, in which he exhibited more feeling than I had believed he possessed, the grand and patient man said:

"There were few men entirely sane, and more women are tainted with insanity and victims to insane delusions than it would be prudent to admit. The caprices of Mrs. Lincoln, I am satisfied, are the result of partial insanity. Wood, have you ever given any attention to the subject?"

"Only in a casual way, Mr. President," I replied.[3]

No other recollections of Abraham Lincoln commenting on his wife's sanity has ever been found. Even those men considered his closest friends, men whom Robert consulted in 1875–76, never pretended to know the dead man's thoughts on the subject. Indeed, Leonard Swett even asked in 1876, "If Mr. Lincoln could speak to us what would he say?"

Introduction

1. Martha Freeman Esmond to Julia Boyd, Chicago, May 10, 1875, published in Herma Clark, "When Chicago Was Young," *Chicago Tribune*, November 23, 1930, H1.

2. Reed refers here to eleven-year-old Willie Lincoln who died in 1862, and seventeen-year-old Tad who died in 1871. Four-year-old Edward "Eddie" Lincoln had died in 1850 from tuberculosis.

3. For the full examination of these events, see Emerson, *Madness of Mary Lincoln*, and Neely and McMurtry, *Insanity File*.

4. "Clouded Reason: Trial of Mrs. Abraham Lincoln for Insanity," *Chicago Tribune*, May 20, 1875, 1; "Mrs. Lincoln: The Widow of the Martyred President Adjudged Insane in County Court," *Chicago Inter Ocean*, May 20, 1875, 1; see also chapter 2.

5. The Bradwells were known crusaders, as abolitionists, feminists, and legal activists. Myra Bradwell also was the founder and publisher of the *Chicago Legal News*, a highly influential legal newsletter.

6. Robert Lincoln to Ninian Edwards, Chicago, December 21, 1875, Folder 2, Box 2, Mary Todd Lincoln Insanity File. (See chapter 8.)

7. Robert Lincoln to Rev. Henry Darling, November 15, 1877, Folder 38, Box 6, Lincoln Collection, Lincoln Miscellaneous Manuscripts, Department of Special Collections, University of Chicago Library.

8. At least fourteen members of the Todd family (direct and extended) have been identified as suffering mental illness, including Mary's brothers George, David, and Levi. See Emerson, *Madness of Mary Lincoln*, 101, 188–89; Burlingame, *Abraham Lincoln: A Life*, 1: 535–40; Berry, *House of Abraham*.

9. Lutz White, "Now and Then," *Aurora Beacon-News*, January 8, 1933, 6.

10. William Herndon to Jesse Weik, January 8, 1886, printed in Hertz, *Hidden Lincoln*, 130.

Chapter 1. April 1865–May 1875

1. David Davis to Miss Addie Burr, July 19, 1882, Adeline Ellery (Burr) Davis Green Papers.

2. Robert Lincoln to Mary Harlan Lincoln July 15, 1871, quoted in Helm, *True Story of Mary*, 293–95.

3. Arnold, *Life of Abraham Lincoln*, 439.

4. Foy and Harlow, "Clowning through Life"; see also chapter 13.

5. Trial testimony of Dr. Willis Danforth; see also chapter 2.

Chapter 5. Suicide Attempt

1. Baker, *Mary Todd Lincoln*, 326.

2. For an excellent examination of the event see Hirschhorn, "Mary Lincoln's 'Suicide Attempt.'"

Chapter 6. May–July 1875

1. Bellevue Place Sanitarium Advertising Brochures, n.d., 2 pages, and 1895, 15 pages, Batavia Historical Society, Batavia, Ill.; "Mrs. Lincoln: A Visit to Her by 'The Post and Mail' Correspondent: How She Passes the Time at Dr. Patterson's Retreat," *Chicago Post and Mail*, July 13, 1875; Ross, "Mary Todd Lincoln," 10.

2. Ross, "Mary Todd Lincoln," 10.

Chapter 8. September–December 1875

1. Dr. Andrew McFarland to Robert Lincoln, September 10 and 11, 1875, Folder 20, Box 2, Mary Todd Lincoln Insanity File.

Chapter 10. Trial of 1876

1. Edwards's second letter is nearly identical to the first and so not included here. It contains only one interesting statement, "I have just returned and was pained to hear of your mother's treatment to you." Ninian Edwards to Robert Lincoln, Springfield, June 17, 1876 (2), Folder 17, Box 2, Mary Todd Lincoln Insanity File.

Chapter 12. October 1876–June 1882

1. Helm, *True Story of Mary*, 298.

2. Robert Lincoln to Rev. Henry Darling, November 15, 1877, Robert Todd Lincoln Papers.

3. "Mrs. Lincoln's Illness," New York Times, October 31, 1880, 5; "Mrs. Lincoln's Health," New York Times, July 22, 1881, 3; "New York: The Health of Mrs. Abraham Lincoln Not Improving," Chicago Tribune, January 15, 1882, 6; *Congressional Record*, 47th Cong. 1st sess., 1882, 13:402.

Chapter 13. Posthumous

1. "The Funeral," *Illinois State Journal*, July 19, 1882, 6; "Laid to Rest: The Last Sad Rites Paid to the Remains of Mary Lincoln," *Illinois State Journal*, July 20, 1882, 1.

2. Florence Snow to Rosemary Ketcham, July 1939, in Snow, *Pictures on My Wall*, 71–72.

3. Unfortunately, Swett's article was never published, and no notes or drafts have ever been found.

4. Herndon and Weik, *Herndon's Lincoln*.

Appendix

1. Keckley, *Behind the Scenes*, 104–5. Emily Helm recalled a similar incident of Mary's hysteria and Abraham's comforting her and leading her to the window from which could be seen the asylum. Louis A. Warren, "Mrs. Lincoln's Mental Collapse," *Lincoln Lore* 1124, October 23, 1950.

2. William Herndon to Jesse Weik, Springfield, Ill., January 2, 1882, Group 4, Microfilm Reel 9, Frame 1753–54, Herndon-Weik Collection.

3. *Washington Sunday Gazette*, January 16, 1887, clipping in Folder "Barbee File, et al.," Box 71, Randall Family Papers.

Bibliography

Archives

Barton, William E., Collection of Lincolniana. Special Collection Research Center, University of Chicago Library, Chicago, Ill.

Batavia Historical Society, Batavia, Ill.

Davis, David. Family Papers. Abraham Lincoln Presidential Library, Springfield, Ill.

French, Benjamin Brown. Family Papers. Library of Congress, Washington, D.C.

Green, Adeline Ellery (Burr) Davis. Papers. Rare Book, Manuscript and Special Collections Library, Duke University, Durham, N.C.

Hay, John. Papers. John Hay Library, Brown University, Providence, R.I.

Herndon-Weik Collection of Lincolniana. Library of Congress, Washington, D.C.

Lincoln Collection. Abraham Lincoln Presidential Library, Springfield, Ill.

Lincoln Collection, Lincoln Miscellaneous Manuscripts. Special Collections Research Center, University of Chicago Library. Chicago, Ill.

Lincoln Financial Foundation Collection. Allen County Public Library, Fort Wayne, Ind.

Lincoln Collection, Louise Taper. Privately owned.

Lincoln, Mary Todd. Correspondence with Myra Bradwell, August 2, 18[76]. Privately owned.

———. Insanity File. Lincoln Financial Foundation Collection, Allen County Public Library, Fort Wayne, Ind.

Lincoln, Robert Todd. Family Papers. Library of Congress, Washington, D.C.

———. Letterpress Books. Abraham Lincoln Presidential Library, Springfield, Ill. (abbreviated as LB in text, followed by volume, microfilm reel, and page numbers separated by colons).

———. Papers. Chicago History Museum, Chicago, Ill.

Randall, James G., Family Papers. Library of Congress, Washington, D.C.

Taft, Horatio Nelson. Diary, 1861–65, vol. 3. Library of Congress, Washington, D.C.

Newspapers

Boston Globe
Chicago Courier
Chicago Evening Journal
Chicago Inter Ocean
Los Angeles Times
Lowell (Mass.) Daily Citizen and News
New York Evangelist
New York Observer and Chronicle

Chicago Post and Mail
Chicago Times
Chicago Tribune
Illinois State Journal
Illinois State Register

New-York Tribune
Pomeroy's Democrat (Chicago)
St. Louis Globe-Democrat
Washington Sunday Gazette

Books and Articles

Arnold, Isaac N. *The Life of Abraham Lincoln.* 1884; repr. Lincoln: University of Nebraska Press, 1994.

Baker, Jean H. *Mary Todd Lincoln: A Biography.* New York: W.W. Norton & Company, 1987.

Berry, Stephen. *House of Abraham: Lincoln and the Todds.* Boston: Houghton Mifflin, 2007.

Burlingame, Michael. *Abraham Lincoln: A Life.* 2 vols. Johns Hopkins University Press, 2009.

Congressional Record. 47th Cong. 1st sess., 1882.

Emerson, Jason. *The Madness of Mary Lincoln.* Carbondale: Southern Illinois University Press, 2007.

———. "New Mary Lincoln Letter Found." *Journal of the Illinois State Historical Society* 101, no. 3–4 (Fall/Winter 2008): 315–28.

Foy, Eddie, and Alvin F. Harlow, "Clowning Through Life," *Collier's* 78, no. 26 (December 25, 1926): 15–16, 30.

Helm, Katherine. *The True Story of Mary, Wife of Lincoln.* New York: Harper and Brothers Publishers, 1928.

Herndon, William H., and Jesse William Weik. *Herndon's Lincoln: The True Story of a Great Life.* 3 vols. New York: Belford, Clarke & Company, 1889.

Hertz, Emanuel. *The Hidden Lincoln: From the Letters and Papers of William H. Herndon.* New York: Viking Press, 1938.

Hirschhorn, Norbert. "Mary Lincoln's 'Suicide Attempt': A Physician Reconsiders the Evidence." *Lincoln Herald* 104, no. 3 (Fall 2003): 94–98.

History of Sangamon County, Illinois. Chicago: Interstate Publishing, 1881.

Keckley, Elizabeth. *Behind the Scenes, or Thirty Years a Slave and Four Years in the White House.* 1868. Reprint, New York: Arno Press, 1968.

Kunhardt, Dorothy Meserve. "An Old Lady's Lincoln Memories." *Life* 46, no. 6 (February 9, 1959): 57, 59–60.

Neely, Mark E., and R. Gerald McMurtry. *The Insanity File: The Case of Mary Todd Lincoln.* Carbondale: Southern Illinois University Press, 1986.

Owen, Robert Dale. *The Debatable Land Between This World and The Next.* London: Trübner & Co., 1871.

Pratt, Harry E. *The Personal Finances of Abraham Lincoln.* Springfield, Ill., 1943.

Ross, Rodney A. "Mary Todd Lincoln: Patient at Bellevue Place, Batavia." *Journal of the Illinois State Historical Society* 63, no. 1 (1970): 5–34.

Snow, Florence. *Pictures on My Wall: A Lifetime in Kansas.* Lawrence: University of Kansas Press, 1945.

Turner, Justin G., and Linda Levitt Turner. *Mary Todd Lincoln: Her Life and Letters.* New York: Alfred A. Knopf, 1972.

Warren, Louis A. "Mrs. Lincoln's Mental Collapse." *Lincoln Lore,* no. 1124 (October 23, 1950).

Wilson, Douglas L., and Rodney O. Davis, ed. *Herndon's Informants: Letters, Interviews, and Statements about Abraham Lincoln.* Urbana: University of Illinois Press, 1998.

Index

15–16, 52, 127, 217; death of Willie and, 221; debts, 3; declared insane by jury, x, 21, 30, 37–38, 41, 210; declared restored to reason by jury, xi, 180, 183–85; delusions of (general), x, xii, 4, 5, 18–20, 25–28, 32–36, 190, 208, 211–12, 216, 217; delusions of Robert deathly ill, 7–8, 19, 26, 28, 29, 32, 33, 35, 163, 190; demands return of items from Robert, 159–61, 169, 171–74, 188, 191, 193–98; depression of, x, 206, 217; dishonesty of, 90, 94, 100, 104, 115, 168; estrangement from Robert, xi, 202–6; in Europe, ix, xi, 127, 128, 189, 197–98, 202–6; fear of fire, ix, 18, 20, 25, 27, 28, 34, 36, 40, 53, 59, 190, 192, 211; fear of rebels, 25, 29, 30, 40, 190, 192, 211; files petition for control of her estate, 179–82; finances of, 77–82, 152–53, 180–83, 210; funeral of, ix, 12, 208–9; generosity to Robert and Mary Harlan Lincoln, 173, 189–91, 197–98; hallucinations of, x, xii, 5, 10, 17, 18, 19, 22, 25–28, 32–33, 36, 38–39, 40, 52, 87–88, 90, 96, 190, 218; and husband's assassination, ix, 1–3, 23, 32, 40, 48, 52–54, 127, 212, 213, 217; and husband's estate, 3; insanity trial of, x, 13–59; interview with Leonard Swett before insanity trial, 46–47, 61–62, 212–13; lives at Edwards home, xi, 144–201, 219–20; lives in Chicago, ix, 3; lives with Robert and Mary Harlan, 5, 103; medical treatment at Bellevue Place sanitarium, 73, 76, 83, 86, 100, 103, 132, 171, 218; medical treatment of (general), x, xi, 5, 14, 17, 19, 20, 26, 28, 32, 36, 37; medications/drugs taken by, 5, 14, 18, 28, 34, 148, 220; mental illness, symptoms of, x, xii, 4, 5, 10, 13–59, 169, 170, 213–14; nervous breakdown postulated, ix, 6, 128; Old Clothes Scandal, 4, 58, 116, 121, 208, 221; pension for husband's death, 3–4; physical health 5, 6, 7, 76, 91, 128, 147–48, 206, 220, 222; reconciles with Robert, xi, 207; recounts husband's last day, 1–2, 53; relationship with Mary Harlan Lincoln, 5, 20, 36, 100, 103, 104, 173, 188, 189, 193, 197–98; released from Bellevue Place sanitarium, xi, 144; second insanity trial of, xi, 178–85; seeks early release from sanitarium, 92–137; seeks husband's salary remainder, 3, 194; seeks revenge against Robert, 186–88, 191; speaks during insanity trial, 28; spending/clothing mania, 3, 14, 18, 20, 25, 27–30, 32, 34, 36–37, 39, 40, 45, 57, 63, 86, 97, 100, 102, 108, 113, 148, 150, 153, 157–59, 167–69, 172–73, 178, 191, 195, 203–4, 211, 213–14, 216, 219–20; Spiritualism and, 5, 24, 31, 88, 92, 121–22, 133, 137, 149, 153, 156;

suicide attempt, 49, 55, 57, 59, 60–71, 135; suggests kidnapping Robert's daughter, 103; Tad's estate and, 186–87, 190; temper of, 11, 218; threatens Robert's life, xi, 167, 192; Todd relatives believe her insane, 4, 120, 133; unethical conduct as First Lady, 222–23; visits health spas, 5; wants control of her property returned to her, xi, 149–51, 155, 158–68, 174

Lincoln, Mary Harlan (Robert's wife), 4, 30; relationship with Mary Todd Lincoln, 5, 20, 36, 100, 103, 104, 173, 188, 189, 193, 197–98; sorts through Mary Lincoln's belongings, 209

Lincoln, Mary "Mamie" (Robert's daughter), x, 5, 86, 91, 92, 100, 103, 115, 149, 162, 205, 206

Lincoln, Robert T.: allows mother's release from sanitarium, 138–44; bars Bradwells from visiting mother, 117; bitten by mad dog, 219; burns mother's letters, xii, 214–15; conservator of mother's estate, x, xi, 77–83, 94, 118, 134, 150–52, 154, 157–61, 168–73, 175, 177; conservator's report for second trial, 180–84; considers returning mother to sanitarium, xi, 170, 171; consults father's old friends on mother's insanity, x, 9–10, 11, 20, 36, 43, 45, 48, 59, 75, 76, 99, 151–54, 157, 163, 190, 212; consults physicians on mother's insanity, x, 9, 10, 16, 45, 73, 74, 76, 99, 151, 169, 170, 190, 192, 211; consults physicians on removal of mother from sanitarium, 138–40, 142–44, 181; contemporary reputation of, ix, 40, 51, 105, 133, 136, 193, 212; correspondence with David Davis, 44, 153–55, 155–57, 178–79; correspondence with Dr. Richard J. Patterson, 107–8, 117, 120, 138–39, 142, 144; correspondence with Elizabeth Edwards, 102–5, 108–13, 116–17, 122, 145–49, 158–59, 168–74, 177, 203–4, 206, 209; correspondence with Henry T. Blow, 99–101; correspondence with John M. Palmer, 164–65, 166, 175; correspondence with John Todd Stuart, 9–10, 43, 152–53; correspondence with Judge M. R. M. Wallace, 77–81, 159–61; correspondence with Leonard Swett, 210–12; correspondence with Mary Lincoln, 8, 115, 171–72, 188, 193; correspondence with Myra Bradwell, 114; correspondence with Ninian Edwards, 150–52, 155, 158, 161–70, 174–76, 179, 184–85, 196; curator of family legacy, xii, 214; disagrees with mother's release from Bellevue Place, 170; discharge as mother's conservator, 175, 177–84; duty to mother as oldest son, xi, xiii, 51–55, 74, 99, 101, 103, 104, 108, 151, 154, 163, 166, 175, 212; estrangement from mother, xi,

202–6; father's assassination and, 3; files petition of insanity against mother, x, 16, 32, 52, 57, 99, 139; hires nurse for mother, x, 5, 217; inheritance from mother, xii; keeps insanity file, xii, xiv; monetary reasons for mother's commitment, xiii, 19, 29, 35, 50, 152, 190, 193, 213; mother's death and, xii; mother's second insanity trial and, 179–84; mother's suicide attempt and, 49, 60, 64, 66, 70, 71; motivations for insanity trial, 32, 41, 53, 73, 74, 177, 212; moves to Chicago with mother and brother, ix, 3; Myra Bradwell and, 102–5, 107, 108, 111, 114, 129–30, 138; negative historical reputation of, xii, xiii; offers to resign as mother's conservator, 163–64, 166, 170, 175–76, 177; opinions on mother's sanity, 4–5, 9, 20, 36, 59, 100, 103, 104, 114, 115, 153, 154, 169–70, 173, 177, 207, 214–15; presidential candidate possibility, 212; reconciles with mother, xi, 207; refuses to send mother items she demands, 174, 191, 198–99; secretary of war, xi, 207; sends mother items she demands, 159–61, 169, 171–73; separation from wife, 103; studies law, 3; testifies against mother, x, 19–20, 29–30, 35–37, 58–59; visits mother at sanitarium, 73, 74, 83, 88, 91, 92, 104, 111, 114

Lincoln, Thomas (Tad), ix, 3, 87, 90, 96, 103, 127, 128; death of, x, 5, 225n2; effect of death on Mary Lincoln, 5, 15, 52, 127, 217; estate of, 186, 190

Lincoln, William (Willie), 87, 90, 96, 221, 225n2

Loomis, Mason B., 83

Mattock, T. C., 21

McDill, Dr. Alexander, 139–40, 143

McFarland, Dr. Andrew, 139, 143, 144

McMurtry, R. Gerald, xiv

Motley, John Lathrop, 91, 128

Neely, Mark E., xiv

Nicolay, John G., 3, 87

Orne, Sally, 73, 105, 207

Owen, Robert Dale, 89

Palmer, John M., 150, 162, 166, 167, 170, 175; correspondence with Robert Lincoln, 164–65, 166, 175; hired by Mary Lincoln in 1876, 174, 178–79

Patterson, Richard J., x, 22, 31, 38, 39, 63, 67, 70, 77, 84, 92, 94, 102, 110, 113–17, 123, 126, 129, 130, 139, 145, 170, 194, 211, 216; argument with James Bradwell, 119, 120, 123–25, 135, 137;

bars Bradwells from visiting Bellevue Place, 118, 141; consulted before Mary Lincoln's insanity trial, 10, 45, 78; correspondence with Myra Bradwell, 106, 107; correspondence with Robert Lincoln, 107–8, 117, 120, 138–39, 142, 144; letter to the *Chicago Tribune*, 134–36; medical background, 72, 76, 83, 89–90, 132; opinions on Mary Lincoln's mental health, 100, 104, 108, 118, 134–35, 138, 141; opinions on release of Mary Lincoln from sanitarium, 108, 125, 129, 131, 134–35, 139, 142, 143; supposedly signs certificate of recovery for Mary Lincoln, 125, 129, 134; treatment of Mary Lincoln, 73, 76, 83, 86, 100, 103, 132, 135, 171, 218

Phillips, David L., 187, 200

Pinkerton National Detective Agency, 45, 63, 65, 78

Rayne, M. L., 84, 88, 122; newspaper articles about Mary Lincoln, 84–88, 120–22

Reed, Rev. James A., ix

Remann, Josephine, 120, 171, 209

Roberts, Marshal O., 178

Roosevelt, Cornelia (Van Ness), 201

Roosevelt, James John, 201

Sayre, Dr. Louis A., 206

Scammon, Charles, 188

Scammon, Jonathan Y., 188

Seward, William, 127

Sickles, Gen. Daniel, 57

Smith, Ann Todd, 112, 113, 146, 195

Smith, Clark Moulton, 112, 113, 151, 152, 159

Smith, Dr. Charles Gilman, 10, 45; insanity trial testimony, 21, 30, 37

Squair, Frank, 66–70

Stackpole, Thomas, 222

Stanton, Edwin M., 223

Stimson, Lena, 218–19

Stone, James P., 20, 30, 37

Storey, Wilbur F., 93, 185

Stuart, John Todd, 9, 11, 12, 42, 98, 103, 109, 151, 157, 161; advises Robert Lincoln on mother and mother's commitment, 9–10, 11, 20, 36, 45, 48, 59, 75, 99, 151, 152, 157; believes Mary Lincoln insane, 10, 43, 44, 46; correspondence with Robert Lincoln, 9–10, 152–53; does not attend Mary Lincoln's insanity trial, 43–44; receives letter from Mary Lincoln, 114; receives request from James Bradwell, 94; supports Robert Lincoln's legal actions, 11, 43, 51, 99

Sturgess, William, 93

Sumner, Charles, 55

Swett, Leonard, 9, 42–44, 60, 113, 123, 136, 196, 223; advises Robert Lincoln on mother and mother's commitment, 9–10, 45, 151–54, 157, 160, 161, 163, 169, 189, 212; correspondence with David Davis, 11–12, 44–50, 71; correspondence with Ninian Edwards, 189–93, 194–99; correspondence with Robert Lincoln, 210–12; interview with Mary Lincoln before insanity trial, 46–47, 61–62, 212–13; Mary Lincoln's anger at, 187, 193–94, 196, 199–200; and Mary Lincoln's first sanity trial, 13, 14, 16, 21, 22, 24, 30, 32, 37, 38, 44–50, 54, 61–63, 69, 70, 75, 212–13; on Mary Lincoln's insanity, 45, 46, 48, 154, 190, 192, 198; and Mary Lincoln's second sanity trial, 179, 182; opinion of Robert Lincoln, 192, 212; prepares article about Mary Lincoln insanity trial, 210–13; suicide attempt of Mary Lincoln and, 49, 64, 71; threatens to commit Mary Lincoln himself, 193

Swing, David, 136–37, 138, 199

Swisshelm, Jane Grey, 5

Taft, Horatio Nelson, 1–3

Todd, Levi O., 204

Townsend, J. S., 20, 37

Turner, Justin, xiv

Turner, Linda Levitt, xiv

Turner, Samuel M., 13, 14, 17, 18, 24, 26, 28–30, 33, 35, 39, 46

Tyndale, Sharon, 87

Van Valkenburgh, Le Grand, 215

Wakeman, Abram, 110, 116, 214–15

Wallace, Frances "Fannie" Todd, 159, 174, 195, 201

Wallace, Judge Marion R. M., 139, 153–54, 163, 166, 210; correspondence with Robert Lincoln, 77–81, 159–61; presides over Mary Lincoln's first trial, 16, 32; presides over Mary Lincoln's second trial, 180, 182

Weik, Jesse, 213

White, Lutz, 218, 219

Wilkie, Franc B., 93, 111, 130, 187; interviews Mary Lincoln at sanitarium, 102, 107, 111; newspaper article on Mary Lincoln, 126–30

Wilson, J. C., 9

Wilson, J. J. S., 8

Wood, William P., 222–23

Wooster, W. H., 20, 37

Jason Emerson is an independent scholar living in Cazenovia, New York. He is the author of *The Madness of Mary Lincoln, Lincoln the Inventor,* and *Giant in the Shadows: The Life of Robert T. Lincoln.*

The University of Illinois Press
is a founding member of the
Association of American University Presses.

Designed by Jim Proefrock
Composed in 10.5/13 Bulmer
with American Scribe display
at the University of Illinois Press
Manufactured by Thomson-Shore, Inc.

University of Illinois Press
1325 South Oak Street
Champaign, IL 61820-6903
www.press.uillinois.edu